Church Administration

PROGRAMS • PROCESS • PURPOSE

Robert N. Bacher
Michael L. Cooper-White

Fortress Press
Minneapolis

CHURCH ADMINISTRATION
Programs, Process, Purpose

Further supportive materials for this book are available at www.churchadm.com.

Cover images: © PhotoDisc by Getty Images; © JupiterImages
Cover design: Abby Hartman
Book design: Jessica A. Puckett

Library of Congress Cataloging-in-Publication Data
Bacher, Robert.
  Church administration : programs, process, purpose.
    p. cm.
  ISBN 978-0-8006-3742-2 (alk. paper)
  1. Church management I. Cooper-White, Michael. II. Title.
BV652.B27 2007
254—dc22   2006024556

The paper used in this publication meets the minimum requirements of American National Standard for Information Sciences — Permanence of Paper for Printed Library Materials, ANSI Z329.48-1984.

Manufactured in the U.S.A.

11   10   09   08   07   1   2   3   4   5   6   7   8   9   10

Contents

Preface: Riding Time to the End!

Time like an ever-rolling stream,
Soon bears us all away;
We fly forgotten, as a dream
Dies at the op'ning day!
—Isaac Watts, "O God, Our Help in Ages Past," alt.

Perhaps as never before in the history of the world and the Christian church, we who live in the early years of the twenty-first century know that time indeed keeps rolling along. With precise atomic clocks, we can measure time with incredible precision to the nanosecond. In the windows of the digital clocks that grace our night stands and automobile dashboards, we monitor time's incremental click-click-click in ways not so apparent to earlier generations, who watched its flow as second hands swept across the face of a wrist watch or grandfather's clock. In spite of the wonders of modern technology, however, no one has realized the dream of inventing a time machine that can halt, reverse, or speed up the passage of time—nor will such a machine ever be designed. For time is the ongoing, unceasing, and irreversible forward march of history.

Yet, in another sense, time does hold still. At least in addition to its one-way horizontal movement, time is intersected vertically by the One who is the same yesterday, today, and forever. Many of us have learned—in a sermon, Bible class or casual chat with a pastor or seminary professor—that in the Greek New Testament there are two distinct words for time. *Chronos*, from which our English words "chronology" and "chronometer" derive, denotes time that can be measured by a clock or by the daily, monthly, and yearly movements of the sun, moon, and stars. *Kairos*, by contrast, points to the deeper significance of time—to its vertical or intersecting and intersect-able nature. Often referred to as "God's time," *kairos* is the word employed when the Bible speaks of the "fullness of time."

In relationship to *chronos*-time, we human ones often feel ourselves to be victims, as did the great hymn writer Isaac Watts, who spoke of time bearing us away into the oblivion of death. If the only marking of time is chronological, then indeed there is literally no ultimate future for us. But for those who cling to the hope of eternity, of a kairotic future beyond clocks and calendars, time is not the bearer-into-oblivion, but rather the way-unto-fulfillment. For those who can see beyond the timepiece, there is an ultimate sense of peace with God and with oneself. While such a peace is personal, it is not merely individual; it belongs to communities, congregations, and even institutions. Such a sense of time is gift and grace. Indeed, all time—both the momentary and the eternal—is a gift from God.

For those who so understand time in these profound and mysterious dual meanings, the future is seen from two vantage points—from behind and from beyond, as seasons yet to come and as a time wherein God has already staked a claim that cannot be reversed. How we live in the present is governed by the way we view the future—as the holder of fearful threats or as coming at us with adventurous opportunities. If seen as threat, then we face the future in fear and trembling, already victims of the perpetrators lurking in the darkness who are bent on doing us harm. But if we see the future as exciting adventure, as time already redeemed by God, then we can understand ourselves as actors called by God into God's great redemptive mission of saving (restoring shalom to) the entire cosmos.

Translating the grand themes of time's dual nature into daily life—and, more particularly and specifically, into churchly communal life—we are faced with tasks to be done, schedules to be established, resources to be garnered, activities to be planned and carried out, budgets to be balanced, schedules to be established, staff to be hired, inspired, and encouraged. In short, we are handed the work of administration! For some in the church, that very word is to be avoided as something tainted or unholy. When it must be done, administrative work is viewed as a necessary evil at worst, bothersome and unrewarding drudgery at best.

The basic premise of this book, the foundation on which we seek to build, is that church administration is a profoundly holy calling, that activities commonly called administration are part and parcel of most ministries, and that one whose work is primarily administrative is no less a faithful servant than those who mostly preach, teach, or counsel. Our English word administrator comes from two Latin roots, *ad + ministrare,* meaning literally "one who ministers to." Thus there is no fundamental distinction between administration and other tasks or manifestations of ministry. To ad-minister is to "add ministry" in any arena, whether ecclesiastical or more secular. It is time for the church to reclaim the holiness of vocations that involve a major measure of administrative work. According to this viewpoint, administration in many arenas—both churchly and "secular"—while burdensome on some days, might be joyful on most.[1]

Because time—a gift of God from creation onward—has been reclaimed in Jesus Christ through the power of the Holy Spirit, we who are borne away by its unrelenting forward march are at the same time bearers of its meaning and shapers of its form and functioning. In that sense, while time rides us as a hard taskmaster drives her steed, we also ride the time as we are entrusted with the reins by the One on whose fields and meadows all time-riders travel.

It is our bold claim that in the very daily demands of ad-ministering a church in one of its expressions—parish, judicatory, national office, agency, or institution—one called to leadership discovers *kairos* in the midst of *chronos,* eternity embedded within momentary duties, the divine hidden amid the mundane. And if such leaders rise to and embrace their administrative callings, they will on occasion capture a feeling or catch a glimmer of the reality of being both borne and bearers, those driven and those called and compelled by God also to sit in the driver's seat for a season.

"Riding time to the end" is an audacious heading for a preface! It could be misunderstood as utter arrogance to presume that we ride and give any direction to *chronos,* let alone serve as agents of the working out of God's good *kairos* in history. But by so entitling this preface to a book about administrative callings in

---

1. For a more thorough treatment of administrative work as part and parcel of spiritual life and ministerial vocation, see: Michael L. Cooper-White, "Administrative Leadership as a Calling of the Spirit," Brooks Schramm and Kirsi Stjerna, eds., *Spirituality: Toward a 21st Century Lutheran Understanding* (Minneapolis: Lutheran University Press, 2005), 147–162.

ecclesiastical settings, we express our belief that the work of setting tables where faith communities feast on holy food, and serving as stage managers for theaters in which the divine drama of salvation is worked out amid the daily lives of ordinary folks, is indeed work unto *kairos*-eternity. But it is work that must be done in *chronos*-time. It is temporal, passing away, yet its temporality does not lessen the importance of doing it well. It is always unfinished, so we indeed keep riding time until the end. In *On Religion*, John D. Caputo writes:

> If the religious sense of life is sometimes thought of in terms of eternity, under the influence of Plato, my advice is to rethink it in terms of time, as a temporary way to be, a way to ride the waves of time, trying to catch its swells while trying not to end up like a drowned rat.[2]

In this book we attempt to cover many of the key topics of interest to those serving in or preparing for administrative leadership. While some areas and examples will be most applicable in parish administration, our hope is that colleagues currently engaged in or aspiring to leadership in church-related agencies and institutions will find valuable insights and guidance for their work as well. We hope the volume will be a helpful textbook for students and their professors in classroom contexts and equally a valuable teaching tool and reference resource for busy administrative practitioners. Beyond sharing good managerial principles and insights from the broad field of administrative practice, our intent is to weave throughout the chapters biblical themes and examples from the history of God's people. In other words, we intend in this book to incorporate a *theology of administration.*

No single volume can address adequately all aspects of the complex and multi-faceted areas treated in the chapters that follow. In many areas, references cited will provide additional resources that further elaborate on key themes and topics. While somewhat arbitrary, the ordering of chapters is intended to offer the reader a brief historical overview of ecclesiastical administration; then provide

---

2. John D. Caputo, *On Religion* (London and New York: Routledge, 2001), 15.

a framework for pondering governance, board work and board-staff relations, planning, budgeting, fund-raising, and general oversight, including personnel matters. Ensuing chapters offer background information and practical suggestions with regard to exercising effective leadership through good communication, dynamic teamwork, and ever-expanding networks. Two topics that would not even have occurred to most authors of church administration materials in previous generations—conflict and legal matters—round out the book, followed by some personal reflections on how a faithful and effective steward-leader might embrace church administration not just as the necessary work but also as my holy calling.

The two of us together have been blessed with opportunities to engage in more than seven decades of ecclesiastical administrative work—as parish pastors, judicatory and national church executives, and consultants to a host of church leaders and organizations in areas of strategic planning, fiscal management, creative use of conflict, and other topics as well. Our callings have included personnel supervision and support for hundreds of coworkers engaged in complex communal workplaces. Our teachers have been legion, including students involved in courses on church administration at Gettysburg and Philadelphia Lutheran Seminaries. Particularly noteworthy are students of the 2006 Gettysburg Seminary course 3.521 (Church Administration, Leadership and Polity) who "field-tested" most of the chapters. Likewise meriting special acknowledgment are several persons—all outstanding administrators in their own right—who kindly read all or portions of manuscript drafts and offered their helpful feedback and suggestions: Shirley Bacher, Emried Cole, Pamela Cooper-White, Phillip Harris, Lita Brusick Johnson, Jennifer Peters McCurry, Eric Shafer, John Spangler, and Marty Stevens.

Acknowledged with gratitude is permission from the New Pig Corporation of Tipton, Pennsylvania, to describe the RealResults® approach to planning included in Chapter 4. Cited frequently are websites of several church bodies, chief among them the Evangelical Lutheran Church in America (http://www.elca.org), and we thank all involved in the design and posting of their vast array of helpful resources.

We hope readers will find helpful the many workbook forms we have created, adapted, and imported into the appendices. They can structure and facilitate your work. We have also created a companion website for the book, at www.churchadm .com, where we have lodged more forms and checklists, study materials, and an interactive feature for mutual conversation and consultation about these topics. Please visit!

We are grateful for the assistance from the editorial staff at Fortress Press, particularly Scott Tunseth, Michael West, and Jessica Puckett, and we are indebted to Augsburg Fortress CEO, Beth Lewis, who urged us to write the book. Hearing of our project, many colleagues, particularly at the Lutheran Theological Seminary at Gettysburg, have encouraged us to persist. We are also indebted to Nancy Vaughn, who typed multiple versions of manuscripts for some of the chapters. Finally, each of the coauthors acknowledges the other as a respected colleague, lively conversant, and fast friend.

In offering this treatment of church administration, the authors acknowledge the limitations of our own social location. Privileged by race and gender within a predominantly middle class and diversity-challenged North American denominational system, we have nevertheless had the opportunity to work in partnership with richly diverse and gifted colleagues whose values, perspectives, and styles of working have challenged and changed us. Our attempts to be broadly inclusive in sharing insights about administrative leadership notwithstanding, all readers will need to engage in a measure of translation, seeking to adapt, apply (or sometimes perhaps even reject) our insights and suggestions for each ministry context.

One means of getting outside the sphere of our own limited social location has been a re-reading of some of Dietrich Bonhoeffer's work during the year commemorating the centennial anniversary of his birth. Readers will find Bonhoeffer's work cited with some frequency, second only to scriptural references. The great German theologian's martyrdom stands as a sobering reminder (for surely Adolf Hitler and the Nazis were efficient organizers) that administration can be used for the most egregious evil as well as for great good. Administrators should always ask themselves, and be critiqued by others, "Are we not just doing things well, but are we doing the *right things?*" Bonhoeffer also inspires through his own recognition of the call to grasp onto the time that is given us, and ride it to the end. Just months before his execution, when if ever the focus might have been on eternity, he wrote of the importance of keeping on with mundane earthly tasks:

The difference between the Christian hope of resurrection and the mythological hope is that the former sends a man [sic] back to his life on earth in a wholly new way. . . . The Christian, unlike the devotees of the redemption myths, has no last line of escape available from earthly tasks and difficulties into the eternal. . . . This world must not be prematurely written off. [3] *yes*

Each of us has been blessed over the years with administrative callings rich in "earthly tasks and difficulties." For several years we served together in the Office of the Presiding Bishop of the Evangelical Lutheran Church in America, entrusted with marvelous opportunities and major responsibilities by Bishops Herbert Chilstrom and H. George Anderson. Together with a handful of other colleagues, we shared the privilege of guiding the day-to-day work of a wonderfully diverse servant corps of persons occasionally branded harshly by some critics as "bureaucrats." To all these faithful, dedicated servants of God, and to our families, who have patiently awaited our homecomings from long days at the office or landings from yet another road trip, we dedicate this book. To all who read it, we extend our hope that you will gain helpful insights, and respond to our invitation to continue the conversation and share your wisdom as you ride and bide the time in your own callings.

---

3. Dietrich Bonhoeffer, *Letters and Papers from Prison* (New York: Macmillan, 1971), 336–37.

CHAPTER 1

Administration's Biography: A Holy History

"But we have this treasure in clay jars [RSV and KJV: "earthen vessels"] so that it may be made clear that this extraordinary power belongs to God and does not come from us."
—*2 Corinthians 4:7*

This book claims that administration and governance are enacted when two or more persons engage in a common purpose under the human condition of temporality—the ongoingness of time. The ecclesiastical history that follows displays the results of faithful followers of Christ attempting to "ride time" prompted not of arrogance and desire to control the exigency of time but birthed from the persistent heeding of God's call. Each period of history to be reviewed shows how the insights of administration in the world have been creatively adopted and adapted for fruitful and competent administration by and in the church.

The Christian story engenders a community. That community occupies space and time. It takes on organizational shape not always the same but constantly in response to how God's call is heard and heeded during certain periods of history.

The goal of the community is not to do administration well. The goal is to be faithful to God's call or, using Paul's language from 2 Corinthians, to rely on the extraordinary power of God—not on our abilities, administrative or otherwise. Administration in the church distinguishes between "treasure" and "clay jars." The clay jars, that is, ourselves (and our artifacts) are engaged in a holy calling, because

God sets us free to be faithful to God's call. That faithfulness is carried out under specific historical, cultural, and social conditions. When God's people express that faithfulness in the world of time and space, a concern for effectiveness arises. When effectiveness is pursued, administration and all that goes with it are inevitable.

Administration has a vocabulary: purpose, coordination, participation, policy, planning, power, authority, conflict, budgeting, structure, leadership, teams, process, bureaucracy, training, roles, evaluation, research, personnel, constituencies, environment, and publics. The brief history of administration in the Christian community that follows identifies the origins of this vocabulary. This history has several features: (a) it is illustrative rather than exhaustive (that would require another book), and is weighted toward the modern period; (b) it closely follows the administrative history of other sectors—private, public, social—because the church has adopted and adapted administrative theory and practice from the world for its own use; and (c) it is a holy history, as these "gifts" from and of the world have been received to serve holy purposes; they focus on the "treasure."

Ecclesiastical Administrative History: Time Traveling

Ancient Greek culture treated transitional moments with great respect. These moments understood as thresholds were so important, both as barrier and point of change, that the god Hermes was assigned to them to guide and advise threshold-travelers. *Threshold* is a more helpful concept for comprehending this particular history than, for example, *phase*, because threshold emphasizes both continuity and change.

The history that follows is not a series of sharp demarcations accompanied by the cry "out with the old, in with the new." In fact, administration, including in the church, has suffered from the thoughtless adoption of new administrative techniques just because they were new. This hopping from fad to fad has left many of the faithful with motion sickness and sometimes loss of confidence in leaders. Threshold seems appropriate because it captures new developments without attempting to discredit old ones. Ecclesiastical administration seems to have traversed seven major thresholds; they are used here to describe our journey through time.

Bible Times and Afterward

The interpretive principle the authors are using (see chapter 2, "Godly Governance," and chapter 3, "Boards: Blessed Balladeers") is a creative reading of the biblical texts for administrative practices with full knowledge that administration is not a primary concern. "But these [signs] are written so that you may come to believe . . ." (John 20:31), not have efficient administration.

There are certain patterns of administration in the Bible, however, and they are instructive even though they should probably not be translated directly into the twenty-first century church (though some have tried to do so and are still trying).

In the Old Testament, the exodus, the rebuilding of the temple, and the wisdom and prophetic literature are illustrative of how "administration" was carried out. As the people of God exit Egypt on the way from bondage to freedom in the new land, they take a census, camp in "regiments," and following God's command, travel in those same administrative units, organized by clan or ancestral house (Num 1:2; 2:1; 2:34). Apparently, statistical analysis and organizing by criteria such as similarity of function, location, history, or process are not new. Likewise "seamless" is a term of current usage to describe an administrative process from start to finish that exhibits no breaks or dysfunctions. Read Nehemiah 3. The rebuilding of the city walls was accomplished by teams working so close to each other on different parts of the wall, for example, the Sheep Gate or Fish Gate, that they formed one perfectly coordinated work force to complete the task in the face of formidable political opposition! In marvelous repetition, this chapter of Nehemiah employs the phrases "next to them" or "after them," naming all forty-four groups engaged in forty-four tasks.

Read Prov 16:1; 16:3; and 16:9 for a theological corrective to overzealous planning of the kind that claims complete certainty and control in the midst of unwieldy organizational and societal forces, "The mind plans. . .but God directs." There is also a word about personal commitment to planning (Prov 16:9). The "wheel within a wheel" image of the prophet Ezekiel has been used by some church administrators as an ancient reference to systems theory. The two of us defer from such a direct reading of the text, but look at Ezek 1:16, 17, "When they moved they moved in any of four directions without veering as they moved." This prophetic vision had an interdependent quality with all the parts (wheels, living creatures) tied together.

The New Testament presents the calling and formation of a group gathered around Jesus. The Twelve were summoned to new tasks and new lives (Matt 10:1-4, Mark 3:16-19, Luke 6:12-16, Acts 1:13). These Twelve were given specific instructions (Matt 10:5-42) on authority, territory, task, time line, rejection, conflict, and equipment. The work unit was "two by two" (Mark 6:7).

Theologian and administrator alike have found guidance in reading about the ways the early Christian community understood itself: "They devoted themselves to the apostolic teaching and fellowship, to the breaking of bread and the prayers" (Acts 2:42). The congregation in which one of us is a member reflects in its mission statement this verse when it promises to equip one another through worship, learning, witness, service, and support.

As the community moves on in time and increased responsibility, the circle is expanded by seven members who engage in food distribution (Acts 6:1-7). Hands were laid on them as a sign of authority and continuity. The issue of how the work (and its administration) *continues* to develop over time as new challenges and opportunities are met, becomes more apparent in any organization, the fledgling Christian community included: "The word of God continued to spread; the number of the disciples increased greatly in Jerusalem, and a great many of the priests became obedient to the faith" (Acts 6:7). An expansion in numbers, territory, and responsibility necessitates corresponding administrative arrangements.

Two incidents are especially revealing about what the community believed, did, and how they made corporate decisions.

Decision Making (Acts 10–15)

The community faces several new situations. The Word has spread and taken hold. More than a single congregation has become involved. Cornelius, the believing Gentile, is placed in their midst. But some "came down from Judea" and taught, "unless you are circumcised according to the custom of Moses, you cannot be saved" (Acts 15:1). Who is the mission for? Who is to be included? Who decides? "The apostles and elders met together (in Jerusalem) to consider this matter" (Acts 15:6).

The main *features* of decision making as witnessed in Acts 10–15 are:

- the assembly of believers plays an active role
- leaders interpret, state, propose, narrate, and pray
- leaders are honored and respected, not worshiped (balance of authority)
- silence and prayer are essential to discernment
- opposing views are given "agenda time"
- personal and pastoral communication of decisions are made
- visitors are commissioned from one part of the church to another (church operates in a wider area, not just local)
- re-reading the Scriptures in the light of experience, James affirms Peter's testimony to salvation for all through "the grace of the Lord Jesus" by reinterpreting the words of the prophet Amos (Acts 15:6-18)
- Scripture has a normative role in decision making and discernment
- there is an understanding of narrative as communal memory
- visions and dreams are shared, used to test and check, give meaning
- the poor are remembered and helped
- God's power is discerned in the patterns of everyday life

In and through these processes, the community seeks a theological outcome: to determine God's intention in the situation. Is Yahweh a local deity or Lord of all? Having found a communal answer to the question, they proceed to develop corresponding strategies for preaching, fellowship, and exercise of authority.

Fund Raising (2 Corinthians 8-9)

> The two letters which emerge before the eyes of the reader show an apostle Paul deeply embroiled in church administration, fiscal problems, and ecumenical strategizing (if that horrible word can be admitted). Here the great theologian that he was reveals himself to be involved with the toughest parts of church leadership: the raising of money for the needy; the establishing of voluntary cooperation among very different people, despite distances and fragile communication; the reconciliation between

churches in different lands and cultures; and last but not least, the preservation of the church as a Christian institution.[1]

Gathering funds in one part of the church for use in another is evidently not new. Second Corinthians 8 and 9 make the case for feeding the hungry in Jerusalem, and Paul wants the money to come from the congregations across Asia Minor. As with most matters of church administration, more is at stake than proper technique. Paul's experience with Christ and the emerging Christian community would not allow him to ignore the need. Nor could the responsibility be delegated. Paul had to lead, and he did so by emphasizing: generosity grounded in grace and joy (8:1, 2, 5, 9; 9:1), zeal not coercion (8:8; 9:2, 7), partnership (8:3, 4; 9:13), visitation (8:6, 16-20, 22-24), challenge (8:10), comparison with the giving of others (8:1, 10-12), fairness (8:13, 14), a contractual agreement (9:13), and thanksgiving (9:11-15). Not bad guidelines for church fund-raising!

As the community experienced the loss of those who had direct connection to Jesus and to those who in turn had contact with them, they faced new issues. Is the movement meant to last more than one or two generations? Having decided (Acts 10–15) to spread out with the gospel for all people, how would they keep in touch? How would discipline be maintained? What teaching was authentic and what was not?

They also encountered questions about leadership. Jerome, an early church leader, formulated the principle, "There can be no church assembly without a leader or team of leaders."[2] The nature of unity raised its head (would Jerusalem and later Rome become centers along the network?). Perhaps the most significant questions emerged around the concept of apostolicity as the community carried on in the name of Jesus. What were the apostolic characteristics of proclamation, liturgy and *diakonia*? The nature of the church: "not isolated entities but bound together in love" and ministry not as status but service—these were on the minds and agendas of God's people in the postbiblical period.[3]

---

1. Hans Dieter Betz, *2 Corinthians 8 and 9: A Commentary on Two Administrative Letters of the Apostle Paul; Hermeneia* (Philadelphia: Fortress Press, 1985), xii.

2. Edward Schillebeeck, *Ministry: Leadership in the Community of Jesus Christ* (New York: Crossroad, 1981), 1.

3. Ibid., 36–37.

At this point, a threshold is reached. The church becomes established and new administrative tasks are attached.

The Empire Strikes Back

Emperor Constantine had an agenda. His Edict of Milan in 313 licensing the Christian cult took on new impetus when he declared himself to be more than defender of the faith; he was a soldier of the cross. What began as a new era of spiritual freedom for all took on the project of a Christian commonwealth.[4]

The faith buttressed by state sanction, law, and even force brought on at least two administrative quagmires. Hierarchical, political, social, and military structures were mirrored by the church. One historian of administration, Donald Wren, claims that the church dealt with its administrative challenges during this period by engaging in what would today be called a search for the appropriate degree of centralization and decentralization, what would be decided in Rome, and what would be allowed, regionally and locally.[5]

Governance during this period ran on the divine right of rulers, the authority of the church, and the vigor and discipline of the military. A modern (until lately) organization chart in the form of a pyramid is derived from the army in-the-field advancing toward the enemy turned on its side (▶ to ▲).

Administrative forms, however, were not uniformly adopted when Constantine's edict was enacted. There is the usual gap (operative today as well) between what is on paper and what takes place "on the ground."[6] A rich diversity of practice over the expanse of Europe and the Middle East continued to flourish during the next two centuries. There was geographical (and psychological) distance between Rome and, for example, a rural parish in Ireland, as there is today between the

---

4. Charles N. Cochrane, *Christianity and Classical Culture* (New York: Oxford Univ. Press, 1957), 177–86.

5. David Wren, *The Evolution of Management Thought* (New York: Ronald Press, 1972), 18–19.

6. We are indebted to Lita Brusick Johnson for this insight.

United States-based Protestant Church "Headquarters" (New York, Chicago, Nashville, etc.) and a congregation in Four Corners, Texas.

A second administrative development is more subtle than mirrored hierarchy, but perhaps in the long run more influential. The historian-politician Eusebius's interpretation of the triumph of the church during this time as "the hand of God" in human history laid the groundwork for an error with us even today—that Christianity is a success-philosophy evidenced by the approximation of the divine in the authoritative rule of the Christian prince.[7] Church administrators are forewarned about the dangers of administrative glory-rides moving from success to success. Administration at its best is congruent with the message of grace and love flowing from the real top of the pyramid, Jesus Christ.

Whether the fifth to the sixteenth century is called "the dark ages" or "the golden years," it was a remarkable period of church history. It was the time of Augustine, Charlemagne, Frederick Barbarossa, Popes Innocent III, Boniface VIII, and the Gregories, the Holy Roman Empire, the Crusades, mysticism, and monasticism. For the purpose of ecclesiastical administrative history, the rise of *religious orders* deserves to be noted as alternative communities that nurtured the faith and provided a degree of safety from the monumental struggle for domination by church and/or state, although some orders were fully involved in struggles between abbots and secular nobles.

A reminder is in order that there always have been, are now, and will be communities of Christian folk who hover around the edges of the official church structure, sometimes picking up a forgotten piece of mission, bringing a needed theological critique, or voicing a set of unpopular (at the time) views. One of us knows a Roman Catholic priest who from the relative safety of his religious order advocates the ordination of women and the marriage of priests. An administrative implication is to appreciate the variety of communities linked in one way or another, formally and informally, to the church organization chart.

The church did not remain established, and there are both tight and loose couplings of church and state around the world today. The church was soon to be cut loose to fare for itself. This movement toward disestablishment marks another threshold.

---

7. Cochrane, *Christianity and Classical Culture*, 184–85.

Reformation and Administration: An Oxymoron?

Administration during the time of the Reformation? How many articles or books are there on the subject? The two of us cannot locate any such material. We suspect this situation has to do with the takeover of existing structures rather than the creation of new ones by Reformation adherents, especially in England and the Scandinavian countries. There is one figure, however, who learned how to address the *new* situation the Reformation events were creating, namely, Johannes Bugenhagen.

Visitors to Reformation sites in Wittenberg, Germany, might miss the statue in the little garden to one side of the city church. There the visitor will find a bust of Johannes Bugenhagen, pastor of this congregation from 1522 to 1558. Less known than his colleagues (he is sometimes called The Third Reformer), Martin Luther and Philip Melanchthon, Bugenhagen has nevertheless been awarded the title "organizer of the Reformation" by his foremost American biographer.[8]

While the focus here is on his administrative acumen, Bugenhagen taught at the university; wrote scholarly biblical studies; served as Luther's pastor, adviser, and confidant (also encourager during Luther's "down times"); conducted the marriage of Katherine and Martin; and preached at Luther's funeral.

Bugenhagen provided feet for the Reformation. He developed church orders for governing the life of the emerging church, visited many town councils (there was still a hefty degree of establishment) in Northern Germany and Denmark, urging them to care for pastors, develop community fund-raising and distribution systems for the poor, and provide quality education for children and young adults. He took the theological genius of Luther and applied it in practical ways at a crucial time in the life of the vulnerable Reformation movement.

Bugenhagen's legacy as an administrator includes the ability to use Paul's distinction between "treasure" and "clay jars." When Luther returned from his exile in the Wartburg Castle, he preached eight sermons in the city church in eight days. Luther was attempting to rescue the new movement from "excesses" of reform led by those who took over during his absence. Luther provided the theology, similar to Paul's distinction, insisting that there be no confusion between "musts" (faith,

---

8. Kurt K. Hendel, "Johannes Bugenhagen, Organizer of the Lutheran Reformation," *Lutheran Quarterly* 18 (2004), 43–75.

gospel, love) and "choices" (everything else). Bugenhagen kept the Reformation on track by developing a set of administrative tenets true to the "musts" (also called "necessities") and which served as an answer to the inquiry, "What, then, should we do?" Addressing some of the thorny problems the Reformation faced, he provided clarity and specific actions on the support of pastors, schools, and the plight of the poor (some of whom were pastors), but failed to establish a pension fund, although not for lack of effort. New initiatives, especially one as significant as the Reformation, require corresponding and creative administrative steps to promulgate and sustain. Bugenhagen deserves more attention. He is named here as a major contributor to the development of ecclesiastical administration.

An Interlude

Before moving to the next threshold, a comment is in order. Up to this juncture, church administration has served very traditional inclinations. The church (and society), even after major shifts brought on by the Reformation both in Germany and England, still operated within certain authority schemes and even authoritarian measures especially around gender, the nature of leadership, and fund raising. The case of Luther's wife, Katherine von Bora, illustrates both the changes and the authoritarian tradition. The delightful byplay between Katherine and Martin provides an interesting study in what was "blowing in the wind" around changes in attitudes toward gender. A wonderful statue of Katy stands next to the Luther House in Wittenberg. She is forcefully striding through an arch, obviously a person in her own right. Yet at Luther's death, Katherine was victimized by the male-dominated inheritance laws.

The remainder of this ecclesiastical history focuses primarily on the New World and illustrates more *democratic* impulses in administrative practice, although there was (and is) a long way to go on gender, race, and authority.

A glimpse of what was to come is provided in the work of an early religious pioneer in the New World, Henry Melchior Muhlenberg. He was a thoroughgoing traditionalist, and his work was sponsored by the nobility in Germany. As he encountered practical administrative needs stemming from the planting of congregations along his travel routes up and down the east coast of the United States, however, Muhlenberg showed a remarkable propensity for a balanced view of authority, especially the relation of pastor and laity. In fact, his intent is probably also aimed at curtailing the ministerial abuse of authority, including so-called pseudo-pastors who operated with self-determined "ordination." In 1762 (25 years before the American Federal Constitution), Muhlenberg prepared a constitution for St. Michael's Lutheran Church in Philadelphia:

> When any important or weighty matter arises in the congregation, of whatsoever kind, whether within or without the church, whether it concerns the parsonage or the school house, the church yard or the burial place, it shall not be decided by the Pastors alone; but it must be carefully and well considered by the whole Church Council, and be approved by at least two-thirds of their whole number, and after that be laid before the whole congregation, and approved by two-thirds of the communicant members of the congregation, especially when it demands contributions from members.[9]

These kinds of participatory arrangements foreshadowed the changes taking place in matters of administration in church and society, changes that blossomed in the United States during the 1920s and 1930s, and whose effects are still being felt today.

The Triumph of Rationality (Temporarily)

The time-traveler making her or his way through the history of ecclesiastical administration encounters a fourth threshold spawned by the increased use of science in academia and everyday life. The Enlightenment in Europe and its effects in the New Republic celebrated the role and use of *reason* to solve problems,

---

9. Faith E. Rohrbough, "The Political Maturation of Henry Melchior Muhlenberg," *Lutheran Quarterly* 10/4 (Winter 1996), 397. This congregation constitution also illustrates how church administration is contextual. Muhlenberg: "There has been repeated and growing demand for an external form of church government suitable to the needs of this land."

meet challenges, and decide truth as well. As industrialization advanced and as commerce changed from a feudal to a national and international system, the factory emerged as a new vehicle for the production of goods and wealth. The factory became the incubator for new administrative processes. A new consciousness about administration was developing and scientific rationality was its driver.

Among the many exemplars of this new mood and method, four are named here: Max Weber (1864–1920), Frederick Taylor (1856–1915), Luther Gulick (1892–1993), and Chester Barnard (1886–1961). The common assumption behind the work of these four and of others who sought to make administration more rational was that it was a *universal* phenomenon, the dynamics of which are basically context-free, and that its underlying principles can be known and applied.

Max Weber called attention to the transition from nineteenth-century "family" capitalism to big governmental departments and large-scale industry organizations. His description of bureaucracy as an "ideal" was largely misunderstood as advocacy, instead of what he intended it to be: a descriptive term. Weber's eloquent descriptions of bureaucracy provided a rational basis for understanding organizations, especially as authority systems seeking ever-greater efficiency.[10] The rigor of scientific method pushes toward context-free truth. That same method employed in the study of administration is expected to uncover timeless principles that are teachable to all. Frederick Taylor's model of administration earned in the 1920s the moniker "scientific management." He developed supervisory protocols based on detailed analysis of the movements of a factory worker shoveling iron ore into a furnace or the ways for the military to keep track of its vast inventory of items. The questions were, "What is the optimal load of ore per shovel movement? How long should it take to shovel X amount of iron ore, and what financial rewards should there be?" Later this approach was called "time and motion study"; its legacy is found today in the field of industrial engineering. Every time an administrative process is examined to increase efficiency by breaking down its component parts for analysis, as in such contemporary improvement

---

10. Max Weber, *The Theory of Social and Economic Organization* (New York: The Free Press, 1947); *The Protestant Ethic and the Spirit of Capitalism* (New York: Charles Scribner's Sons, 1938); Arthur Mitzman, *The Iron Cage: An Historical Interpretation of Max Weber* (New York: Grosset & Dunlap, 1969).

programs like re-engineering or total quality management, you can see old Fred Taylor smiling.[11]

Luther Gulick's study of public administration led him to believe that the universality of administration consisted of seven components: planning, organizing, staffing, directing, coordination, reporting, and budgeting (as an aid-to-memory, he dubbed his model POSDCORB). Manuals of this time, and even later into the decades of the 40s, 50s, and 60s, used this model, or parts of it, to describe the "unchanging" aspects of church administration.[12]

Chester Barnard's book *The Function of the Executive* (twenty-four printings by 1974) shared the basic assumption of universal application but opened up new topics for consideration: authority as reciprocity between leader and led (the theory of authority acceptance), organization as formal and informal systems, the difference between effectiveness and efficiency, the nature of accountability, treating people fairly and with respect, and anticipating the use of systems thinking defining an organization as "a system of consciously coordinated activities or forces of two or more persons."[13]

It is not that the rigors of the scientific method were pursued; rather it was the structure of the method that influenced the practice of administration. A wide variety of problem-solving and planning models stem from this period, the basic outlines still operating today: data gathering, analysis, issue identification, goal-setting, action, and evaluation. The assumption behind the use of these steps in attacking problems and planning futures is that, since the universe is a rational place, proper thinking in a careful and sequential order will yield desired outcomes.

Church administration made widespread use of these models. It was a heady time, pun intended. One of us was involved in a parish development project in the 1970s, the features of which were Looking at Where We Are, Developing Ministry Objectives and Priorities, Deciding on Plans for Ministry, Carrying out the Plans,

11. Frederick W. Taylor, *The Principles of Scientific Management* (New York: Harper & Row, 1911); *Shop Management* (New York: Harper & Row, 1903).

12. Luther Gulick, "Notes on the Theory of Organization," in Luther Gulick and Ludwig Urwick, eds., *Papers on the Science of Administration* (New York: Institute of Public Administration, 1937), 15–31.

13. Chester Barnard, *The Function of the Executive* (Boston: Harvard Univ. Press, 1938 and 1968), 73.

Evaluating Progress, and Going Forward. The church in all its expressions—congregation, middle judicatories, national offices, related institutions and international bodies—pursued versions of the *rationalistic* assumption. It was a great time for initials: Management by Objectives (MBO), Planning Programming, Budgeting Systems (PPBS), and Program Evaluation and Review Technique (PERT).

The church should have known better, given its theology about the human condition, but it seemed to fall into the same traps of over-expectation and hype as other institutions in adopting these systems. The Rational Model seeks out True Believers. The wreckage is considerable on the days *after* a spate of hyper-claims.

But this history is getting ahead of itself. A slight detour is necessary to pick up the fifth threshold that in turn paves the way for the final two.

Human Nature Rediscovered

Hints at the arrival of this next threshold are found in the insights of Chester Barnard and Mary Parker Follett (1868–1933). Describing authority and leadership as reciprocal, that is, cooperation between leader and follower, Barnard was paving the road for an understanding of administration that took seriously the *social* nature of human beings. Follett proved to be ahead of her time by picturing goal-attainment through coordination and cooperation, the resolution of conflict through integration of common interests, and obeying the "law of the situation" as an alternative to "power-over" others. She suffered the charges of being iconoclastic for her accurate anticipation of a more humanistic treatment of employees.[14]

As a research team from Harvard studied the effects of varying degrees of illumination on the task of wiring a bank installation, a funny thing happened. It was the late 1920s, and they were in the Hawthorne Western Electric plant near Cicero, Illinois. Everyone knows that a team of workers can't perform such an intricate job of electrical wiring in virtual darkness. But they did. The counterintuitive discovery was that task performance and amount of illumination were totally unrelated. The dynamics of the *group* and the positive effect of being studied

---

14. Pauline Graham, ed., *Mary Parker Follett: Prophet of Management* (Boston, MA: Harvard Business School Press, 1996), 36–37.

(given attention, later called "The Hawthorne Effect") were the critical variables in "explaining" what happened.

This and other studies and experiences quickly bloomed into a full-blown industry at first dedicated to knowledge about group behavior and then to disseminating the new findings through workshops, conferences, university courses and degrees, consultants, books, articles and T-groups (T stands for training). New attention was given to such topics as groups in the work place, motivation, task groups, job redesign, job enlargement, conflict theory and resolution, inter-group behavior, and the training of group leaders. More recently, this line of administrative practice has led to self-directed work teams and communities of practice (learning groups). From an original interest in understanding and improving group functioning in general, the circle has widened to include groups for a variety of purposes—introduce change, deepen learning, perform complex tasks, coordinate disparate pieces of a process, develop new projects, and create or recreate vision.

It would be hard to over-estimate the effects and use of small-group theory, practice, and training on church administration. Over the next six decades, there was an explosion of group activities in the church: the use of small groups in congregations; the group dynamics of boards, committees, and task forces; improving multiple staff relationships; and more participatory teaching methods in academic and congregational classrooms. A cascade of books, articles, and pamphlets on groups has descended on the church and its leaders. It would be impossible to count the manuals for training group leaders and guiding group development in church settings. The bookshelves of the two of us are resplendent with the publications resulting from the small-group phenomenon.

The sum total of group activity does not, however, capture the fullness of an organization, its identity and mission. That realization led to a different set of concepts and practices for administration.

Systems: The Eternal Dance of the Parts and the Whole

Through most of the twentieth century, administration received its marching orders from three basic ways to comprehend organization: machine, organism, and system.

An organization as a machine leads to such expressions as "well-oiled," "runs like a clock," "keep the train on the tracks," or "running a tight ship." This image or metaphor was popular during the scientific management era and is the image of choice for those who favor well-controlled no-surprise "outfits" (military image).

Organization as organism attempts to overcome the deficiencies of the machine image by attributing more features related to growth, adaptation, or even human capacities such as thinking and imagining. The recent emphasis on organizational health is grounded in this image. Though the New Testament contains around one hundred images of the church, a favored one is church as body. We are bodies. We have bodies, so we connect to this kinder and gentler comparison. There are limits, however; for example, parts of the body do not walk away as do individuals from organizations. The limits of machine and organism images give rise to the third one: system. System relates the parts to the whole in an interactive fashion that does not cancel out the distinctiveness of each part but highlights its role and contribution to the whole. Systems morph into other systems over time. Systems are complex or simple, open or closed. They have purpose, generate corrective feedback, and convert *input* into *throughput* resulting in *output*. Systems thinking points to the "more than" quality of a collective—the whole is more than the total of its parts. A good basketball team builds on the strengths of its individual players and compensates for their weaknesses, becoming something more than can be explained by just adding up the contribution of individual players.

One student of systems suggests that there is an administrative disease called "system blindness." It has four forms: spatial (seeing one part but not the whole), temporal (seeing the present but not the past: Where did all this come from?), relational (seeing the self as an isolated entity, missing relationships, connections), and process (seeing our part without comprehending how the whole system works, leading to turf warfare and groupthink).[15]

Similar to the proliferation of group-oriented materials and training, systems models and thinking have been widely employed in church administration. From many possible examples, here are three. Typical of church administration literature

---

15. Barry Oshry, *Seeing Systems: Unlocking the Mysteries of Organization Life* (San Francisco: Barrett-Koehler, 1995), xii–xiv.

in the 1960s and 1970s is an issue of *The Journal of Pastoral Psychology*.[16] Seven articles give the impression that the church has much to learn about administration from the business world: administration is more about process than structure; administrative skills can be learned; conflict and ways to deal with it need to be more central; and the systems model has more potential for viable church administration than the rationality or group model.

For a thorough treatment of ministry "as a system," take a look at *The Management of Ministry*.[17] Topics are leadership, community, reason for being, organization, and structure. Marketing experts see the "congregational system" as prime territory for the use of marketing concepts and techniques with special attention given to the "environment" of the congregation. One diagram depicts the relevant "publics" of the congregation—sixteen of them![18] A recent development is the employment of MBA graduates of prestigious business schools as marketing experts on the staff of mega-congregations.

Institutions-R-Us

The seventh threshold is a progressive application of the systems model: institutionalization. This threshold is a good example of the crossover effect, namely, that two or even three thresholds can operate at the same time, mutually reinforcing each other. Armed with all the benefits of previous thresholds—rationality, group behavior, systems thinking—it became possible to *build* institutions, complex and widespread enough to cover a large territory, deliver many goods and services, and innovate at astonishing speed. The wisdom and skill to accomplish this have sometimes been grouped under the heading *organizational development* (OD). This collection of experience, research, learning, and training is a

---

16. Alvin J. Lindgren, ed., "Pastoral Psychology and Church Administration," *Pastoral Psychology*, September 1969.

17. James O. Anderson and Ezra Earl Jones, *The Management of Ministry: Leadership, Purpose, Structure, Community* (San Francisco: Harper & Row, 1978).

18. Norman Shawchuck, Philip Kotler, Bruce Wrenn, and Gustave Rath, *Marketing for Congregations* (Nashville: Abingdon, 1992), 95.

formidable force in institution building. Many church administrators received their training in this field and found the concepts and tools easily applicable in their work and callings.

For institution builders, boundaries of nation, coast, ocean, desert, mountain range, culture, politics, and history, though still powerful, are simply challenges to be overcome. Managing across boundaries is the nature of institutional leadership today. One study of leadership contrasts the leader of the village in the valley as protector from "them," the unknown but highly suspicious occupants of the valley on the "other side" of the mountain with today's leader living on "the connective edge" as bridge builder, reconciler across boundaries, real and imagined.[19] The impulse toward church institutionalization made possible by new models, concepts, resources, and skills operated as early as the eighteenth and nineteenth centuries in the United States.

As the American church became more confident in its ability to move beyond survival to faithful effectiveness in the midst of the swirling societal forces of the nineteenth century, a series of leaders emerged who recognized the necessity of institutions to carry out a vigorous and full understanding of Christian witness and mission. Each Christian tradition that has been around for a while on American soil can name and celebrate these leaders. For example, the oldest Lutheran seminary in the United States celebrated its 175th anniversary in 2001. Begun in 1826 by Samuel Simon Schmucker, it has spawned a long line of those who engage in "public ministry."[20] The seminary's current president continues this tradition as he interprets to contemporary students "a full mission at the crossroads" in these words,

> Sun-filled sanctuaries where the Sacrament is served from silver
> vessels on Sunday are no more sacred than soup kitchens where

---

19. Jean Lipman-Blumen, *The Connective Edge: Leading in an Interdependent World* (San Francisco: Jossey-Bass, 1996), 8–16.

20. Frederick K. Wentz, ed., *Witness at the Crossroads: Gettysburg Lutheran Seminary Servants in the Public Life* (Gettysburg Penn.: Lutheran Theological Seminary at Gettysburg, 2001), 41–53.

holy suppers are served in Styrofoam and sipped from plastic
spoons at Saturday's midnight setting.[21]

This institution's location on Seminary Ridge in Gettysburg, Pennsylvania,
is a living reminder of the symbolic and actual role it has played in public life.
During the Civil War's Battle of Gettysburg, the seminary's "old dorm" was used
as lookout and later hospital for Confederate and Union soldiers. Its graduates
have fanned out over the land to serve congregations as well as build institutions
where church and world intersect. Since the organizing of social services by William Passavant in the eastern United States during the mid-nineteenth century,
many of the seminary's graduates have been leaders in social ministry organizations that continue to flourish. Today, nearly 300 of these social-service agencies
band together under an umbrella called Lutheran Services in America (LSA), with
combined budgets equal to Catholic Relief and surpassing the Red Cross.

Another "institutionalizer" in frontier America was Henry Melchior Muhlenberg, who orchestrated the first Lutheran "ministerium" in 1748. Muhlenberg's
initiative (after several failures by colleagues to organize something beyond local
congregations) is now seen as the first "synod" (middle judicatory) that brought
together clergy and laity to consider "regularized, credible ordination of persons
for the ministry, acceptance of the Lutheran Confessions as the basis for beliefs and
practices, and a common form of worship." Muhlenberg stated the rationale in his
opening address: "A twisted cord of many threads will not easily break."[22]

The institutionalizers recognized that congregations and a loose or informal
linkage would not suffice; there had to be places where the church would marshal
its resources in a concerted way for leadership preparation and service ministries.
While these entities were "of the church" they soon began to interface and intersect with other publics, including governmental regulatory agencies and funding

---

21. Introduction by Michael L. Cooper-White in *Leading the Way in Church
and Society* (Gettysburg: Office of Communication, Lutheran Theological Seminary at Gettysburg, 2004), 4.

22. Helmut T. Lehmann, *Missioner Extraordinary* (Wescosville, PA: The
Northeastern Pennsylvania Synod of the Evangelical Lutheran Church in America, 1991), 8.

sources. These institutions today are at the forefront of the church's "boundary spanning" as they hold multiple accountabilities. An academic institution of the church, for example, because of accreditation and its public status, must satisfy not only its churchly constituency but also its counterparts in academia, as well as state departments of education and federal agencies that monitor, for example, financial aid administration. Likewise, social ministry organizations must meet a whole host of regulatory requirements; some of the larger ones have full-time "compliance officers"—and their work does not consist of assuring doctrinal purity! These phenomena are yet another kind of other-ness beyond "loving one's neighbor." This recognition has led church bodies to define themselves theologically and ecclesiastically to include this institutional work as ministry and mission.

> This church shall receive, establish, and support congregations,
> ministries, organizations, institutions, and agencies necessary to
> carry out God's mission through this church; establish support,
> and recognize institutions and agencies that minister to people
> in spiritual and temporal needs; lift its voice in concord and
> work in concert with forces for good, to serve humanity, coop-
> erating with church and other groups participating in activities
> that promote justice, relieve misery and reunite the estranged;
> and establish and maintain theological seminaries, schools, col-
> leges, ministries, and other educational institutions to equip
> people for leadership and service in church and society.[23]

Crossing this threshold took the church back into the *world* institutionally in ways that had not happened since the Reformation. Happening at the same time as crossing this institutionalizing threshold was greater attention to gender and multicultural inclusiveness. Today more and more women and people of color occupy administrative posts. The debate continues about gendered, ethnic, and racial leadership styles. For example, the old classification of nurturing female

---

23. Excerpts from section 4.03 of the *Constitution, Bylaws and Continuing Resolutions of the Evangelical Lutheran Church in America* (Chicago: Evangelical Lutheran Church in America, 2005).

leader versus hard-driving task-attainment male leader are giving way to more mixed characterizations for both sexes. Does gender make a difference? One study found that groups engaged in creative tasks led by a woman do better. Another study done of females and males in the *same* group did not reveal any differences related to task and maintenance functions. One generalization drawn from these and other studies is that operating in an interdependent fashion, while not exclusively a trait of female leaders, is very strong.[24] Katherine Luther would perhaps be remembered differently if she were a contemporary figure.

Administration and Imagination

Seven thresholds have formed the markers for our journey through the history of ecclesiastical administration: the Bible and the immediate centuries afterward, the establishment of the church, Reformation effects, the temporary victory of rationality, new discoveries of human behavior in groups, systems thinking and models, and institutionalization. At every step of this journey, the illustrations provided have shown that the practices of each of these periods have not been left behind. The discoveries and wisdom of each period are still very much with us today. As administration and its holy counterpart, church administration, have progressed, the distinctive breakthroughs in theory and practice of each threshold are still at work.

On what threshold do we stand today? All of those cited, and maybe one more. An example of the direction administrative theory and practice in the early part of century twenty-one takes is found in the work of a handful of theorists (for example, Gareth Morgan and Karl Weick) as they lobby for a more imaginative approach to things administrative. They argue that organizations are not physical objects but social constructions of our making, and therefore can be shaped and guided by communal imagination. They believe that new opportunities and fresh directions are missed as administrators are imprisoned in temporal mental images that bind rather than set free the imagination, talent, and wills of those involved in a collective effort.[25]

---

24. Found in Lipman-Blumen, *The Connective Edge*, 287–92.

25. Karl E. Weick, *The Social Psychology of Organizing* (Reading, MA: Addison-Wesley, 1969).

One advocate suggests that a starting point is to be aware of the rich reper-
toire of images of organized work:

- machines—interlocking parts to reach a well-defined goal
- organism—meeting needs and environmental demands
- brain—information processing, learning, intelligence
- cultures—ideas, values, norms, rituals, beliefs
- politics—interests, conflicts, power plays
- psychic prisons—trapped in preoccupations, thoughts, ideas, beliefs (some unconscious)
- flux and transformation—logic of change, shaping social life
- domination—exploitative aspects of organization, imposition of will on others[26]

The intent of such a list is to loosen up ways of thinking about organizations
and their administration to the end that thinking might match the complexity of
the situation. One implication is an increased emphasis on vision casting and shared
purpose and less on mechanisms to control human behavior. A second implication
is that technological innovation *will* transform the way administrators function.
The two of us are not strong for forecasting, but the future will bring more networked, technology-based communication and organizational systems. There will
be (already is) a strong emphasis on organizational learning, sort of a learn-as-you-
go approach. A recent book on denominational futures makes this claim:

> Very soon, the organizations of national offices (and perhaps
> regional agencies too) may be more virtual ("click") and less
> physical ("mortar"). Perhaps even the physical necessity of a
> central office will diminish. In the future, a new "organizational
> architecture" will emerge tied more to agreed-upon purposes
> than physical space. We think this may be very exciting and call

---

26. Gareth Morgan, *Images of Organization* (Newbury Park, CA: Sage, 1986),
11–17.

for a kind of thinking not yet imagined. At the same time, we are not at all sure about what this means to our conception of a community of people working and living together. "Gathering" together may take new forms, which may well call for new "structures." Is it possible to have a "virtual" church?[27]

Earlier a reference was made to the approximately one hundred images of the church in the New Testament. Ecclesiastical administration could benefit from the exploration and application of this rich and deep reservoir of Christian wisdom. Such an endeavor would prepare the church to receive a great gift: freedom to hear and respond to God's holy call today and tomorrow.

But you are a chosen race, a royal priesthood, a holy nation, God's own people, in order that you may proclaim the mighty acts of God who called you out of darkness into his marvelous light. (1 Pet 2:9)

27. Robert Bacher and Kenneth Inskeep, *Chasing Down A Rumor: The Death of Mainline Denominations* (Minneapolis: Augsburg Books, 2005), 139.

CHAPTER 2

Godly Governance

All power in the Church belongs to our Lord Jesus Christ, its head. All actions of this church are to be carried out under his rule and authority.[1]

Good governance has eight major characteristics. It is participatory, consensus oriented, accountable, transparent, responsive, effective and efficient, equitable and inclusive, and follows the rule of law. It assures that corruption is minimized, that the views of minorities are taken into account, and that the voices of the most vulnerable in society are heard in decision-making. It is also responsive to the present and future needs of society.[2]

How are we going to make an important decision that lies before us? Who will ultimately define the mission and determine the course of our

---

1. *Constitution, Bylaws and Continuing Resolutions of the Evangelical Lutheran Church in America 3.01* (Chicago: Evangelical Lutheran Church in America, 2005), 20.

2. United Nations Economic and Social Commission for Asia and the Pacific: Human Settlements, "What Is Good Governance?" (http://www.unescap.org/huset/gg/governance.htm).

congregation or other ministry? With unlimited possibilities to meet unending needs of countless persons in the community where God has called us to serve, and with very limited resources and energy, how can we make a difference? When there's a crisis, how will we cope, and who will guide us through to the other side of the current conflict?

Asking such questions plunges a group or community into matters that can broadly be defined as *governance*. Literally, of course, to govern means "to make policy" or "to control actions and behavior." Our English word *govern* comes from a Greek verb, *kybernao,* meaning to steer or direct; its nominative form, *kybernēsis,* is used for a ship's pilot or helmsman. Direction setting, with all its complex aspects and multiple dimensions, is the role and responsibility of those entrusted with governance. In a Christian community, the mission is ultimately God's, and the directions set by those in governance should be in accord with Jesus Christ's call to discipleship.

There are as many forms of governance as there are families, communities, congregations, townships, counties, states, and nations. While there are a limited number of basic governance patterns and organizational archetypes, every group or organization has to determine its own processes for carrying out work, resolving problems, garnering resources, and making decisions.

Unless one is creating a new organizational entity from the ground up, upon entering a congregation or joining a faith community, it is important to discover the existing structures and styles for decision making and direction-setting. In most cases, the ultimate authority is an annual congregational meeting where all voting members (however they are defined) receive and approve reports and decide the big issues like budget, building expansion or major repairs. Unless a minister is appointed by the bishop or other ecclesiastical authority, most congregations also reserve to an all-member meeting the election of a pastor.

While a small community can function on an ongoing basis with governance exercised by all its members as a kind of "committee of the whole," in larger contexts some form of representative governance is established whereby policies are determined, planning is carried out, and monitoring of programs and fiscal performance is achieved. In congregations, an elected council, board, vestry, session (or whatever the appropriate ecclesiastical terminology may be) has responsibility for month-to-month oversight of the ministry between annual or semi-annual congregational meetings.

Why Is Governance Necessary?

> "We don't need all this formal business-like stuff, do we? We're just one big happy family and in my family we don't talk about 'governance'—we just love and look after one another."

> "In my mind, being so managerial or bureaucratic has no place in the church. We're God's people and we can trust that God is leading us. Didn't Jesus say, 'Don't worry about tomorrow'? Doesn't that mean we can just take one day at a time and trust that God will guide us?"

> "In our church, we trust our pastor and the other staff members. We know they make good decisions in the best interests of the whole congregation. We do have a board of deacons, but we wouldn't really need to have them and from what I can see they really don't have much to do."

Have you encountered such attitudes and viewpoints in your life in the church? Do you perhaps personally subscribe to these or similar perspectives? Why indeed do congregations and other forms of the church need governance structures and processes?

First, governing structures and processes are needed to select, sanction, legitimize, evaluate, and hold accountable pastoral (or executive) and other staff leadership. Following appropriate processes described in constitutions, bylaws and/or policy documents, those involved in governance choose who will be empowered to exercise leadership in a community of faith. To any would-be accusers who assert that a leader gained his or her position by manipulation or through self-promotion and power-grabbing, the vestry, council, or board can respond forthrightly, "Not so, we chose this person, and we authorize and give legitimacy to our leader."

Forged in a time when much was up for grabs (in large measure because of their challenging and ultimately defying the established authority of the Roman Catholic hierarchy), the Lutheran reformers of the sixteenth century set forth their basic beliefs about theology and the church in a document called the Augsburg Confession (1530). One of its key tenets is that legitimate leadership in the church involves the issuance of a "proper call" by a community of faith (Article XIV)[3]. That is, an inspired individual who feels a spiritual call from God must have that call legitimized through orderly preparation (usually involving a lengthy educational process) and election (the issuance of a call), following proper ecclesiastical endorsement.

While there have been informal processes of assessing "the preacher" since preaching first began, in recent decades more formal periodic pastoral and program staff evaluations have been carried out by many congregations. When ill-conceived or carried out improperly, such "pastoral evaluations" can do more harm than good. But when broadened to include the concept of "assessing our entire ministry as a congregation, including those aspects carried out by the pastor," such *mutual ministry* evaluations can provide affirmation and identify opportunities for a leader's continuing education, as well as ways the entire congregation can better support its pastoral leader.[4]

In the occasional instance of poor leadership performance, or even pastoral malfeasance and misconduct, a key role for those exercising governance is to carry out appropriate measures of coaching, corrective action, or ultimately separation of the leader from her or his ministry in that context. In most traditions, this latter step will generally require the involvement of a bishop or other ecclesiastical authority working in partnership with the governing board. If there is no established legitimate governance authority or if those occupying governance roles abdicate their responsibilities, an unaccountable leader-gone-astray can continue wreaking great harm in the life of a faith community.

---

3. "Concerning church government it is taught that no one should publicly teach, preach, or administer the sacraments without a proper [public] call." Robert Kolb and Timothy J. Wengert, eds., *The Book of Concord: The Confessions of the Evangelical Lutheran Church* (Minneapolis: Fortress Press, 2000), 46.

4. For a description of mutual ministry, see *Pastor and People: Making Mutual Ministry Work; Congregational Leader Series* (Minneapolis: Augsburg Fortress, 2003).

A second critical role for governance in a church or any organization is to steward the overall mission entrusted by God to that community. Initially, as a community is forming, and periodically throughout its life, those charged with governance should engage in prayerful discernment of just what is the mission. This goes beyond voicing broad platitudes and generalities (which unfortunately is the case with many congregational mission statements following months of meetings to craft them!). While "to love God and serve the whole world" is a laudable mission statement, no one faith community can carry it out single-handedly. "To love God, serve several hundred of God's people in the Pico-Union neighborhood, join with others in a number of service ministries, and to advocate for greater justice in two or three critical areas" may indeed be a realistic mission statement.

Over time, a community's mission may well change as the context in which it serves changes, and as the gifts and resources offered by members are also constantly in flux. Accordingly, it is the role of those engaged in governance to reassess the overall mission, make appropriate adjustments, and establish realistic goals. We will say much more about this important aspect of governance in a later chapter on planning.

A third critical role for those involved in governance is to manage things in a time of crisis, especially if the crisis involves the key administrative leadership. An issue of a magazine devoted to those who serve as trustees of theological schools shared stories of seminaries thrown into crisis when their presidents either died or resigned suddenly. Unfortunately, emergency succession planning processes had not prepared the institutions for this "sudden loss of cabin pressure."

But even if a faith community has thought through various scenarios that might render ineffective or absent the head pastor or other key leaders, when such a scenario actually unfolds those granted legitimate governance must rise to the occasion and step into the breach. Likewise, there are situations which, while not removing the spiritual and administrative leadership, are of such cataclysmic import as to require all hands on deck to supplement and support those who normally can handle many things on their own. A fire or natural disaster that kills or injures people or destroys a church's property, or a human-caused catastrophe such as that experienced on September 11, 2001, will cause everyone to be in shock. During such a time, ministers and staff who can normally carry out their designated duties will need propping up, advice, and counsel from the governing board and other seasoned volunteer leaders.

In many arenas, a governance body may feel itself under-utilized and even largely unnecessary for months or even years of "ordinary time." But when a crisis moment occurs, the body will be called into rapid action for the sake of the community's well-being. In this sense, a governing body may be akin to a firefighting crew that is inactive or in light-duty maintenance activities the vast majority of the time. It is a foolish community indeed that allows its firefighting corps to erode or disappear altogether simply because for a season it begins to appear unnecessary.

Governance and Administration

If you are convinced that some form of governance is indeed necessary, even in the smallest faith community, what are the different roles and responsibilities of those who govern (council, vestry, or board) and the staff or administrative personnel? As in almost every area discussed in this book, the first response is, "It depends!" Just as every community or organization will organize its governance in a unique way, so the interplay of those involved in administration and governance will vary considerably.

In broad and general terms, the role of governance is to discern and safeguard the overall mission, establish long-range plans, select and support appropriate staff and volunteer leadership, ensure fiscal integrity, make certain the full diversity of a community is reflected in decision making, and set forth broad policies that affect the entirety of the congregation or organization. Administration's (or management's) role—and this includes pastoral leadership regardless of denominational polity or congregational history and current practice—is to oversee day-to-day activity and program, make decisions based on policies and both short- and long-range goals, and report regularly to the governing body. To use an analogy, it is the role of an airline's board of directors to determine overall corporate goals and objectives, monitor its fiscal health, compliance with laws and regulations, and cheer on managers and the entire organization's workforce. God forbid that board members rush into cockpits and tell pilots how to fly from point A to point B on a stormy night!

Not surprisingly, it is often the activity and work *at the boundaries* that leads to conflict between those called to serve in governance and those they in turn call or hire to administer the organization. Constant judgment calls must be made by those in administration regarding which decisions fall within their clear purview and which must be reviewed with appropriate background information for decision by the governing board. In a congregational context, many areas are fairly clear. While the pastor may consult with a variety of folks about themes for sermons, the minister must prepare and deliver one every Sunday morning. Correspondingly, no clergy we know have sole authority to mortgage a church's property, incur major indebtedness, or withdraw from the denomination over a controversial doctrinal matter. In the big issues, it is fairly clear where and by whom decisions must be made. Likewise, in trivial matters most governing officers do not want to be bothered with decisions that can and should be made by those entrusted with management. In churches, however, this apparently neat distinction seems to break down when the color of sanctuary carpet or the menu for the annual stewardship banquet is at stake!

It is generally in the middle level of decisions that conflict ensues between governing boards and staff or administrators. Such conflict may arise around hiring or termination of staff, with chief administrators (for example, senior pastors) believing they have hire-and-fire authority, while at least some council or vestry members think that all personnel matters must be brought to the governing board. In order to avoid conflict insofar as possible (and it's never going to be absent altogether in a healthy organization, where a certain amount of low-level tensions keep life interesting and the organization flexible), policies may be established to clarify authority. A fiscal policy, for example, may limit a chief executive's authority to exceed budget in any area by 10% unless a situation constitutes an emergency.

Leadership styles and governance-administration roles vary greatly, depending upon a variety of factors. A first is simply the type of governance chosen. In the so-called "Carver model" of policy-based governance, a governing board is very self-restrained, setting broad priorities and establishing policies to guide the leadership of a chief executive. In this model, governing document provisions regarding the governing board are stated primarily in negative phrases: "The board shall not. . . ." Such a governance style may be most appropriate for large and complex organizations, where any degree of micro-managing on the part of board members can do serious damage and undermine the authority of senior administration. The Carver method of policy governance is summarized as follows:

> In contrast to the approaches typically used by boards, Policy Governance separates issues of organizational purpose (ENDS) from all other organizational issues (MEANS), placing primary importance on those Ends. Policy Governance boards demand accomplishment of purpose, and only limit the staff's available means to those which do not violate the board's pre-stated standards of prudence and ethics.
>
> The board's own Means are defined in accordance with the roles of the board, its members, the chair and other officers, and any committees the board may need to help it accomplish its job. This includes the necessity to "speak with one voice." Dissent is expressed during the discussion preceding a vote. Once taken, the board's decisions may subsequently be changed, but are never to be undermined. The board's expectations for itself also set out self-imposed rules regarding the delegation of authority to the staff and the method by which board-stated criteria will be used for evaluation. Policy Governance boards delegate with care. There is no confusion about who is responsible to the board or for what board expectations they are responsible.[5]

At the opposite end of the governance spectrum from the hands-off-by-the-board Carver method is a style wherein the entire congregation or all organizational members must be involved in nearly every decision, even those of minor consequence. Weekly every-member congregational meetings to select hymns for the following Sunday would be an example of such extreme participatory democratic governance. In most church-related organizational cultures a balance

---

5. "The Policy Governance Model" (http://www.carvergovernance.com/model .htm). See also John Carver, *Boards That Make a Difference: A New Design for Leadership in Nonprofit and Public Organizations* (San Francisco: Jossey-Bass, 1997).

is struck somewhere in between staff-dominated and board-controlled decision making. Generally, the larger the organization, the more restrained should be governing board members, recognizing that over-functioning on their part will impede efficient day-to-day operations that require a high degree of decision-making authority for staff.

Governance as Trusteeship and Stewardship

In many non-profit arenas, but especially in churches, those called to the ministry of governance frequently are called "trustees." While "director" or "council member" are perfectly fine titles for those so called, *trustee* may better point to the reality that the one who serves in churchly governance does so as one under authority—the ultimate authority of Jesus Christ, the head of the Church. One so called, then, holds a responsibility in trust from the faith community and ultimately from God.

Trusteeship is a high honor and privilege. One who serves in governance does so humbly as a servant of the servants of God. In pointing to leadership within the community of faith, Jesus said that hierarchical "lording over" should not be the style practiced by Christians. Rather, "through love, be servants one to another" was his counsel (Gal 5:13). Faithful trustees exercise their ministry of leadership, direction setting, and decision making not to aggrandize themselves but to offer support for the entire faith community. In a particular way, they offer support and encouragement to those called as staff—both ordained or commissioned ministers and lay persons employed by the congregation or faith-based organization.

Malcolm Warford has pointed out that "steward is a primary image for leadership and governance in the Christian community. Essential to understanding the office of steward is the recognition that it originates in something beyond itself. At the center of stewardship is the management of resources belonging to God."[6] In exercising a biblical style of trusteeship, those entrusted with governance should

---

6. Malcolm L. Warford, "Stewards of Hope: The Work of Trustees," in *Building Effective Boards for Religious Organizations: A Handbook for Presidents, Trustees and Church Leaders*, ed. Thomas P. Holland and David C. Hester (San Francisco: Jossey-Bass, 1999), 5.

strive for the highest principles of justice and fairness. Making a faith community a safe place free of all forms of abuse, denigration and prejudice in any guise must be a fundamental guiding principle.

How Do Administrators Serve Those Called to Governance, and Vice Versa?

A key role for all staff members, but especially for the lead person, is to provide information and offer resources to those who constitute the governing entities. Providing too much data can confuse and overwhelm busy board/council members who cannot be expected to spend a great deal of time preparing for meetings. Conversely, the staff's intentionally withholding or unintentionally overlooking the provision of important needed information can severely handicap a governing board in making the decisions that are its to determine.

So again, a good administrator frequently asks herself or himself, "Who needs to know about this? What can and must I pass along, without compromising the boundaries of pastoral confidentiality? Can I gather and provide more data that will assist the council to engage in big-picture planning? Am I overwhelming my thirsty governing board by offering them to drink from a fire hose? Should I 'declare myself' on a controversial issue, make a recommendation on a major decision, or just sit back and let the deliberations and debates unfold?"

While many a church or other volunteer organization is blessed with some members who devote a significant portion of their time to its work and well-being, increasingly busy people involved in governance are not able to spend hour upon hour pondering their responsibilities and how the community they govern can thrive. Staff members, on the other hand, spend their entire working lives carrying out the mission of that congregation or organization. They may well be in the best position and have the necessary time (even while driving to appointments, relaxing at home or on vacation) to envision new programs, propose solutions to vexing problems, or assess how well the community is fulfilling its mission. At the same time, the staff's very closeness to day-to-day operations may blind them to big-picture developments and environmental factors that can have a tremendous impact on their ministry.

For their part, an organization's governors (trustees, board members, or directors) do well to offer encouragement and support to the staff they have called to serve among them. One of the key ministries of those engaged in governance is the ministry of encouragement: "Therefore encourage one another and build up each other, as indeed you are doing" (1 Thess 5:11). Warford points to a particular emphasis that ecclesiastical governors should constantly keep before them: to offer frequent reminders to a pastor, president, or other chief executive, as well as her or his senior associates, that their office is a teaching office. He writes, "Teaching should be the primary role of the executive. . . . Though the popular definition of the executive is that of chief administrative officer, a religious perspective on 'organization' will help to illuminate the extent to which this person is essentially a teacher, an educator of the board."[7]

In what areas should a pastor, president, and other staff leaders teach and educate members of the board? In the case of congregations, it is likely that the pastor(s) has the most in-depth knowledge of Scripture, theology, church history, and other areas typically included in a seminary curriculum. By engaging the governing board in regular Bible study and reflection upon the great themes of the faith, with particular insights offered by one's theological and denominational perspectives, the chief staff leader will assist the board in remaining grounded in the most important things. In many arenas, the staff will also have opportunity to monitor trends in the environment, ecclesiastical developments, and other important information that the governing board needs at its disposal to make informed and wise decisions. Serving day-to-day in administration, executives simply have more ready access to critical data such as financial reports, attendance or enrollment records, and the like. While few staff leaders actually consciously withhold information for dubious or outright nefarious reasons, many probably could serve those in governance better by recognizing what information tends not to be within their easy reach.

In a healthy organizational culture, the respective roles and responsibilities of administrators or staff and governing board members are not rigidly fixed. While clarity of functions is important to avoid unnecessary conflict, those who seek to pin things down too much in fixed categories may lose opportunity for creative

---

7. Ibid., 7.

ideas and solutions to emanate from many directions. Overly rigid boundaries may keep out creative winds of the Spirit. On the other hand, boundaries that are too permeable may allow all manner of mischief to intrude.

One specific area where boundary keeping is important is in the matter of supervisory authority and personnel management. When board members allow themselves to become a "listening ear" or even a "court of appeals" for disgruntled employees who don't get what they want from a supervisor, the stage is usually set to undermine legitimate supervisory oversight and appropriate accountability of the lead person (senior pastor in a larger congregation) for the work of the entire team. By the same token, there need to be carefully defined grievance procedures whereby an employee who feels disrespected or even abused can appeal a decision or challenge inappropriate behavior on the part of his or her supervisor to a higher authority, including the governing board's leadership.

Chair and Chief Executive: A Special Partnership

Upon retiring after nearly two decades of service as president of Luther Seminary, Dr. David Tiede reflected with his peer Lutheran presidents about the joys and challenges he had encountered during a challenging era for all leaders in theological education. Tiede pointed to the critical role played in his long-term presidency by three deeply committed and highly competent board chairs. He spoke of their role as readily available "listening ears," offering more objective perspectives from a bit of a distance, and exercising strong leadership in chairing the seminary board.

In similar fashion, many pastors and other church administrators point to strong congregational presidents or council, vestry, or session chairs as making life both easier and more enjoyable. Conversely, in conversations over coffee at many a clergy gathering, one can hear tales of woe from those not so blessed with strong lay leaders. In some cases, a weak or unengaged board chair simply fails to carry an appropriate measure of leadership. Sadly, in a few, the chief elected governing elder or board chair is postured in an oppositional stance, challenging the chief administrator's every move and musing.

Wise administrators cultivate a close (but not too close) relationship with the one chosen by the community as its chief elected officer. Being proactive in communicating frequently with the board chair, keeping him or her informed regarding all aspects of the community's life, should keep the chief governor from being surprised. Offering discussion items and working together in shaping agenda for board meetings is another key dimension of a healthy administrator-chair partnership. Strategizing together how to help each member of the board become and remain engaged in areas of her or his interest and competence is another important aspect for fostering good governance and healthy community life.

In times of difficulty or crisis, especially when conflicts may have legal implications or when soured or inappropriate relationships have crossed the line into abuse, and when grave harm has been or may be caused to one or more of God's children, a strong partnership between staff and key governance leaders is crucial.

When the relationship of chief administrator and congregational president or board chair is marked by common commitment to a shared vision, open and honest communication, and an easy camaraderie, the entire community will tend to emulate this spirit of partnership. Trust between key leaders begets trust within the entire "system" of the congregation or organization. Both board chair and pastors or senior administrators do well to offer each other frequent expressions of gratitude and support. Those who serve as staff may need occasional reminders that they are paid for their work, whereas volunteers engaged in governance may be contributing hundreds of volunteer hours, taking precious time away from their families or even using work vacation days to fulfill their stewardship as trustees.

Governance in the New Testament Church

In order to gain a sense of the nature of governance practiced among the earliest Christian communities, one must engage in a fair degree of creative reading "behind the texts" of the New Testament. That is to say, it was not high on the agenda of the authors of biblical material to provide a comprehensive description of how the early church conducted its decision making and direction-setting processes.

Leadership in New Testament times was highly charismatic in nature. As he initiated his public ministry, Jesus wandered about as an itinerant rabbi/teacher, and issued "calls" to various individuals who responded by joining in his itinerancy.

Spirit-imbued with God-given charisms, Jesus' invitation to discipleship could not be denied by those who followed. Nor was he systematic or scientific in his leadership selection process! Job openings entitled "Disciples" were not posted, nor did the disciples submit resumes detailing their qualifications for spiritual leadership and church planting.

While we cannot learn a great deal from the New Testament gospels or epistles about how to carry out effective governance in the complex context of the twenty-first century, perhaps we can discern the most important thing. Direction setting and decision making were exercised always within the context of prayer and discernment of the Spirit's leading. Jesus was frequently going off on his own to pray, but increasingly he and the disciples may have prayed together. During the days when Jesus wandered the Palestinian countryside with the disciples, he appeared to have determined where they would go, whom they would visit, and how work would be carried out. Again, however, the textual material is sketchy at best. Perhaps the decision to send out the seventy two-by-two in their initial missionary forays (Luke 10:1–16) was suggested by a small committee of the disciples themselves and implemented by Jesus. In other words, there may have been a much higher degree of "shared governance" going on than is readily apparent from the gospel texts.

Not long after the resurrection and ascension of Jesus, the first apostles appear to have organized themselves in some fashion. A close reading of the book of Acts suggests that an organizational structure, methods of regular communication with one another, and arenas of decision making were determined quite early in the dawning days of the Christian era. The councils at Jerusalem, early assemblies or convocations where representatives of the various emerging local communities gathered to resolve problems and issue normative teaching, had to be preceded by notifications and invitations, agenda setting, and leadership selection.

In Acts 15, the pressing question of whether or not Gentile Christian boys and men had to become circumcised was central on the agenda of the Jerusalem church council. Some primitive rules of engagement appear to have been established for the debate that was about to ensue: "The whole assembly kept silence, and listened to Barnabas and Paul as they told of all the signs and wonders that God had done through them among the Gentiles" (v. 12). Following their setting forth the perspective that surely the gospel was for more than Jewish-born believers, James quoted some scripture and posed to the assembly his conviction that the Gentiles turning to God need not be troubled with circumcision. We can imagine that lively debate persisted until, finally, consensus (reported as being unanimous) was reached that James' perspectives would prevail. A brief written communiqué was prepared for broad dissemination, and individuals were deputized by the assembly to carry the decision to various communities. Among the Gentile believers, it was received with relief and great joy.

What Might This Mean for Today's Godly Governance?

In the classic pedagogical style set forth by Martin Luther in his Small Catechism, the bold faith assertions of the creeds, commandments, and other key Christian doctrines are followed by Luther's blunt question, "What does this mean?" Reflecting on the biblical governance process distilled from a close reading of Acts, we might ask the same question vis-à-vis churchly governance in our time. What meaning might we glean from the way the early church carried out its direction setting and decision making at the Jerusalem council and elsewhere?

First, good governance in any arena is *highly participatory*. As far as possible, all who have a stake in decisions should be invited to share their perspectives, offer their ideas, and engage in discussing proposals or solving problems. A second insight from the decision-making process in Acts 15 is that *orderly processes* need to be established whereby discussions are held and decisions are made. Determining who will conduct a meeting, the rules of procedure for debate, and how mutually respectful dialogue will be carried out—especially pertaining to highly charged and controversial issues—are tended to in preparation and as a governance process unfolds. Third, once decisions are made, *clear communication* of the corporately held outcome is offered to all who need the information. Not every decision will be unanimous. Individuals who dissented may feel free to share how they cast their vote, but the decision of the body is the one that stands and should be articulated by all involved in governance—even those who disagreed with the ultimate outcome.

Most important of all, governance in communities of faith is *carried out in communion with the One for whom the community exists*. Prayerful discernment, while never a guarantee of harmonious deliberation and unanimous consensus-building, centers a community about its founder. As with every other aspect of a faith community's life, its governance processes should be spiritual—part and parcel of that community's life in the Spirit.

How can these overarching principles be translated into practical shaping of a congregation's or other church organization's governance processes? Those who shape and plan governance processes should give attention to how they may be carried out in a spirit of *prayerful discernment*. Many church councils or governing boards devote at least a small portion of time at each meeting to Bible study and corporate prayer. *Communal reflection* on some of the great historic or contemporary texts of Christian theology can supplement biblical study and help a governance group keep in mind the big picture of the church's God-given mission. Allowing sufficient time for *unhurried discussion and deliberation*, especially involving conflicted issues surrounded by strong feelings, is another component of godly governance. At the same time, permitting interminable delays in hope of unanimity can allow a governance process to be manipulated and dominated by one or two strong-willed individuals incapable of committing themselves to a greater communal decision. *Fair and even-handed treatment* of all discussants, guaranteed through having at least broad principles and rules of procedure spelled out in governing documents or policies, is another key to good governance.

St. Paul's encouragement to the Ephesians, while perhaps not explicitly offered as principles for godly governance, sets forth a spirit to be emulated by all those whose calling includes participation in a faith community's direction setting and decision making:

> I therefore, the prisoner in the Lord, beg you to lead a life worthy of the calling to which you have been called, with all humility and gentleness, with patience, bearing with one another in love, making every effort to maintain the unity of the Spirit in the bond of peace. (Eph 4:1-3)

CHAPTER 3

Boards: Blessed Balladeers

The board of directors is a curious beast. For all its collected heads, it often fails to see straight. Its staple nourishment seems to be the boring meeting and its byproduct the complicated resolution. The undisciplined, undomesticated Board tends to prowl around aimlessly, alternately baring its teeth or settling into a snooze. It has been known to devour its young.

Yet, there's common agreement that the board of directors should inspire, sustain, and drive an organization forward. It should resemble a lioness: ferocious in the pursuit of its goals, yet tender and nurturing toward its offspring. And, of course, it must set a noble example within the community.[1]

We all have known colleagues who express dread when their board, vestry, council, session, or whatever the governing group may be called is about to meet. Perhaps you, the reader, regularly or on occasion have similar apprehensive, negative, or downright hostile feelings about your governing board. Some boards are worthy of such fear and dismay on the part of those who report to them. Poorly organized, unclear about their purpose, and unfocused in their meetings, boards can do more harm than good in a church or other setting.

---

1. Fred Setterberg and Kary Schulman, *Beyond Profit: The Complete Guide to Managing the Nonprofit Organization* (San Francisco: Harper & Row, 1985), 11.

Occasionally, mean-spirited board members adopt an adversarial stance regarding pastoral or other staff, seeing their role as offering criticism, saying no more often than yes, protecting the congregation against newfangled ideas that could bring about change, and otherwise making life miserable for a creative pastor or chief executive. And, every so often, here and there, manifestations of downright evil inclinations rear their heads to the extent that a board acts like a beast spewing bile and general unpleasant disruption that can severely cripple or eventually kill an otherwise healthy community.

At their best, by contrast, boards are deeply committed faith communities in their own right, peopled with the most mature members who set aside all self-serving motives and make every effort to support the health, mission, and forward positive movement of the congregation or organization. Over against the bilious beast as metaphor for a board gone awry, a faith community's board at its best might be thought of as a chorus of blessed balladeers. A ballad is a folk poem, usually set to music, that tells the story of a people, its history, hopes, dreams, and deepest yearnings. A board that fulfills its intended purpose does many things— provides comprehensive oversight, monitors programs and fiscal health, engages in garnering resources to carry out carefully delineated plans, and selects and supports staff leaders in a dynamic and mutually satisfying partnership. Above all else, however, a good governing board tends the mission of the faith community, discerns, refines, and rehearses its covenant with God and the community. Each member is a balladeer in her or his own right, and the voices of all members blend together in a powerful chorus that sounds forth the songs to which the entire community dances on its missionary journey.

In chapter 2 we looked at principles and some practical suggestions regarding good governance in ecclesiastical organizations, congregational and otherwise. As we pointed out, in any governance pattern or structure, except that of very small communities that operate by committee-of-the-whole, there is likely to be a governing board of some variety. Such a group, normally elected by an annual meeting of all members, serves as a representative body of the whole community, carrying out the governance function between gatherings of the full membership.

In this chapter we seek to explore some best practices gleaned from a variety of church-related boards that we have observed, served on as members, or consulted with over the many years of our collective experience. We offer some practical tips for new member selection and orientation, board leadership development, meeting preparation and conduct, and overall oversight of the congregation's or organization's life.

For the sake of simplicity, we will not strive for all-inclusive language in discussing the role of the governing board. Depending on denominational affiliation and organizational culture, one's board may be called vestry, church council, session, trustees, or another term. The authors will trust the reader to substitute appropriate nomenclature; generally, we will use the generic "board" to describe the entity that sets policy and conducts the business of the congregation or church organization.

The Board: Learning Its Role and Rhythms

For a new leader, understanding the role of the board and how one relates to it is an early and primary task. Ideally, the board's self-understanding and how it relates to a pastor, chief executive, and other staff will have been explored in a search or call process. In many congregations, the governing board will itself serve as the search/call committee. Other churches will delegate initial candidate screening to a search or call committee, with the board becoming involved at a later stage in the process of engaging new pastoral leadership. In still other traditions, the board has no direct involvement with a new leader until she or he is on the scene, having delegated the search and hiring entirely to another group or committee. In that latter case, the wise candidate may request a session with the board prior to accepting a position, recognizing that a call or search committee likely has very limited authority and cannot speak on behalf of those charged with governance.

Over the years, we have seen many leaders in a new position falter and stumble early on in a ministry simply because they assume the board's role is identical to that in the last parish or other setting. As no two congregations or organizations have the same overall governance style and processes, so too, none will have identical understandings of the work, authority, and role of the board. Even among churches of the same denomination, there will be considerable variety as to meeting patterns, agenda items, and the degree to which the board is a hands-on working group or a more hands-off oversight body that sees its role as delegating almost everything to committees and staff.

If at all possible, attending a board meeting prior to actually assuming office can be very helpful to a new leader. Having the opportunity to watch the board in action and observe how its leaders interact can be invaluable in preparing to assume a new ministry. While such an arrangement may not be possible in many or most situations, a leader new to a ministry might reach an agreement with key leaders that he or she will be in primarily an observer role for the first couple of board meetings, thereafter assuming a more engaged leadership stance.

Seeking personal conversations with key board leaders—officers and others who may be identified by knowledgeable insiders—can be another means whereby a new leader begins to gain familiarity with the board's culture, norms, climate, and self-understanding. If regular or occasional retreats are part of a board's lifestyle, a new leader will be blessed if one can be scheduled early in her or his tenure. In such a relaxed setting, perhaps with the help of a skilled facilitator, the courtship between board and pastor/leader/CEO can proceed at a much brisker pace than would otherwise occur. Engaging in some light activities and playful exercises can be illuminating, for example, asking board members to speak metaphorically about how they see their role ("Our board is like. . .") or bringing along physical objects that remind members of the board. There are many fine board development instruments and exercises that also assist a board to sharpen its own self-identity and clarify its roles and style of governance. A retreat also affords opportunity for each board member to deepen her or his self-understanding and where she or he can make contributions for the sake of the whole board's cohesive work. Members can ask of themselves: "What gifts and expertise do I bring to the table? How can I contribute to this board's mission and functioning?" Sharing answers to such self-questioning among all members can help the entire board grasp the scope of its talents, and also point out any areas that might need shoring up in searches for future board members.

It is also important to remember that, just as individuals grow and change over time, so boards are dynamic living organisms in their own right. Especially as members rotate off and are replaced by new members bringing different gifts, interests, and talents, a board will change. The context and conditions amid which a board serves will also change its activities, work style, and self-understanding. If a faith community is thrust into crisis—resulting from a fire or natural disaster, sudden illness, death or incapacitation of the pastor or other key staff—the board's role may change dramatically overnight.

Board Members: Nobodies Apart from the Body!

One of the richest sources for the development of imagery and language about board existence and activity is the Pauline passage about the body of Christ (1 Corinthians 12). As an individual Christian cannot live into the fullness of discipleship apart from the church, the body of Christ, so a member has no standing on behalf of the congregation or organization apart from corporate action of the body that is the board. In *The Corporate Person*, board development expert Harold Everson traces the history of corporate action to early Christianity: "Incorporation is a concept that grew out of the Christian theological principle of the Corpus Christi, the 'body of Christ,' a way in which the Christian church has traditionally defined itself."[2]

For persons unaccustomed to serving on boards, or even for many long-time volunteer board members, frequently there is a lack of understanding of this corporate nature of board existence and action. In brief, "the basic principle is. . .'without the board, you're not the board.'"[3] Individual board members do well to remember, "Because trustees operate as a body—a community of leadership—no trustee acts apart from the support and authorization of the whole board."[4] Individuals bring their personal opinions and convictions to board meetings and also leave with them. But from the perspective of board existence and activity, the board can speak and make decisions for the congregation or organization only as a collective body.

This corporate nature of the board has profound implications for communication, particularly outside board meetings. While members should not be muzzled or discouraged from offering their personal perspectives on important issues, they must be very careful when articulating the position of the board, which frequently will be different from that of some individuals. In some congregational or

---

2. Harold Everson, *The Corporate Person: The Nature of Volunteer Boards, Their Culture, and Corporate Personality* (Minneapolis: Fortress Press, 1998), 1.

3. Ibid., 9.

4. Malcolm Warford, "The Calling of Stewards: Recruiting and Supporting Seminary Trustees," in *Good Stewardship: A Handbook for Seminary Trustees*, ed. Barbara E. Taylor and Malcolm L. Warford (Washington, DC: Association of Governing Boards of Universities and Colleges, 1991), 78.

organizational cultures, it is permitted or even encouraged for a board member to say, "This is what we decided by majority vote; personally I disagreed and felt we should have gone another way." Recognizing that such public statement of personal opinion can be divisive, particularly when dealing with controversial matters, other boards arrive at agreements that, outside of board meetings, members should be very cautious in stating personal opinions.

Regardless of an organization's norms relative to members offering personal perspectives, clear understandings should be set forth concerning who speaks for the board. Typically, the chair or lead staff person is authorized to speak officially, interpreting the board's corporate decision internally within the broader organization or externally to public media and other constituencies.

While discussion may be freewheeling and largely unrecorded in many board cultures, at least major decisions should be formalized into official motions, with minutes documenting the board's decision or declaration. Precise recording and permanent preservation of board actions in official minutes by the secretary will safeguard against confusion and misunderstanding of exactly what occurred. Those interpreting the board's decisions do well to refer to and even quote verbatim from the minutes. In some matters with legal and financial implications—for example a decision to purchase real estate or establish bank accounts—certified copies of official minutes may need to accompany applications or other documents, thereby certifying that the corporate person which is the board has acted.

Choosing and Calling New Board Members

It has been said that over time any organization will be only as strong and healthy as its board or governing council. That being the case, the selection of board members is critical for the life of a faith community. Depending upon local culture and customs, a pastor/CEO may have little or no direct influence in such selection. In most congregations, governing board members are elected at the annual meeting from a slate of nominees proposed by a nominating committee or some other group. In many cases, all those nominated are elected, whereas in other settings multiple candidates are nominated, and some are excluded by a process of balloting until the required number are elected.

In the selection of members, those responsible for identifying, recruiting, nominating, and electing do well to consider the needs of the board at a given time. To serve most effectively, a board should have among its members a broad array of gifts, experience, and abilities. In an increasingly richly diverse world, a board ideally will have a similarly good balance in terms of gender, racial-ethnic composition, and other aspects of diversity. In general, a board will function well if it has a good blend of creative-idea persons and those who tend to be practical and pragmatic. In order to minimize conflicts between persons with differing inclinations and leadership styles, some boards have found it helpful to engage a consultant who might lead them in examining personal styles by using such tools as the Myers-Briggs personality inventory.

Boards of large and complex church-related institutions and agencies can best steward their heavy responsibilities if they include persons with financial expertise, knowledge of regulatory requirements, fund-raising commitments, and connections to multiple constituencies. In today's litigious climate, having a lawyer or two on one's board can be a blessing too. After assessing its current "intellectual capital" and the array of needed gifts and experiences, a nominating committee or other selection group may need to target certain individuals and stress to them and to the electors the high need for their service.

Even if formal processes preclude much direct influence on selection by those currently in office, leaders will do well to give attention to the nurturing of potential governing board members. An encouraging word spoken here and there ("You should be open to serving on our board"), public praise for the gifts and talents of committed individuals ("Wouldn't Jane be a great vestry member?") can be ways of exerting informal influence in the nomination and election process. Such encouragement should not escalate into "picking the pastor's people," where boards become a mirror image of and rubber stamp for the leader's visions and proposals. Conflict can erupt in an organization if it is perceived that chief administrators are "stacking the deck" with yes-persons in board member recruitment.

In order to enable potential board members to consider their possible calling to service in governance, as well as to remind all trustees/directors of their responsibilities, a written job description should be developed and reviewed from time to time. In some cases, the duties of board members may be sufficiently spelled out in bylaws so they can simply be shared with those being asked to consider board service. But generally a more detailed position description will delineate exactly what is expected of board members in terms of time commitment, roles, and responsibilities. Such a description should also set forth what the board member can expect in terms of support and resources provided to enable effective board service.

Offering public recognition of the importance attached to board member selection is another way of signaling to the entire congregation or organization the key stewardship of those who serve on the board. Including prayers for the nominating committee and election process, as well as for individual candidates, can be a way of engaging the entire faith community in asking God's blessing upon those willing to serve. And a formal rite of installation into office of those elected will remind them and the entire community that board service involves a spiritual calling.

New-Member Orientation

Being new kid on the block is not an experience reserved for kids! Throughout life, we all continue moving into new territory where things are unfamiliar and the rules unknown to us. Many newcomers to the boards of faith communities experience considerable frustration and occasionally even quit after a short time simply due to a lack of an intentional and comprehensive orientation process. Where it is done well, thorough new-member orientation will equip board stewards for long, fruitful, and rewarding tenures of service.

What are the essential ingredients of a new-member orientation process? This will vary greatly, depending upon the nature of the board as well as the experience and comfort level of new members. In a small, family-style congregation, where all current participants have been members their whole lives, little formal orientation may be necessary or expected by those elected to serve on the church council. Even there, however, sitting down for a session or two before new members join the board can be helpful in bringing them up to speed on the work of the board. Providing meeting minutes from at least the previous year or so, together with any printed annual reports and other materials, will enable the new members to do some homework and avoid feeling out of touch as they begin their service. In larger and more complex congregations or organizational entities, new member orientation may require several sessions and the provision of an extensive corpus of policy documents, budgets and audit reports, and organizational charts.

A good place to begin in any orientation process is to focus on the mission of the faith community. This might involve Bible study and at least a brief review of a church's basic faith tenets and local traditions. It should include the provision and a brief overview of the organization's constitution and bylaws, the road map by which any faithful board must navigate on its journey of governance. If one exists, a careful rehearsal of the mission statement should be offered to new board members, perhaps even encouraging them to memorize it as a way of gaining focused clarity about the mission and purpose. Certainly, if they are not already, new board members should be added to all-important mailing lists, email distributions, and all other communication channels whereby the faith community transmits important messages.

Those involved in providing orientation will need to be judicious in what information to provide, neither overwhelming new board members with too much data nor underestimating their need for a basic body of knowledge in order to be able to hit the ground running at their first meeting. Providing new members of an airline's board of directors with all the pilots' operating handbooks for all the aircraft in the fleet would be overkill! By the same token, withholding from them the quarterly profit and loss statement and balance sheet would be irresponsible. After conducting a few rounds of new-member orientation, leaders will determine the best approach and right amount of material to be provided. And, of course, inasmuch as all members are unique individuals, the introduction to board service should be tailored and individualized as much as possible.

Recognizing that individuals absorb information and learn in different ways, any educational process, including new board member orientation, should be delivered in as many media and with as much creativity as possible. When the authors served together as liaisons from the Evangelical Lutheran Church in America's Office of the Presiding Bishop to the Church Council (governing board) and a variety of boards that provided oversight to programmatic churchwide units, we developed together with a third colleague and outside consultants a comprehensive process of board orientation. In addition to a three-ring binder handed to each new board member, various exercises and multi-media presentations were included. Among them was an exercise in which council or board members were spread out in a large room where they could join in creating a human organizational chart depicting the rather complex nature of the Evangelical Lutheran Church in America's church-wide governance and programmatic structures. A ball of twine was tossed from one to the other as we described governance patterns, reporting structures, oversight responsibilities, and the like. By the time each group concluded the exercise, they understood and empathized with us when occasionally things would seem to be all tied up in knots!

Who should be involved in new board member orientation? Again, this will vary depending upon the history, culture, size, and complexity of the congregation or organization. In small churches, the orientation for new church council or vestry members probably occurs rather informally, perhaps in a pastoral call that might include the council president visiting one or two new members in their homes. In larger entities, a group setting involving several newly chosen board members might be planned and conducted by board officers together with the president or chief executive and other key senior staff members. In any case, to reinforce the importance of the presiding officer's role and underscore that in some sense the board has a life of its own apart from staff, the board chair should have a key part in planning and conducting orientation for new members.

In providing a comprehensive introduction to the pressing issues and current aspects of a board's life and work, a wise board chair and CEO will want to give the new members opportunities to interact with a wide range of others. So enabling multiple conversations will ensure that the new board member is not just afforded the benefit of perspectives that inevitably will be shaped by the views, prejudices, and hobbyhorses of one or two key leaders.

Some organizations have found helpful a kind of buddy system, in which each new board member is paired with a seasoned veteran who is intentional in assisting the newcomer get up to speed on both issues and how the board functions. In some cases, having the new member sit next to this buddy at the first few meetings will provide her or him with ready access when an item under discussion isn't clear, or when the new member can't remember where the bathrooms are located!

Once again, local culture will dictate which measures are helpful and which might seem contrived or even comical. Providing nametags and nameplates for council meetings in a small congregation where all the members are already on a first-name basis would seem rather odd. On the other hand, not doing so for a national board where new members will know few if any of the other members at first meeting is insensitive and unhelpful to all concerned.

Fiduciary Responsibility, Conflicts of Interest, and Risk Management

Another important area that should be addressed in the recruitment and orientation of new board members is that of a director's or trustee's fiduciary responsibility. Often narrowly misconstrued to refer only or primarily to matters financial, fiduciary responsibility is actually broad-ranging and signifies the board's final accountability for the total well-being of the entity served. When all is said and done, the governing board has direct or delegated (by the annual congregational meeting, a churchwide assembly or judicatory convention) responsibility to ensure that the organization's mission is fulfilled, that sufficient resources are gathered and stewarded, and that its values are upheld and advanced in the process.

Etymologically, the word "fiduciary" comes from the Latin *fiducia*, "trust." It means literally "to be a person of trust or a trustworthy person who holds in trust that which belongs to others." As a board member, a person is called to act on behalf of something greater than his or her self-interest—to serve the whole of the congregation or organization, not simply to represent certain interest groups.

If there is a common pitfall we have observed in board members of many organizations, it is that they feel they are chosen primarily as representatives of certain perspectives or constituent groups. When one comes to serve on a board, that individual is still everything else she or he is in life—a worker, perhaps a parent, spouse, registered member of a political party, community citizen. But none of those other self-identities and personal interests can prevail over acting in the best interests of the organization served as a board member or director.

This becomes particularly a challenge for many who serve on a congregational council or board of some other church-related entity. It is not unusual to hear a council or vestry member say, "In my role representing the Sunday school. . . ," or, "As a concerned parent of children in the church-sponsored pre-school. . . ." To be sure, representing one's other commitments and involvements can be part of the value brought by a board member. But, in the final analysis, that board member cannot make decisions based exclusively upon what is best for the Sunday school or pre-school but must take into account the entire big picture of the congregation's mission.

It is not uncommon for board members to feel great personal internal conflicts when there are competing interests that make it difficult to act solely or primarily on behalf of the organization served. If a board member has a child enrolled in the pre-school, voting to raise tuition will have a very personal impact and may be a difficult decision. Or if one has a good friend or relative who operates a construction business, it may be challenging to weigh bids from several building contractors fairly in determining whom to engage for the new sanctuary construction. In cases where they exist, such conflicts of interest should be made known publicly to one's fellow board members.

Many organizations, including church-related ones, now require all board members to sign and file annually a document known as a Conflict of Interest Disclosure. In writing, a board member is asked to list any other involvements that are likely to conflict with her or his service in the best interests of the entity served. In the above cited examples, it would be simple on such a disclosure form to note, "I have a child in the church-operated pre-school," or, "My sister operates one of the firms that may bid on our new building." Such conflicts of interest often dictate that on certain issues a particular board member may have to recuse (sit out) himself or herself. Having made a public disclosure will offer other board members opportunity to remind and privately confront a member whose objective judgment might be clouded by personal interests. (For a more extended treatment, see chapter 12. See also Appendix A for a sample conflict of interest declaration.)

In the current climate in which public organizations, including churches, function, those who serve on their boards may incur significant risks. There are probably very few of us who do not know someone who is being or has been sued for something or other. Increasingly, when mistakes are made, when persons are or feel they have been injured in some way, a lawsuit is filed. Also increasingly, such lawsuits may go beyond suing a corporate entity to also naming those who serve on its board of directors. Recognizing that this is the case, any organization should give attention to reasonable protection against unnecessary personal exposure for those who serve in its governance roles. Concern for those who serve in governance is part of an overall strategy to provide prudent "risk management" for the organization. Many if not most comprehensive insurance packages for an incorporated entity, including ecclesiastical ones, provide what is commonly referred to as "directors and officers" coverage. This means that should the unfortunate circumstances develop that lead to a lawsuit, appropriate legal counsel will be provided by the insurer.

In chapter 5, on fiscal management, we offer additional comments regarding the importance of audits, good accounting practices, and other matters that fall under a governing board's oversight.

Tips for Good Meetings

Good meetings don't just happen. As with an outstanding musical or theatrical performance, athletic contest, academic lecture, and most other accomplishments, the success of a board meeting depends on preparation that begins long in advance of the event itself. In the case of a board meeting, agenda preparation should begin several weeks in advance. Reviewing minutes of previous meetings can be a reminder of follow-up items that need to be given attention; such minute perusal likewise will signal agenda matters, likely under "old business" (or what might be better termed "previously discussed items," since none of us likes to discuss matters old and stale).

Depending on the governance patterns and committee roles and responsibilities, agenda building may include consultation with chairs to determine items discussed in committee that are ready for full board attention and decision making. In some organizations, a call for agenda items is issued to every board member (doing so has become more streamlined and easy with the advent of email). Still other agenda items may surface from the staff, given their involvement in every aspect of the congregation's or organization's life. The actual development of the agenda often involves a face-to-face, telephonic, or email exchange between board chair and the pastor/president/CEO.

Following its preparation, the agenda, together with important documents, should be distributed in advance to all board members. Depending on the scope of a board's work, the quantity of material might range from just a few papers in an envelope to weighty documents mailed in UPS boxes. When the Church Council of the Evangelical Lutheran Church in America meets, for example, its agenda materials frequently are equal in thickness to the Chicago telephone directory! The purpose of advance materials distribution is to enable board members to give careful and prayerful preparation for the meeting, reviewing ahead of time reports, proposals, financial statements, and other important documents.

We are convinced that good ecclesiastical governance occurs in the context of prayer and faith-sharing. Meetings should begin with a time of devotional reflection, include prayer moments perhaps interspersed throughout, and conclude with an invocation for God's continuing guidance. Likewise, we believe that almost every board meeting should include some aspect of board development, offering an opportunity for members to learn more about the organization, external dynamics in the broader environment, trends likely to affect the ministry, and personal sharing of insights gained by members in their many arenas of life and service. Providing board members with an occasional "treat" such as an outside speaker or workshop leader (for example on personal faith issues, spiritual formation, or practical life skills) can offer non-financial rewards and convey to board members how much they are valued. While such board development or learning time can occur at any point in a meeting, putting it up front on the agenda after opening devotions signals its importance and also ensures it will happen when folks are likely to be at their highest energy and attention.

Every board will find its own rhythm for reviewing and approving minutes, receiving reports, discussing important proposals and problems, and moving on to making decisions. Some find it helpful to divide the agenda into categories such as "For Discussion," "For Decision Today," and "Looking Ahead." Others follow a more traditional agenda flow: Approval of Minutes, Pastor's Report, Treasurer's Report, Committee Reports, and Special Items. A good chair might introduce the meeting with a brief overview, citing those items that in her or his judgment are the most important, in what areas decision must be made at this meeting, and where advance discussion of matters to be decided at a future date will be most important. Likewise, at the end of the meeting, a brief summary offered by the chair or another designated critical observer can help the board members grasp the high points and leave with a sense that important things have occurred and their time has been well spent.

While many boards operate with an informal style and natural flow, some find it helpful to attach time allotments to agenda items, with a designated time-keeper signaling when time is running out and a decision must be made. Particularly for boards of large and complex entities with wide ranging responsibilities, keeping on task with a timed agenda may be crucial. Establishing firm beginning and ending times can be helpful in keeping board members engaged, motivated, and convinced their time is valued. Such matters as these, of course, can be highly contextual and cultural as well. In some cultural contexts, rigid adherence to a timed agenda would be perceived as inhospitable and insensitive to the need for generous amounts of time simply engaged in fellowship and personal connecting. (See Appendix H for an example of a timed agenda.)

The person in the role of chair carries a heavy burden but also has great opportunity to facilitate the work and witness of the board. The chairperson can seek to draw in the silent sitters who undoubtedly have much to contribute but may feel uncomfortable in sharing. On occasion, "going round the table" and giving each person opportunity to speak, especially on "hot" issues or difficult matters, is a wise strategy. Striking a balance between maintaining good order, often by following Robert's Rules of Order, and allowing leeway by avoiding heavy-handed legalistic meeting conduct, is another challenge for the chair. A wise chair will sense when a group may be stuck and unable to move forward, perhaps suggesting a spontaneous brief break, or asking if a matter should be deferred to a subsequent meeting. Inviting the board to divide into small groups for a few moments can also interrupt lethargy or avert unproductive conflict.

A good meeting is not over when it's over! That is to say, in addition to official minutes, which typically are reviewed only by board members, a brief written summary may be very helpful in communicating broadly key decisions made and discussions held by the governing board. In congregations, typically a "Church Council Highlights" column in the parish newsletter is such a means of communication; increasingly, a similar summary on the website provides prompt communication to a broad audience. In the case of particularly important decisions deemed newsworthy, the preparation of a press release or even hosting a news conference may be important post-board activity. We offer more about communication in chapter

8. Following up on all decisions made and directions set may fall to a combination of board member volunteers and staff, again depending upon the nature, structure, and style of the particular community of faith.

Board Goal-Setting and Self-Assessment

In many organizations the board holds everyone accountable except itself. That is to say, many boards do a good job of planning, monitoring progress, and helping the organization move forward toward its goals. But far too many do not apply such practices to the most important group of all in the organization—themselves. While some would argue that the board's role is purely oversight, and that in one sense everything the entire organization does is a measure of the board's achievements, such an analysis may be avoidant behavior on the part of board members.

It is our belief that good boards set goals for themselves and periodically evaluate their progress toward the established goals. Some of the easier to define may be numerically quantifiable, such as, "We will raise $20,000 this year through board member fund-raising activity, with 100% participation in personal giving," or, "Board member meeting attendance will exceed 90%, with 85% of our meetings ending at the hour established on the agenda." Many board members may find it helpful to set their own personal goals in terms of community life involvement, personal outreach, or nurturing of fellow members. A composite of all the personal goals may shape an overall map of the board's course for the next period of time.

While the nature and scope of boards' work varies tremendously, every board should give perpetual special attention to one matter: supporting the staff, particularly that one called by the board or entire faith community as chief pastor, president, or director. Any time a board engages in a process of staff evaluation, particularly assessing the performance of its chief executive, it should simultaneously examine its own performance, especially in the matter of support for those called to staff ministries. If the concomitant question to "How is she doing?" is not "And how are we doing in supporting her?" a board's assessment fails to honor the principle that "we have this ministry together."

When a Board Goes Bilious

This section is one that we hope only a handful of readers will need to consider. The vast majority will find that church boards of all sorts are constituted by dedicated, generous, visionary, and committed congregational or organizational members. Most colleagues will find themselves supported by and in partnership with a group of blessed balladeers frequently chanting songs of good news.

Sadly, however, even in the church there are times when a board goes awry. Sometimes, despite careful recruitment, strong orientation, wise nurturing, and mentoring, a board can be held hostage by a few or even one or two disturbed or deeply self-centered individuals who cannot find it possible to put first the mission of the gospel and faith community. Generally, with a bit of patience, some mild interventions on the part of the chair and pastor or CEO, poorly functioning board members can be brought around to productive positive contributions. But on occasion a board becomes dysfunctional and begins to undermine rather than advance the community's mission. If deep interpersonal and intra-group conflicts erupt, behavior can become downright bilious, spewing unhealthy dynamics in all directions. In such a sad state of affairs, life will be miserable for most if not all members—and particularly for those called to executive staff responsibilities.

What to do? The temptation is to rush to despair and contemplate hasty departure, to begin planning one's exit from a community whose board has become unsupportive. There may be times when, after repeated efforts to help a board get back on track, for one's own mental health, family well-being, or other factors resignation is the wisest course of action. We believe, however, that some of the most important ministry on the part of a pastoral or executive leader can occur in the context of paralyzed, ineffective, or downright damage-inflicting board behavior. Sticking it out under such circumstances may be extremely difficult, but giving in to destructive behavior will further reinforce negative patterns and convince those who are acting out in inappropriate ways that such behavior will be tolerated.

If a leader finds herself or himself dealing with unhealthy board dynamics, the first advice is: don't try to endure it alone. Find allies, either inside or outside the organization, who can be good sounding boards and commiserate with your frustrations, and offer objective analysis of what's going on and how positive interventions might occur. Recognize that individual and collective negative behavior may have little or nothing to do with you and your leadership.

Studying the history of a board's behavior may also provide helpful insights in the midst of conflict. Are there discernible patterns over time that might offer some clue to why the board finds itself in disarray? Going back over years of meeting minutes, annual reports, and talking with a few trusted long-time members might reveal such cycles. One of us once consulted with a congregation whose council was in a horrendous conflict. Member was pitted against member. It seemed as though at times the entire council could only agree in common disappointment with and opposition to the pastor. As the consultant studied the history of this particular faith community, it became apparent that every five years or so this pattern seemed to repeat itself. Upon further reflection and careful listening, it was discovered that this group of folks placed a high premium on the very Christian value of forgiveness. And of course, the only way to enjoy forgiveness is to have a big fight every so often! Simply naming this repetitive cycle and posing the possibility that there would be other values worth raising to higher priority seemed to help the board and the entire congregation move to new patterns of interaction.

If the board's dysfunctional dynamics or bilious behavior is of such destructive nature that no amount of patient coaching and counseling on the part of a leader will make a difference, the only course of action may be to call for intervention from the outside. In congregations, at such a point the bishop or other judicatory leader likely will need to become involved. She or he may have limited authority and training or skills to make much positive headway in helping steer the board in a positive direction. Depending on the denomination's polity, it may be possible for the bishop, district superintendent, or other authority to place a congregation under special oversight for a time until the unhealthy internal dynamics can be remedied.

Our assessment, based on decades of working with and observing many boards enduring seasons of distress, is that there is a tendency to give in too soon to destructive behavior. The typical pattern for bishops and others in oversight is to suggest that the pastor, president, or CEO resign. In most cases, the pattern likely will repeat itself with leader after leader. A better solution may be to call for the resignation of elected board leaders. On one occasion, one of us recommended that the entire board be dissolved and a new board convened with all new members.

Anecdotal evidence from all denominations suggests there is a relatively high drop-out rate for former church board members, particularly those who have served during a season of heavy conflict and turmoil within the board itself. Providing pastoral care to board members, especially those who may become targets of misplaced anger or frustration vented by peers, can be critically important for their spiritual well-being, as well as to insure that they remain committed members of the faith community.

Boards in the Bible

For the most part, leadership in the Bible, particularly in the Old Testament, is understood as being exercised by charismatic individuals called and drawn into covenant with God. There is little evidence that Abraham and Sarah answered to a council or that the great liberator Moses was a chief executive accountable to a board of directors. The great kings of Israel and Judah, figures like David and Solomon, appeared to loom larger than life. While there are references to what may have been some type of council of advisers, it is clear that monarchs like Kings David and Solomon did not report to boards of directors! The prophets of Israel appeared generally to find themselves in opposition to the reigning powers of kings and other rulers; once again, their calls and commissions came directly from God. No matter how much one seeks to read behind the obvious events recounted in the great prophetic literature, it seems impossible to imagine a scenario of Isaiah or Jeremiah meeting with their prophetic governing boards. Nevertheless, numerous Old Testament references to "elders" imply that indeed forms of shared leadership existed. Perhaps the kings and prophets were more accountable to (and even selected by?) others than is readily apparent from a cursory reading of biblical texts.

In the New Testament, one can begin to discern emerging governing structures. As the Church gained momentum, and as fledgling faith communities began to burgeon with stunning conversion rates, organizational matters started to take on increasing importance. As noted in Chapter 1, the Acts of the Apostles is our primary window into the community life of the early church. Through a close reading of Acts, it becomes apparent that the New Testament church emerged within a context of governance by councils. By all evidence available to us, the Roman Empire had developed fairly sophisticated administrative structures and exercised governance with a tight control over its citizens exerted by a combination of civilian and military authorities. A well-developed taxation bureaucracy had been put in place to garner resources for Caesar. In Acts 4:5 we read, "On the morrow their rulers and elders and scribes were gathered together in Jerusalem, with Annas the high priest. . . ." In many other places, the Gospels and Acts speak of the Sanhedrin, councils of the Pharisees, and other secular and religious governing groups. It is only natural to assume that as it grew and began to institutionalize, the fledgling New Testament *ekklesia* patterned its organizational life after those in the surrounding culture.

Some form of decision-making body begins to appear fairly early in Acts. As the Christian movement began to flourish, the apostles huddled (6:2ff.) and summoned others to organize a cadre of the first deacons for ministries of service. Very soon, some form of council also initiated a primitive form of strategic mission planning. For example, in Acts 8:14 it is reported that, "Now when the apostles at Jerusalem heard that Samaria had received the word of God, they sent to them Peter and John. . . ." Whether it was a regularly convening body or ad hoc one-time convention, some form of a deliberative body had begun to assess the current situation, consider their resources—human and otherwise—and engage in enough planning to send a delegation.

By the middle of Acts, references to "elders" (*presbyteroi*) begin to appear (cf. 15:6), providing first indications of what we know emerged into a threefold ministry of deacons, presbyters (elders), and bishops. In Acts 15, we have a report on what appears to have been the first major convention of the early church. Called to resolve burgeoning theological disputes over the necessity of circumcision for male Christians, the Jerusalem council exercised governance in both practical and theological matters. In one of the first ecclesiastical attempts to carry out a communication strategy, the apostolic decree eliminating a circumcision requirement was transmitted in an orderly fashion (15:22ff.) The apostles and elders obviously began to hold other conciliar gatherings for decision making. These early councils sent delegations to outposts of the church and to new mission fields.

Inasmuch as the latter half of the book of Acts is a travelogue that chronicles the journeys of Paul and his encounters on the road, we are given little additional insight into governance patterns and the character and style of the early Christian boards and councils. But we may assume that they harked back to the words of the Lord as he had coached his disciples into servant leadership with a high level of mutual respect and an avoidance of overly hierarchical patterns by which some sought to accrue power unto themselves at the expense of their colleagues. We can be confident that, as tensions and conflicts arose, some recalled the Master's exhortations to "love one another" and to remember that "the first shall be last and the last first." As they encountered one problem after another, as they coped with limited or nonexistent resources for their mission, as they faced persecutions and even martyrdom for faithful exercise of their ministries, surely they remembered Jesus' parting promise: "And remember, I am with you always, to the end of the age!" (Matt 28:20).

CHAPTER 4

Planning with Passion

"For time was just a line, a gift we saved, a gift the future gave."
—Harry Chapin, singer, storyteller

This chapter is about ways to shake loose the gift the future gives and sometimes withholds. That gift is an incomparable freedom to act by becoming sufficiently loosed from the past to do what seems right in the present moving toward a future full of hope and expectation (Jer 29:11). The gift is available for a person, group, congregation, institution, or international entity.

Planning is about action-in-time. Planning is not about planning. Yet, how numerous are the planning projects that become ends in themselves, whereby a feeling of accomplishment is reached when the planning is complete rather than the action it is designed to effect. What follows is meant to be helpful in thinking about planning, and creating and using planning tools and models that avoid the planning trap, that is, planning becoming full of itself rather than the action it claims to birth.

Planning Prompts

What prompts planning? Why is it so ubiquitous? Some say rapid social change. The organization that does not plan falls behind and gets out of position to capitalize and optimize on evolving situations. Others locate the urge to plan in the necessity to cope with ever-expanding amounts of information. There is not a paucity of information; rather we are overwhelmed by information signals. What parts of the aggregate are important and essential for us? What disasters can be averted, or which opportunities can be seized? While these responses are useful in understanding the imperative to plan, they do not take into account the human desire to be effective within the stream of time. Recall Isaac Watts's words, "Time like an ever-rolling stream soon bears us all away" (see the epigram to the Preface).

Nor do the responses speak to the situation of the church-related organization as it seeks to hear and act on God's call within that same stream of time. A study of planning that was conducted in a church setting says it well: "Planning is related to not letting the world happen to you"; and "Planning is being active, not reactive."

Temporal Structures of Everyday Life

Humans, at least most of us, are very pragmatic. Everyday life is organized around what two social philosophers call "the 'here' of my body and the 'now' of my present." The "here" takes precedence over the "there" and the "now" over the "then." Yet the "here and now" do not exhaust relevant interests and concerns; therefore, everyday life consists of caring for the immediate and somatic, as well as the important but distant.[1] It is easy to identify with the following excerpt from a diary:

> Long-Range Goals:
>   1. Health—more leisure
>   2. Money
>   3. Write book (play?)—fame!!!??
>   4. Visit India
> Immediate:
>   Pick up pattern at Hilda's

---

1. Peter L. Berger and Thomas Luckmann, *The Social Construction of Reality*, Anchor Books (Garden City, N.Y.: Doubleday, 1967), 22.

Change faucets—call plumber (who?)

Try yoghurt??[2]

Human effectiveness happens within time. No one has "all the time in the world" to act. A sense of mortality arrives in two ways: the awareness that I will die or that my organization may fade ("time runs out") generates anxiety about finitude and limits. But time not only "runs out," it also "flies by." Thus a sense of *timing* is also important. Human effectiveness is carried out within the structure of temporality. We speak of "being in the right place at the right time," of "an idea whose time has come." We say, "I just can't seem to find time to do the things I really want"; "This congregation doesn't seem to have a future"; "Time waits for no one." The moment that was just now and with which I was becoming familiar is gone, never more to return. This movement from the "not yet" to the "now," and on to the "no longer" has been called by theologian Emil Brunner "the deepest source of the world's sorrow."[3]

What prompts planning? you may ask again. Planning may indeed be prompted by a refusal to cave in to the transience of time in all its irreversibility and inevitability. Planning is a human activity designed to enable individuals and organizations to combat the tyranny of time. Planning is one means of actualizing effectiveness within the everyday structures of life. As suggested in the Preface, it is an attempt to ride time even as it soon bears us all away.

Passion for Planning

Given a more powerful (and, we hope, more interesting) explanation of the widespread phenomenon of planning, it may be clear why this chapter is entitled "Planning with Passion." Passion seems appropriate for three reasons: it connotes an emotion commensurate with the combative quality of struggle against time; it positions planning as a major human activity that is far more than following a

---

2. Taken from the "Diary of a Lady," quoted in *The New Yorker*; cited by H. Igor Ansoff, *Corporate Strategy* (New York: McGraw-Hill, 1965), 43.

3. Emil Brunner, *Eternal Hope* (Philadelphia: Westminster, 1954), 43.

mechanical sequence of steps (although it is that too); and it calls forth one's own best efforts and talents if the planning is to be effective.

A participant at a conference in the United States asked a world-renowned professor of planning from Berlin University, "How do you understand your role as a planner and teacher of planning?" The answer: "I am an encourager, a passionate attendant to hope." The audience seemed surprised and not a little disappointed at the response. Surely there was some technique, concept, or even trick a planning practitioner could learn from this learned teacher. The wisdom of the answer, however, is found in comprehension of the human dynamics of action-in-time described above. Put another way, the results planning seeks are not only in the *what*—goals, opportunities, direction, vision, long-range analysis—but in what happens to the *who*—engendering hope, encouraging human effort and faithfulness, full use of talent and creation of significant communities of competence with more than ample common purpose and action.

There is a significant spiritual dimension as well. The German theologian Jürgen Moltmann relates passion to theology and planning:

> In the medium of hope our theological concepts become not judgments which nail reality down to what it is, but anticipations which show reality its prospects and into future possibilities. In 1516, he [Luther] writes of the 'earnest expectation of the creature' of which Paul speaks in Romans 8:19 . . . believing hope will itself provide inexhaustible resources for the creative, inventive imagination of love. Thus [hope] will constantly arouse the 'passion of the possible.'. . . [C]reative action springing from faith is impossible without new thinking and planning that springs from hope.[4]

An administrator says, "let's plan." A marvelous confluence of forces, emotions, hopes, dreams, anxieties, self-images, histories, theologies, and whatever get activated. For the church administrator, under a holy calling, a creative passion

---

4. Jürgen Moltmann, *Theology of Hope* (Minneapolis: Fortress Press, 1993), 34–35.

is involved, because the subjects, the gospel and the church, are cared for so passionately and resolutely.

Twin Templates of Planning

Before some specific advice and models for the practice of planning are described, its two crucial dimensions must be emphasized. Though obvious, attention to these two increases the chance of good planning, while neglecting one or both spells disaster.

Template One

Planning is *thinking* about action-in-time. Psychologist, sociologist, and theologian agree that mental operations involve four broad categories:

> There is the *empirical* level in which we sense, perceive, imagine, feel, speak, move. There is the *intellectual* level in which we inquire, come to understand, express what we have understood, and work out the presuppositions and implications of our expression. There is the *rational* level in which we reflect, marshal the evidence, pass judgment on the truth or falsity, certainty or probability, of a statement. There is the *responsibility* level in which we are concerned with ourselves, our own operations, our goals, and to deliberate about possible courses of action, evaluate them, decide, and carry out our decisions.[5]

Good planning provides concrete ways these four levels of thinking can happen. Look at the steps of any planning model that appears later in this chapter ("Menu of Models"). The steps are a mirror image of the thinking process, and that mental activity takes place within the fascinating and sometimes frustrating dynamic of time.

---

5. Bernard Lonergan, *Method in Theology* (New York: Herder and Herder, 1972), 9.

The object of planning is to create a space in time or perhaps more accurately a *gap* between *reality* and *vision* and then to identify rationally determined ways to close the gap. More recently, vision has been the winner in church administration and administration in general, especially as leaders or potential leaders are expected (or required) to "have a vision." Vision casting is important. Vision, especially when owned by all the actors involved in a collective process, serves at least five vital functions. Vision

- attracts adherents
- gathers them together, creating a sense of "we"
- unites in a shared future
- grounds in reality and pulls toward possibility
- "sees" what is not there but could and should be

But reality is making a comeback. One recent study of vital business organizations and how they got that way finds that these organizations have people who "confront the brutal facts."[6]

After experiencing his much-anticipated visit to Rome at the age of eighteen, Dietrich Bonhoeffer, German pastor, teacher, theologian, and Confessing Church leader in Nazi Germany, wrote in his diary, "But reality is, quite certainly, more beautiful than fantasy."[7] Bonhoeffer's later theology, perhaps not incidentally, sought to rescue the church from an idealism too easily co-opted by the Nazi program into a *realism* shaped by the incarnation of Christ and a careful analysis of the situation at hand. Vision *and* reality, not either/or, makes for effective planning.

Template Two

Planning is a *social* activity. It is done with others. As much, if not more, attention needs to be paid to the ways people have access to and participate in the process

---

6. Jim Collins, *Good to Great* (New York: Harper Business, 2001), 65–89.

7. Dietrich Bonhoeffer, *The Young Bonhoeffer 1918–1927;* Dietrich Bonhoeffer Works 9 (Minneapolis: Fortress Press, 2003), 83.

as it does in the more rational, knowledge-based aspects of planning as think-ing. The social interaction involved in planning runs from soft (small family-like congregations talking about their dreams and hopes) to hard (large social ministry organizations or universities crunching data about student enrollments, needs and issues of the communities served, educational trends, housing needs, and financial expenses and income). One scholar states that organizations have "publics with opinions" (adversaries, clients, suppliers, advisers, controllers, and friends).[8]

Information vital to the desired results of the planning can be gathered from participants (internal) and publics (external) through a variety of means, such as interviews (in person and telephone), surveys (mail and e-mail), focus groups, histories, trends, vision and mission statements, data gathering meetings and conferences, and the results of previous studies, planning projects, and conflict episodes.

Another important aspect of planning as *social* interaction is the role played by a planning group. A small but as representative as possible (gender, age, eth-nicity, experience, new members, "old guard") group of six to ten persons for the planning leader (whether pastor, executive and/or consultant) to work with is essential. Stacking this group with the power elite or the executive's friends guarantees conflict and power grabs. On the other hand, the right group not only contributes to the outcomes but also communicates the process and results to the rest of the organization. Consideration of the two templates of planning—think-ing and social interaction—leads to a definition of planning as *thinking about action-in-time with important others.*

Because it contains what seem to be the essential powerful features of effective planning (imagination, constructing an attractive future, being beckoned, and rational preparations), consider this succinct description:

> I project, that is to say, I cast something forward into time.
> What do I cast? My imagination, which jumps to a time not
> yet accomplished and builds something there, a *signum* (Latin
> for sign), and this construct beckons and exercises a present

---

8. Bertram M. Gross, *Organizations and Their Managing* (New York: The Free Press, 1964), 113–166.

attraction to me. Thus actions by coming before this imagined
future are determined by it and prepare it rationally.[9]

Change the singular, "I-my-me," to plural, "we-ours-us," and it is possible to
grasp the power, passion, and perils of planning as an administrative activity.

Prepare to Plan

Probably the most neglected step in planning is preparation. The ground must be
prepared to receive the seed. Here are five ingredients of preparation.

1. *Aftermath.* The "leftovers" from a previous planning episode may help or hin-
der initiation of a new process. The literature on planning is stocked with examples
of failed planning, which in turn become an obstacle to be overcome in motivating
persons to try it again. Planning difficulties include inadequate preparation, weak
process, lack of support from leaders, shallow analysis, lack of significant information, unclear objectives, spotty participation, the "paralysis of analysis," fatigue,
delayed action. All or any of these can then become the memory that pollutes the
next attempt. Inquire about past planning projects and learn from them.

2. *Making the case.* Find answers to the question "Why?" What are the reasons for doing this planning? Is there new leadership who wants to undertake
some new directions? Are there major changes in the wider environment of the
organization that require consideration and new responses? Planning related to
increased collaboration among theological education providers is underway in
some denominations. This collaboration now has a ten-year history of significant
accomplishments. Planning helps to answer the questions, "Now what? What
new opportunities are emerging? What new threats are on the horizon?" Reasons
for planning can also be related to the enhancement of unity. Are opinions too
scattered? Can common action be developed? Or is planning needed to improve
governance practices or design a new structure? Make the *reasons* clear and transparent; no "hidden agendas," which usually are uncovered anyway and become
barriers to receiving "the gift the future gives."

---

9. Bernard de Jouvenal; the source of the quotation is not known.

3. *Power shifts.* Who will lose power as the planning proceeds toward implementation? Who will gain power? Power shifts are one reason people resist planning. They see ahead past the process and imagine (perhaps wrongly) that their influence will wane while that of others will grow. Honesty is the best policy. Trying to satisfy everyone probably will not work, but sometimes new coalitions can be created that support or even lead the process.

4. *Conflict.* Conflict as an expected part of doing administration will be treated in chapter 11. Note now only that conflict *will* result from planning—unless you are in a completely homogeneous everybody-agrees organization. It is hardly likely that there is such an outfit. Therefore, expect conflict and follow steps to address it. Conflict can debilitate a planning process but it can also energize one.

5. *Theological objections.* Jesus instructed, "Take no thought for the morrow," or, in another translation, "So do not worry about tomorrow, for tomorrow will bring worries of its own. Today's trouble is enough for today" (Matt 6:34). Does planning disregard Jesus' teaching? It does if it loses its *offering* quality, that is, as an offering to God, as a response to Christ, and as an embodiment of the activity of the Holy Spirit. Throughout this book are biblical and theological perspectives on administrative practices, including the final section of this chapter, "Planning in the Bible." These references are attempts to link church administration to theology. They are our offerings to address objections and to develop a theology of administration that is faithful, informative, inspirational, and that guides administration by and in the church. This material can be used to formulate sound responses to planning objections.

Outline of a Planning Proposal

Preparing a proposal to undertake a planning process is a critical step. Here is an outline of a real proposal.

1. Background leading to the need for a proposal
2. Desired results of the proposed planning
3. Several premises (assumptions) on which the planning is based
4. Statement of conditions for doing sound planning
5. Outlines of the proposed planning process

6. A timeline for the process

7. Ways to evaluate results and monitor progress

8. Description of roles for essential groups and persons in the planning process

9. A brief assessment of the readiness to do planning with suggestions for preparation

10. An estimate of financial costs (direct expenses of the process and person days) and other "social costs," if relevant

What Happens?

A planning process can be described as a series of sequential steps—preparation, internal and external assessment, analysis, directions and goals, implementation, and evaluation. These sequences can be compressed into as few as three steps and as many as twenty-three! An example of the former is a process for Action youth groups in congregations—Awareness, Critique, and Try (ACT). The twenty-three-step process is from a federal government bureau with seven layers of authority. In basic form, these two processes are the same, only adapted to their specific institutional settings.

Another way to depict a planning process is to go deeper into the dynamics of what happens as the sequential steps are followed. There are at least four "levels" at work: instrumental, interpersonal, substantive, and symbolic.

Level 1: Instrumental

The first task is to provide/decide on the mechanics of the planning process. Effective forms, timelines, and instruction on how to plan do not guarantee a planning process will go well, but ineffective ones can produce aggravation and pull attention away from much more important matters. Experienced planners seem to have a bag full of concepts and techniques adaptable to the given situation.

A workable framework for planning is absolutely necessary. A framework for a national church program unit consists of six tasks expressed in a single (run-on?) sentence: (1) Drawing data from the groups involved, (2) in the areas of special relevance, (3) the cabinet (highest staff authority) works to perform, (4) analyses and first-cut planning (external, internal, issues, and alternatives), (5) to provide policies and guidelines on specific topics, (6) for the groups involved. A framework provides some mental "hooks" that double as communication devices and learning aids.

Factors that shape customizing are also part of the mechanics of planning: knowing and appreciating the history of planning in this specific setting, the perception and memories of members or staff about previous planning efforts, the planning skill level of participants, the goals of the executive or pastor, the interpersonal style of the organization, and the realization that individuals came to the planning project with certain predilections. There seem to be True Believers (planning is a very useful way to bring people together through the creation of a shared future); Politico-Doubters (real decisions are made through the use of power and authority, planning is window dressing for politics); and Friendly Missourians (if you can demonstrate to me that planning will make some real difference, count me in).

Planning needs support and endorsement by those in leadership. That may call for carefully nurturing the process from infancy to maturity (passing through adolescence, of course) and "stepping to the plate" through personal investment of time and talent, demonstration of honesty, integrity, and personal values.[10]

Level 2: Interpersonal

Planning usually happens in groups; therefore the ability to understand and lead groups tending to both tasks and group maintenance is important. Conflict among persons and even inside individuals seems inevitable and even desirable if the planning is addressing significant change and critical issues. An entire chapter in this book is devoted to conflict. Sometimes people feel left out. Providing realistic but significant access to and participating in the planning process is one way planning produces action, because a certain consensus is created about what needs to be done. One planning theorist, Warren Ziegler, connects participation to human agency:

---

10. On the relation of leadership and planning, see Michael L. Cooper-White, *On a Wing and a Prayer: Faithful Leadership in the 21st Century;* Lutheran Voices (Minneapolis: Augsburg Fortress, 2003), 29–42.

> The notion of participation, or of participatory planning . . .
> is thus to be understood as the development of opportunities
> for a reconsideration by persons of the ways in which they can
> reacquire a belief in their own potency.[11]

Different personality types also experience planning in a variety of ways. For example, some "see" reality clearly, while others are better at imagining a future. Communication in planning groups can be enhanced by sharing these individual differences, perhaps through some assessment instrument. Witness congregational planning that ignores the pastor or goes against her wishes, or from which the pastor excludes himself, assuming that the whole thing would blow over and life would return to normal, and you will see the conditions being created for conflict. Determining the role of the pastor, executive, and/or staff is critical. It need not be the same in all situations, but it should be clear and agreed to by the relevant parties.

Finally, the interpersonal level includes encouragement and hope, especially by those who lead the process of the kind previously identified in this chapter. As a person in a church-related institution doing some strategic planning said, "When you think of people and planning together, it is important to be optimistic about people. They desire to become more capable. We sometimes underestimate them." One theory of human development is that humankind has moved from *fear* of the unknown to *hope* as more control is gained through scientific knowledge and technological advances. At the rational level, certainty rules, that is, until it fails to deliver. "In our time, where the failure of rational certainty has brought back fear, only renewed hope is capable of giving gracefulness and balance to the lives of humans and human systems."[12]

Level 3: Substantive

Planning also leads its adherents into the wonderful world of ideas and information. Wisdom can be shared by recommending relevant articles, papers, and books to those

---

11. Warren Ziegler, "Planning As Action: Techniques of Inventive Planning Workshops," Educational Policy Research Center (unpublished manuscript), 55.

12. Erich Jantsch and Conrad H. Waddington, *Evolution and Consciousness: Human Systems in Transition* (Reading, Mass.: Addison-Wesley, 1976), 232.

who are planning together. Expanding the knowledge and wisdom base can only help by rescuing the process from a strictly mechanical feeling by providing *substance* for new direction or affirmation of old ones. Pastors sometimes provide books to a planning group on mission, theology, parish revitalization, or community data and trends. Wisdom has a threefold nature in the Bible: wisdom of ultimate things, practical wisdom like knowing what to do, and critical wisdom that makes judgments to choose the path from A to B.[13] Every effective planning group seems to have someone who is wise in one or more of these three ways. Some people have a knack for seeing below the obvious or finding hidden treasure and meaning in vast arrays of data.

A more formal step is the *environmental scan*. This is a systematic investigation of mission-relevant short- and long-range information gathered from internal participants and those persons, groups, institutions, and even society that are important to the organization. While forecasting the future has fallen on hard times in an increasingly complex world, looking at the long-range implications of present issues and needs is possible and desirable.

There is evidence that suggests that, for nonprofit organizations, positioning according to the latest trends may be self-defeating. More important may be probing histories for effective actions, especially in times of crisis, determining what practices are critical to effectiveness in mission, and strengthening identity, which by definition has to do with the durable features of the organization over a longer period of time. Identity and mission and their interplay may be the clue for churches that last. Non-profits, including churches, perhaps need to position themselves less in space (environmental scanning) and more in time (our reliable past propels us into a useable future: we did it before, we can do it again),[14] or at least keep a balance between the two.

Level 4: Symbolic

We are not sure what to call this level, but we know it exists and is a powerful part of effective planning. In one sense, this level already has been explored in

---

13. William Barclay, *New Testament Words* (Philadelphia: Westminster, 1974), 258–61.

14. See Robert Bacher and Kenneth Inskeep, *Chasing Down a Rumor: The Death of Mainline Denominations* (Minneapolis: Augsburg Books, 2005), 168–70.

the foregoing section of this chapter on planning as thinking about action-in-time with others. Planning ushers persons into deeply personal matters related to time—regret, dreams deferred, opportunities lost maybe forever, entering some new life stage like retirement, failed relationships, previous effective planning projects or failed ones. Some also see planning as a chance to "get it together," that is, mastering the situation, taming the untamable, rationalizing the irrational.

Faith issues also come to the fore. Is God trustworthy? Can I be forgiven? Is this congregation an expression of God's community of faith or does it resemble a private club? Does this church-related university have a future? What is God calling us to be and do?

Planning as action-in-time raises questions of faith and life, unity and mission, future and past, and being together. What are the skills summoned by significant planning projects?

Cheaper by the Dozen

Journeying across the terrain created by a planning exercise requires certain skills if effectiveness is to be achieved. Those listed below do not seem to be present in any one person, but a team or group can exhibit them all. Skills can be pooled.

1. Starting up planning: the ability to introduce, explain, and interest others in engaging in planning.
2. Providing the mechanics of planning: the ability to provide models, forms, timelines, and instructions for doing planning.
3. Maintaining planning: the ability to assist the evolution of planning from infancy to maturity.
4. Working in groups: the ability to help groups to engage in planning by attending to task and group maintenance needs.
5. Handling conflict: the ability to deal constructively with conflict that arises among individuals and groups as planning progresses.
6. Encouraging/engendering hope: the ability to offer personal encouragement about the future, its effects, and the capacity to "change things."

7. Obtaining and interpreting information: the ability to gather and interpret information relevant to planning.

8. Developing practical ideas: the ability to locate and apply or create "program" ideas that are attractive and usable.

9. Developing evocative symbols: the ability to "raise up," that is, formulate and identify language and visual symbols (especially biblical and theological ones), which seem to motivate action and enthusiasm and shape organizational identity.

10. Retrieving the past: the ability to describe and interpret significant past events and conditions which serve to affirm and "cleanse" the past for its role in planning the future.

11. Envisioning the future: the ability to develop and describe broad and specific possibilities for the future.

12. Confronting mortality: the ability to help individuals or organizations deal with a sense of mortality (I or we will "not last forever") through understanding, significant action, and the promises of God.

The Planning Process: An Unending Cycle and Unbroken Circle

As planning is contemplated, it is important to recognize that it is not as much a linear process (moving from point A to B to C and ultimately to Z) as it is circular and cyclical. Just as we are never done with breathing or eating or sleeping, so a planning process carried out in a dynamic context is never finished. Nor does it proceed sequentially in neatly predictable steps. Along the way in a planning process, life happens! Planning is accomplished in the midst of a constantly changing context and continually evolving environment. Planning might be thought of as measuring an ice cube with a hot ruler: the very act of seeking to measure changes the thing itself. Experienced planners use metaphorical images like "building the plane while it's already in the air and flying" or "eating the cake while it's still in the oven and the recipe hasn't quite been found yet." Planning is dynamic. One of childhood's playthings that has endured from generation to generation serves as a visual aid in teaching about planning—a Slinky. Tweak an extended Slinky at any point and the whole thing moves. Set it on a course down a stairway and it will never end up quite where expected.

Because the nature of a dynamic planning process tends to be circular and multi-dimensional, it is difficult to picture or display on a page in a book. The following description was developed for a board-orientation booklet of the Evangelical Lutheran Church in America and depicts a typical planning process involving multiple steps and four discrete phases or aspects. Strategic planning involves casting the long-range visions and imagining overarching goals that may take years or even decades to achieve. Tactical planning brings us into the shorter time frames and more modest questions: "To land a person on Mars in 2020 (the long-range strategic goal), what do we have to do this next year in order to take several key steps forward?" In the implementation phase, we take the steps identified in tactical planning, while not losing sight of the long-range strategic objectives. And constantly along the journey, we ask ourselves, "How are we doing? Where are mid-course corrections needed? Should some of our tactical plans be modified in light of new information or changing conditions?"[15]

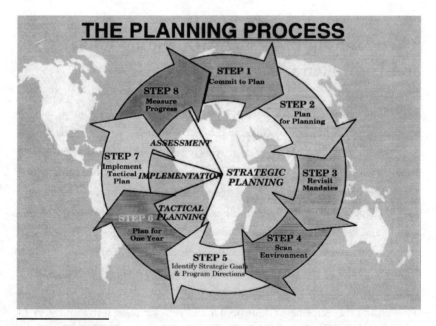

15. Cinda B. Rierson and Kathryn Heidrich, *Equipped to Serve: Steering Committee Basics* (Chicago, IL: Evangelical Lutheran Church in America, 1997), 10.

A Menu of Models

What is the best approach to planning? "It depends" sounds tentative and uncertain but may be the best answer, as there is no one right way to plan, no perfect process, no surefire approach that will guarantee a successful outcome of exciting visions, clear objectives, careful assignment of implementation responsibilities, and ultimate attainment of both short- and long-range goals. There are multiple approaches to planning, a vast array of resources, and a broad network of consultants available and eager to assist a community or organization in its planning.

The following is a short "menu" of several approaches that have proved helpful in a variety of contexts. Commentary is provided for the less familiar models.

Model A: In a Congregation: Scenario Development

Following several months of discussion and prodding by the pastor and lay president, the congregational council voted to conduct a planning process. The stated objective was "to prayerfully chart a course toward our future in light of our overall mission, *making Christ known in the Adams-Morgan neighborhood and sharing in the wider work of the Church in our diocese and around the world.*"

Council leaders were persuaded to proceed with an approach suggested by a member, Jason, whose military background and current profession as a consultant relied heavily upon developing "scenarios" for the future and then identifying short- and medium-range goals that would enable a business, military unit, or organization to proceed toward its long-range goals.

As the planning process began under Jason's leadership, he asked members of the Planning Committee appointed by the council to convene small groups of members in informal settings, where the simple question was posed: "Where do you think St. Sofia Church should be going, and how might our congregation look ten years down the road?" After several months, during which a dozen or more of these sessions were held, members of the Planning Committee came together in a day-long retreat.

"Your job this morning," said Jason following devotions and some team-building time designed particularly to enable relatively new members to get better acquainted, "is to open your minds and seek to discern where the Spirit of God might be leading St. Sofia. I ask that you review your notes from all those cottage-meetings we've held, attempt to summarize what you've heard our members saying, and take seriously their perspectives as we begin casting a vision for our future. But remember also, as we've discussed previously, our future cannot be bound solely to the present visions of current members, since we hope to be a growing congregation. If we hope to attract several hundred new members over the next decade, we need also to consider their needs and what they might say if they are asked the same questions we've posed our current members. And inasmuch as we desire to serve here in Adams-Morgan and more broadly, we need to be mindful of the needs and hopes of people in our neighborhood and city as well."

Guiding the group in its visioning expedition, Jason went on: "Now, for the next hour or so, I want each of you to go off individually and ponder all you've heard these past months from our conversations. Keep in mind the projections about what's likely to occur in St. Sofia's neighborhood and our fair city, based upon our studies of demographic data and what we've heard from city planners and others who spend their days wondering and worrying about the future of this community. Out of all that learning and listening, then, I want to ask that each of you develop a scenario for St. Sofia Church in the year 2017. Describe in detail what you envision our parish looking like in 2017 in the following specific areas: membership (numbers, ethnicity, age, etc.); staffing (how many? broad job descriptions); worship life and programs (how many services, what kinds of offerings for both members and the broader community?); budget and benevolence (how much for ourselves, how much for "mission" beyond the congregation?); buildings and property (will we need to expand, renovate, or perhaps even move our ministry to a new locale?).

At the conclusion of the hour-long session, in which St. Sofia's key lay leaders and staff had developed their personal scenarios for the future, Jason gathered them back together just before lunch. "You all go down the street to our favorite coffee shop and enjoy a leisurely lunch while I review your individual scenarios and attempt to synthesize them into a cohesive summary." Jason did as he promised. When the planning committee members returned from lunch, he handed each a one-page summary scenario, a digest of which follows:

It is the year 2017. St. Sofia Church, a member congregation of the recently formed Episco-Luthero-Presbygational

Church of the USA (ELPCUSA) has a baptized membership
of 2000 souls, with average Sunday worship attendance of just
over 1000, who praise God at one of our five weekly services
(three on Sunday; one Saturday evening and one Wednesday
noon). We are blessed to have two full-time clergy, two bivo-
cational ministers who also work in other professions, a full-
time youth and family minister, a volunteer coordinator, two
office administrative staff, and two part-time custodial staff.
In the course of a typical week, at least fourteen small groups
meet to enjoy a variety of programs or discussion groups or to
plan and conduct our several service ministries. Our recently
completed new multipurpose sanctuary has become a community gathering point for concerts and other special events
sponsored jointly by St. Sofia and the Talents-R-Us organization formed by local artists a few years ago. Our benevolence,
which supports a half-dozen local service organizations and
provides over $150,000 annually to the ELPCUSA, represents
more than 15% of our total budget. St. Sofia recently entered
a partnership with the nearby seminary of our new denomination, serving as a teaching congregation in which seminarians experience a dynamic and growing parish, and assisting
the seminary in launching a new leadership training academy
for staff and volunteers serving in dynamic urban parishes
throughout the country.

When Jason finished reading his summary scenario, a lively discussion ensued
for the next two hours. With some further tweaking, the Planning Committee
felt comfortable and excited to forward the scenario called *St. Sofia 2017* to the
church council for its discussion. Following the council's consideration during its
next two monthly meetings, the scenario was distributed to all committees and
task forces responsible for various areas of St. Sofia's ministry. It was published in
the parish newsletter, with encouragement for all members to discuss or email
their comments to members of the Planning Committee. As planning went on,
every group and committee was asked to develop short-range plans for the next

two years that would enable St. Sofia to begin moving toward the envisioned future described in the *St. Sofia 2017* document. At the conclusion of the eighteen-month planning process, a reporter invited by the Planning Committee to one of its meetings ran an article in the local newspaper under the headline: "St. Sofia: A Church on the Move that Knows Where It's Going."

Model B: A Seminary Board Retreat

Board members were divided into three groups—Past, Present, and Future—for dialogue and for answering the questions below. After reporting back, the whole board worked on Action. The strengths of this model are dealing with all the aspects of time (for example, the importance of nonprofits looking at history and tradition for reliable strengths to move forward) and engaging governance leaders in significant conversation about the institution's performance. A weakness is that the work of the three separate groups may become disjointed. That can be overcome by comparing differences, similarities, distinctive features in the three reports during the retreat and afterward.

Past

Principle: The past is retrieved, recollected, honored, cleansed, and reappropriated for use in seeing the future. Also the past as heritage, tradition, or legacy contains pluralism, fecundity, and rhythm as necessary ingredients to move ahead.

Background: Nonprofit Research—"traditionality," probe for accomplishments in times of adversity. Walter Brueggemann, *Deep Memory, Exuberant Hope*: tradition as memory. Diana Butler Bass, *Strength for the Journey*: the past is honored and reappropriated at the same time.

Leadership: Nan Keohane as Duke University President "stuck her neck out" by building on tradition, using the past as a foundation to move forward, "one Duke, not an old Duke and a new Duke" (*Duke Magazine*, 2004).

Application 1: Share seminary stories of past accomplishments in times of adversity.

Application 2: What about the "traditions" of the seminary is useful for moving ahead?

What about the "traditions" of the seminary functions as obstacles to moving ahead?

Present

Principle: Though "fleeting," the present situation is assessed for strengths and weaknesses, and agreement is checked for reliability in moving ahead.

Background: What up ahead just moved past us on the way to becoming what was? There is some dispute that there is a "present," only futures that evolve quickly into pasts.

Augustine saw it differently. "What now is clear and plain is that neither things to come nor past are. Nor is it properly said, 'There are three times, past, present, and to come'; yet perchance it might be properly said, 'There be three times; a present of things past, a present of things present, and a present of things future.'" (*Confessions*, Book 11)

Application 1: What is good about the seminary's present situation: What needs improvement?

Application 2: Do you see similarities or differences in the way the present is assessed by the seminary's constituencies? What are they?

Future

Principle: The future is "seen" not as prediction or projection but in casting the imagination usually closely connected to intention.

Background: The language used about the future by persons attempting to create or realize a shared future includes

- clarity
- agreement
- hopes, fears

- expectations
- issues
- dreams
- visions: what do you "see"? coming soon? a long way off?

Application 1: What do you see for the seminary three years from now?

Application 2: What do you see for the seminary ten years from now?

Action

Principle: There are basically two patterns of action to affect a shared future. One is immediate, perhaps obvious, action. It needs to be done. The other is more rationally prepared, using well-known sequential steps.

Background: For psychological and philosophical reasons ("I would rather act, reflect and improve, act again") or the demands of the moment ("the building is on fire"), one pattern of action is to do it and ask questions later. The other pattern follows the rational model: description, data gathering, analysis, options, action, and evaluation. It is also important to distinguish among actions by individuals, groups (teams, departments, units) and entire institutions.

Application 1: What actions should be taken now (present to two years)? By whom?

Application 2: What actions should be taken in an intermediate time frame (two to five years)? By whom?

Application 3: What actions should be taken in a long-range time frame (five to ten years)?

Model C: Structural Mapping

In another seminary, a board member who makes his living as a strategic management facilitator and coach offered to lead a planning effort utilizing a process he designed called *structural mapping*. In this approach to planning, designated as *Real Results*, an overarching desired future state is envisioned by key leaders following environmental scanning, information gathering, and various constituent focus group conversations. Each dimension of the current state of affairs in an organization or institution is assessed in terms of whether it is currently adequate (+) or inadequate (-) in contributing to movement toward the envisioned future state, and also the degree to which things are improving (+), staying the same (0), or getting worse (-) in each area.

Following some preliminary assessment, a map toward the future begins to evolve. With the ultimate goal clarified, key structural elements that must be attended to begin emerging. The gaps between where things are today and where we want them to be at some specified time in the future are then expressed in what are called *dominant tensions*. These dominant tensions must be given ongoing attention, with sub-maps developed in each area which chart a course toward resolving the tensions (bridging the gaps) and achieving the desired futures. As maps are developed for each identified key dominant tension, a vital component is the identification of key constraints that may inhibit progress toward the ultimate goals. If such constraints cannot be eliminated, they must be taken into account as leaders guide the organization toward interim way stations en route to the ultimate goal.

As the organization begins implementing steps to resolve the dominant tensions, that is, close the gaps, between current reality and the desired future state, ongoing monitoring occurs. Every working area in the organization is guided by its map toward the future. In staff meetings, while developing periodic or annual reports to supervisors and a board of directors, those charged with responsibility in an area measure their progress by reference to their guiding map.[16]

A Sample Structural Mapping Exercise

We recognize the urgent needs of the Church for more ordained ministers and other theologically trained leaders who can serve congregations and church institutions. Over the next decade, the Seminary will grow from current 300 to 400 or more stu-

---

16. Larry Webber introduced the authors to the RealResults® approach to planning.

dents. We regard our current recruitment processes as inviting
and hospitable; nevertheless, overall they are deemed inadequate. Likewise, while excellent courses are offered by superb
faculty, course delivery and methods need an expanded and
enhanced menu. The three dominant tensions that need to be
addressed to grow the Seminary's student body and graduate
numbers are identified, and each is followed by preliminary
strategies to begin bridging the gap between current reality and
our desired future state. Accountability is assigned in each case
to an individual leader and/or responsible team.

TENSION #1 **Expanded Course & Delivery Options**	TENSION #2 **Long–term Fiscal Sustainability**	TENSION #3 **Proactive Applicant Recruiting**
Desired Future	**Desired Future**	**Desired Future**
We offer an increased number of post–first graduate degree courses, along with more options that will appeal to ecumenical students. Our required courses are offered more frequently, and we utilize "block" and intensive formats. Our "distance" and offsite delivery options are significantly expanded.	More resources are available to support the expanded student body. The Seminary contains costs within balanced budgets; endowment grows steadily to $200M by 2026. Tuition remains affordable, miminizing further growth in graduate indebtedness.	As the heart of a compre-hensive marketing strategy, we are physically present at various gatherings where potential applicants are in attendance. Our applicant pool is expanded to 150 per year; with greater selectivity our admissions rate is 75%, with 90% acceptance.
GAP	**GAP**	**GAP**
Current State (-) A broad array of courses are offered, but limited access keeps some students from enrolling in our excellent degree programs. We attract relatively few enrollees for post-first degree, and are at 12% non-Lutheran.	**Current State (-)** Budgets are balanced, but income from synods, national church & annual fund is flat; endowment has been stagnant for three years. Higher tuitions will increase student debt load.	**Current State (-)** Good paper and website self-presentation by Seminary; but we lack in face-to-face encounters with prospective students. Project Connect is assisting current efforts. Admissions rate is 95%.
Accountability: Faculty and Scholarship & Leadership Formation Team (Dean)	**Accountability:** Asset Mgmt and Resource Devel Team (VP Advancement)	**Accountability:** Enrollment & Seminary Services Team (Director of Admissions)

Model D: Augusta Victoria Hospital, East Jerusalem

Can planning be done under the highly uncertain conditions of life in East Jerusalem? "Yes, in fact it has to be done," was the conclusion of board and staff of the Lutheran World Federation hospital (founded in 1950). This planning model moved the hospital into much-needed specialties and brought the medical staff, employees, and board into agreement about future directions. This is an example of doing planning in the face of financial uncertainties, political upheaval, threats of violence, and unionized employees. This hospital turns no one away for financial or any other reasons. The motto for the board became, "We haven't enough money, so we have to think."

The flow of the planning (see diagram next page) moves from Internal Assessment, External Assessment, and Analysis of Strengths, Weaknesses, Opportunities, and Threats to an identification of Strategic Issues. The development of scenarios became a very important step in addressing the uncertainty of the situation. Scenarios gave the staff and board the advantage of thinking before events occur. For example, "If the hospital ends up inside Israel, then these are the important responses," or, "If the hospital is inside a new Palestinian State, then this is what should be done." "If it becomes harder for patients and staff to get through Israeli checkpoints, then. . . ." What have been the results of using this model? In a land where victories are sparse, this hospital now has the best kidney dialysis program for children, a new fully functioning cancer treatment center for Palestinians, and daily bus service for patients and staff to counter the effects of the Separation Wall being constructed by the Israelis.

Model E: Traditional

Using a steering committee to guide the process and several analytical tools (for example, determining the interaction of mission, strengths and weaknesses, opportunities and threats), this model is typical of what is available in planning literature (see, for example, *Strategic Planning Workbook for Nonprofit Organizations*, St. Paul, MN: Amherst H. Wilder Foundation, 1997).

Step 1:   Get organized
Step 2:   Take stock (situation analysis)

Step 3:   Set direction: critical issues, goals, scenarios, or alignment (integra-
          tion of resources, structure, programming, mission)

Step 4:   Define and adopt the plan

Step 5:   Implement the plan

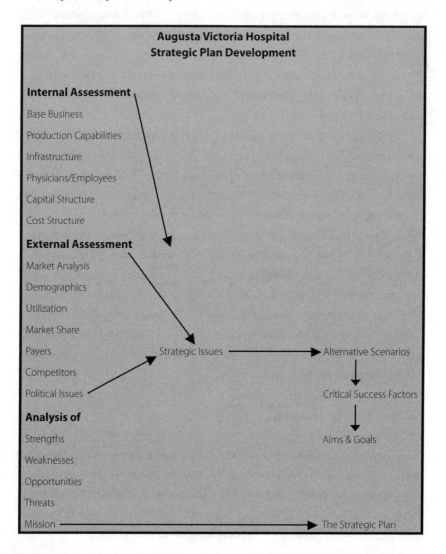

Model F: Agency Model

Similar to Model E, this approach is used widely in public organizations such as government agencies (from John M. Bryon, *Strategic Planning for Public and Non-profit Organizations* [San Francisco: Jossey-Bass, 1991], 311 pages).

Step 1: Initiating and agreeing on a strategic planning process

Step 2: Clarifying organizational mandate

Step 3: Clarifying organizational mission and values

Step 4: Assessing the external environment (stakeholder analysis)

Step 5: Assessing the internal environment

Step 6: Identifying the strategic issues facing an organization

Step 7: Formulating strategies to manage the issues

Step 8: Establishing an effective organizational vision for the future

The models above illustrate two important conclusions about planning. First, they all have similar core features. Second, they are adapted to their context. There is a creative component to planning—making it fit the situation.

Follow-up Is Essential

This chapter on planning would be incomplete if the absolute importance of follow-up were not underscored. There is a tendency to let down after a period of planning, especially if it has been comprehensive, that is, with input from a large variety of groups and extensive data-gathering in the community. This letdown should be expected. People need a break, a pause to catch their breath, and this need should be affirmed, but not to the loss of the wisdom and agreement gained. Therefore, implementation should be undertaken as a secondary process (planning is the first) with its own timeline, responsibilities, groups, and evaluation. St. Peter Church was involved in planning over a ten-month period following the call of a new pastor. The excitement, vision, and support were palpable! But they got tired. The wise lay leaders of the congregation and their new pastor recognized the letdown, used the time to communicate the new vision and insights, properly thanked everyone involved, and waited, but not forever. Two months later, new implementation groups with specific instructions, new deadlines, and an overall lay coordinator were begun. Results were achieved, and planning was not remembered as "planning for planning's sake."

Planning in the Bible

There are two ways to read The Acts of the Apostles. There is ample evidence that the early disciples believed and proclaimed the work of the Holy Spirit among them. Clearly, God is the agent and the persons are passive, at best assigned the role of acknowledgment. For example:

- An angel of God releases Peter and John from prison in order to preach (5:19-20).
- Peter is released from imprisonment a second time (12:6-17).
- An angel of the Lord and the Spirit guide Philip (8:26, 29, 39).
- The Holy Spirit selects Paul and Barnabas for mission in Antioch (13:1-3), forbids Paul's preaching in Asia (16:6-7), and drives Paul to Jerusalem (20:22).

Divine and human agency are somewhat more balanced in:

- The election of Matthias (1:15-26)
- The decision to continue preaching (4:23-31)
- The choosing of the seven (6:1-6)
- The acceptance of Paul as a disciple (9:26-30)

There is, however, a certain *inevitability* to the decisions and actions. "It has to be this way," the texts seem to say, "nothing could stop or alter the outcome." Arriving at chapter 10, however, and continuing through the end of chapter 15, it is a little surprising and even encouraging to find divine and human initiative blended and intertwined, encouraging because that experience seems closer to ours.

As the early Christians made and implemented corporate decisions, certain qualities associated with planning occur. For example, they looked at what *was* (circumcision required of the faithful), what should or could be (God's grace meant for all), set policy (God's grace *is* for all), and then planned accordingly by adopting strategies of proclamation, service, worship, church leadership, organization, and communication. It is a thoroughly theological process but is what also could be called a *theologically informed and inspired planning process*. We are just not used to thinking of planning in this way. Maybe we should.

Does the term "plan" or "plans" appear in the Bible? Yes, in several places. See Jeremiah 29:11, "For surely I know the plans I have for you, says the Lord, plans for your welfare and not for harm, to give you a future with hope."

Or, as suggested in chapter 1, read Proverbs 16: "The plans of the mind belong to mortals but the answer of the tongue is from the Lord" (v. 1). "Commit your work to the Lord, and your plans will be established" (v. 3). "The human mind plans the way, but the Lord directs the steps" (v. 9).

These verses from Proverbs recognize and affirm the way human beings are made: our minds construct plans. The mind activates the four levels of thinking—empirical, intellectual, rational, and responsible—and seeks to counter the tyranny of time. The mind plans actions not yet achieved and, when wedded with hope, creates powerful possibilities, which, if enacted, build a future beneficial to human beings and faithful to the God who created the human mind in the first place. Such plans are not unfaithful unless they are attempts to replace the Creator or control the Creator's world, that is, to use planning to "be like God" (Genesis 3:5), to be Creator, not creature. As an *offering*, however, plans made before God and with God find their place: the mind plans but God answers, establishes, and directs. Thanks be to such a God who creates minds among God's creatures capable of such plan-making and who receives the product, corrects, cleanses, and makes it fit for carrying out God's intention for God's world.

Some church liturgies include the prayer, "We offer with joy and thanksgiving what you have first given us—our selves, our time, and our possessions, signs of your gracious love. Receive them for the sake of him who offered himself for us, Jesus Christ our Lord. Amen."

> The future's gift arrives in time.
> God gives a future with hope.
> Our minds plan with hope.
> We offer our plans to God in joy and thanksgiving.
> And then we take action!

CHAPTER 5

Budgets and Balance Sheets:
Deeply Doctrinal Documents

*He was accompanied by Sopater son of Pyrrhus from Berea, by
Aristarchus and Secundus from Thessalonica, by Gaius from Derbe,
and by Timothy, as well as by Tychicus and Trophimus from Asia.*
—Acts 20:4

The Apostle Paul made an appeal for money in 2 Corinthians. What did he do
when the money began to arrive? Paul has been lifted up as an example of early
church administration in action as he attempted to gather money for the poor in
Jerusalem from the churches across Asia Minor (see "Bible Times and Afterward,"
in chapter 1, above). Just as his fund-raising principles and techniques (2 Cor 8-9)
are instructive for the church of today, Paul's concern for honesty and safe transport
following the gathering of the money are also worth noting. The story can be followed
in Acts 20:4 and 24:17. Without the security of electronic bank transfers, he avoided
suspicion by taking with him the representatives of the congregations (Acts 20:4)
from which the money was gathered. Today's CEOs and CFOs making headlines
with greedy and illegal financial practices could learn a thing or two from Paul!

The community of faith needs money to operate. As it gathers, counts, stores,
and dispenses, a process occurs that we call financial or fiscal. This chapter is about
that process. Given the highly significant and even symbolic role money plays in
American society, this process has to be done well.

The objective of this chapter is twofold: (1) to offer a series of admonitions
about things fiscal that cut across church-related budget and finance tasks and (2)

to include some suggestions about making things more interesting, as budgets and financial reports can be exceedingly boring. An admonition is a gentle or friendly reproof; counseling against fault or oversight; warning. In the New Testament, an admonition is a counsel or urging about something important to the body of believers. Paul admonishes the Ephesian elders about factions "to warn everyone with tears" (Acts 20:31). What follows, then, are seven admonitions, gentle and friendly "reproofs," counsel, warnings that are designed to avoid tears (as much as possible) shed over financial matters, and to clear up and brighten those eyes that tend to glaze over at the sight of numbers neatly arrayed in columns.

Budget and finance work performed within the church community seems to be one of those responsibilities that seldom generates much appreciation beyond an occasional "thank you." If, however, it is not done well, accurately, and honestly, then it becomes a source of difficulty and sometimes of conflict. Tending to budgets and balance sheets, therefore, is of the utmost importance and deserves our best effort.

We intend this chapter to be useful to the person who does budget and finance work and also to the one who oversees such persons. Possibly you are a pastor or treasurer of a congregation, a CEO, or finance director of a church-related organization such as a social ministry organization, university, or camp. Or you may be a student preparing for these roles. We hope that the best wisdom drawn from experience and those who write about such matters in other sectors—public, private, and social—will set the table for a helpful approach.

There are seven admonitions: (1) connect fiscal matters to mission, (2) clarify authority and put checks and balances in place, (3) establish transparency assurances, (4) build budgets better, (5) report accurately and regularly, with variety, (6) audit accounts authentically, and (7) treat finance and budgets as vicarious ministry.

Connect Fiscal Matters to Mission

Relate budget and finance matters to beliefs, mission, and ministry in a variety of creative and soundly theological ways. The subtitle of this chapter, "deeply doctrinal documents," is designed to drive home the assertion that budgets and balance sheets are about beliefs. We contended in chapter 1, above, that the goal of the Christian community is not to do administration. This claim is never truer than when applied to budgets and finance. At the end of the day, it is not fiscal matters that determine our faithfulness to God's call but, if done well, attention to such things can surely help.

We use the term "belief" here in two ways: (1) budgets are an expression of how we apply what is believed ("I believe in God the Father Almighty . . . and in Jesus Christ, his only Son, our Lord, who . . ."), and (2) belief about who we are as God's called and sent people in this place at this time. Belief and budget are a mismatch if the congregational budget provides little for evangelism while asserting, "We are an outreach people . . . ," or if an educational institution pronounces, "We are a university for all people regardless of race, ethnicity, gender, or financial means . . . ," but the budget calls for a tuition increase of ten percent but no change in scholarship aid.

A positive approach to the relation of belief and mission to budget and finance is to interpret them continually as means to an end. Accurate records are kept not to "run a tight ship" (machine metaphor, see chapter 1) but out of love, love for the mission and the God who assigns it to us.

Imitation of the actions of Paul in 2 Corinthians 8-9 leads to a treatment of money as a means to an end, not an end in itself. In volunteer organizations like United States–based denominations, the work is funded by a rerouting of some portion of personal income to the religious organization and its work, or the organization dies. Paul's straightforward appeal to the Corinthians was to give to a great need (the alleviation of hunger in another part of the world—Jerusalem) based on God's generosity and love—not because it would bring great rewards to the giver, but because it was needed and was an expression of the mission. Some corners of American Protestantism seem to be engaged in a "reward theology" that sounds not much different from the rampant "me-ism" of society; the gift is given in order to receive something rather than as a response to the already received gift of grace in Jesus Christ. "I do not say this as a command . . . for you know the generous act of our Lord Jesus Christ" (2 Cor 8:8a, 9b).

There are two dimensions, then, to this first admonition. First, treat budgets and finance as ways to get there, that is, as a means to mission fulfillment. Second, if the mission is not clear and supported, then do some implementation and planning (see chapter 4, "Planning with Passion").

An annual budget makes much more sense and may draw more enthusiastic support if it is interpreted as a way to achieve the goals of the organization. For example, "This budget closes the gap between mission and action as a called and sent people in two areas: support for evangelism and for the work of the wider church; for outreach here locally and joining hands with others worldwide." "This budget, however, does not address deferred building maintenance over the last two years. This we will have to cover in next year's budget." The leader as an interpreter invites the congregation or church organization to understand and take ownership for the mission by describing challenges and opportunities over time. "This year . . . last year . . . next year," captures the journey through time. Fellow time-travelers are respected, invited, included, and admonished to be members of the community hearing and heeding and then re-hearing and re-heeding the call of the Lord of all time. What is budget and finance stuff? Busy work or a way to serve?

Clarify Authority and Put Checks-and-Balances in Place

Clarify the authority given to budget builders and finance managers in your oganizational system to do what they are expected to do. Every church-related organization has statements of permission, responsibility, and expectation. Typical for a congregation would be:

1. The Congregation Council shall be the board of [trustees] [directors] of this congregation, and as such shall be responsible for maintaining and protecting its property and the management of its business and fiscal affairs. It shall have the powers and be subject to the obligations that pertain to such boards under the laws of the State of _____, except as otherwise provided herein.

2. The Congregation Council shall not have the authority to buy, sell, or encumber real property unless specifically authorized to do so by a meeting of the congregation.

3. The Congregation Council may enter into contracts of up to $_____ for items not included in the budget.

4. The Congregation Council shall prepare an annual budget for adoption by this congregation, shall supervise the expenditure of funds in accordance therewith following its adoption, and may incur obligations of more than $_____ in excess of

the anticipated receipts only after approval by a Congregation Meeting. The budget shall include this congregation's full indicated share in support of the wider ministry being carried on in partnership with the synod and churchwide organization.

5. The Congregation Council shall ascertain that the financial affairs of this congregation are being conducted efficiently, giving particular attention to the prompt payment of all obligations and to the regular forwarding of benevolence monies to the synodical treasurer.

6. The Congregation Council shall be responsible for this congregation's investments and its total insurance program.[1]

The Association of Governing Boards of Universities and Colleges includes in its guidance for financial affairs:

A. Financial performance
    1. Assurance of sound financial management
    2. Positive financial performance
    3. Balanced sources of revenue
    4. Balanced expenditures
B. Financial condition
    5. Increase of institutional assets
    6. Prudent use of debt leverage for needed assets
    7. Maintenance of strong financial condition
C. Endowment management
    8. Increasing total return on endowment
    9. Allocating return on endowment between current and future needs[2]

The giving of authority in budgeting and finance matters, regardless of the type of church organization and its size, should include five areas:

1. **A separation of responsibility between those who receive the money and those who dispense it.** In a congregation the person who receives and counts

---

1. *Constitution, Bylaws and Continuing Resolutions*, Evangelical Lutheran Church in America, 2005, C12.05.

2. Quoted in Thomas P. Holland and David C. Hester, eds., *Building Effective Boards for Religious Organizations* (San Francisco: Jossey-Bass, 2000), 194.

grant authority in
finance matters

the money is sometimes called the financial secretary while she or he who stores and dispenses typically has the title of treasurer. Even in the smallest family-like congregations, these two activities should not be carried out by the same person. Much grief has resulted from not honoring this basic split of functions. Stated another way, no one person or group should be in charge of money gathering, storing, counting, and dispensing from beginning to end. The principle of checks and balances, so foundational among governmental entities in a democracy, applies also to church systems. This principle is needed not for lack of trust; it is a guarantee (as much as possible) that inappropriate or even dishonest practices will not happen. A seemingly innocent practice by a middle judicatory treasurer of doing the bookkeeping in his home rather than at the church office led to dire consequences. Several years after the practice began, embezzlement was discovered, criminal prosecution ensued, and widespread publicity erupted.

Bank draft (checks) authorization procedures need to be clear and within the assigned authority. One example (not embezzlement but rather a *power* issue between pastor and congregation): "Who authorized this $40,000 sound system for the sanctuary?" the treasurer asked, "I didn't." The requirement of two signatures on a check was met in this congregation by the pastor and the office secretary (for convenience!). The pastor attempted to push through his new worship program by circumventing the authority of those who were opposed, leading to loss of confidence in the pastor and a rather messy congregational fight.

2. **Identifying the groups or persons involved.** Developing a national church organization's annual budget of nearly 100 million dollars involves several groups with varying types of authority. The overall authority is derived from the bishop who holds responsibility for budget development; the Church Council (highest legislative authority between national assemblies) and its Budget and Finance Committee for spending authority; the Churchwide Assembly (highest legislative authority) for final approval; and the executives of the program units who prepare and revise their budgets based on income estimates and spending authority; and the reception of advice from the Treasurer's Office. Sound complicated? Not really, when everyone pulls together and not against each other, and the process provides the appropriate checks and balances needed for an organization of this size with worldwide responsibilities.

3. **Developing the timeline.** In a congregation the cycle of budget development and reporting is usually annual. For example, "The Congregation Council

shall prepare an *annual* budget" for submission and approval by a congregation meeting. In some national church systems, the budget is for two or three years, determined by the frequency of the assembly or convention. Within such a pattern, the Council grants spending authority for one year and makes adjustments if it falls below or exceeds projections. Time intervals will also be treated below under the budget development process.

4. **Reminders about other authorities.** The faith community exists in time and space. It is, therefore, subject to authority other than its own internal ones. Usually that is determined by the state in which the congregation or organization is located. "It (the board of trustees) shall have the powers and be subject to the obligations that pertain to such boards under the laws of the State of _____, except as otherwise provided herein." The specifics of these obligations can be spelled out by a professional in nonprofit or church (not always the same) legal and financial matters, such as a tax attorney, certified accountant and/or incorporation specialist. Sometimes tax accountants are not aware (or do not fully understand) the housing allowance for clergy which is authorized by federal government legislation. This is an area where denominational offices can be of help, usually available on a website or through a toll-free telephone number.

Some local tax authorities collect property tax on "non-church" property, usually defined as other than "the worship area." Without getting into a theological debate about the definition, it is important to be aware of such regulations and even question them informally or file official objections. One approach some congregations and church-related organizations have taken is to voluntarily make a contribution to local government for fire and police and other relevant services. One denominational publishing house, though not required to do so, makes an annual donation to its municipality, an act that receives favorable treatment in the local media and helps to create a "good will" relationship between publisher and city. Likewise, the seminary served by one of the authors contributes to its municipal government and in other ways demonstrates its good citizenship.

5. **Definition of the relation of the designated leader to the governance board in matters of budgeting and finance.** Most authority-giving statements delineate responsibility between the pastor or CEO and the governance entity— the council, board, or committee. This clarification is often very explicit, as in the churchwide office example above; the bishop is responsible for the budget, and the

chief administrator works on the bishop's behalf with the other named groups to get it done. In the congregation example cited above, however, the pastor is not named (except if she or he is president of the council) in the budget and finance processes. In some business corporations, the CEO and CFO are both responsible and report to the board of directors. While this can make for some interesting dynamics between CEO and CFO, from a board point of view, this arrangement puts some assurances in place about fiscal integrity through checks and balances.

Some persons in church-related organizations or congregations could not care less about financial matters. For those people who may be supportive in a variety of ways—prayer, volunteer time, positive attitude, and worship attendance—budget and finance should be conducted in as simple and unobtrusive manner as possible. Others, however, care deeply for things financial. For these people there should be appropriate access, participatory decision making, and on-top-of-the-table process and procedures. The faith community needs both types of folks, and leaders should be aware of the different "need sets" involved.

Establish Transparency Assurances

Pay attention to attitude, technical detail, and information provided for a nothing-to-hide transparent financial system. "Transparency" here refers to how things financial are to be conducted by organizations; a financial system is to be transparent, meaning, quite literally, that one can see through it.

What has happened? While the standard of doing budgets and finance in an honest way has always been there (remember Paul and the churches in Asia Minor), several events have pushed the concern for honesty to new heights. From society, the corporate scandals of shady and downright criminal financial practices have received much media attention. The public consciousness has and will be exposed to these phenomena for a long period of time. Stories of "clever" ways to accelerate the recording of income before its reception and the delay of expenses and debt boggle the mind and lay siege to our sense of morality. The federal government has passed legislation titled the Sarbanes-Oxley Act (SOX), which raises the bar for financial practices in business corporations and hopefully puts in place curbs designed to prevent what has been happening. While some corporations whine about the new "bureaucratic" requirements, others use the new regulations to strengthen their already healthy and honest systems. Texas Instruments, for example, created an opportunity for its staff to learn about TI's financial concepts and practices as they prepared the new documentation.

The church has contributed its own examples. Some televangelists have presented the image of wrongdoing through poorly managed financial systems and by taking a percentage of income to the ministry. The Episcopal Church (USA) is recovering from the embezzlement, conviction, and imprisonment of the national treasurer when $2.2 million was found to be missing. To their credit, Episcopal leaders have responded not only with new financial checks and balances and structural reforms in management and supervision but in the manner they handled this bad news with clear and honest communication.[3]

As societal and church misadventures have contributed to the environment in which organizations operate, it has become more important than ever to develop transparent ways of carrying out fiscal matters. How is that done? There seem to be three components: attitude, attention to technical detail, and clear and explanatory information.

The *attitude* needed is that everything possible will be done to achieve transparency. This attitude probably begins with leaders—pastor, executive, financial officers—and volunteers who work with budget and finance. An aspect of being a leader is setting a tone or climate for the congregation or organization. This role applies especially to the financial area. "We have nothing to hide" is the sound of this attitude in action.

Some people are probably not meant to tend financial matters because they just don't like detail. Not only should the t's be crossed and the i's dotted, but the numbers should add up correctly! Meeting the requirements of local, state, and federal laws and regulations in church financial affairs was previously discussed. This task calls for research, understanding, and then carefully putting into place responsibility for the smallest of details. *Attention to technical detail* is one factor that develops confidence that things are being done right and that therefore there is nothing to hide.

---

3. David A. Roozen and James R. Nieman, eds., *Church, Identity and Change: Theology and Denominational Structures in Unsettled Times* (Grand Rapids: Eerdmans, 2005), 207–9, 227–34.

The third piece of transparency enhancement may be the most neglected after attitude and attention to detail. *The kind of information and its transmission* about benefits, balance sheets, income forecasts, expenses actual and budgeted have much to do with the perception created and judgments made by members, colleagues, those in leadership, and the public at large.

There are two ways to create doubts and breed suspicion: give too little or too much information. The motivation to keep things simple is worthy—but not if it appears that "the whole truth" is not being told. Presenting only a budget with income and expense to a congregation or governing board for approval without a balance sheet that gives a more complete picture of all assets and liabilities may be sufficient for some, but others may conclude that something is being held back, perhaps for the proverbial rainy day. Decision makers deserve the whole story as they exercise their responsibility in a conscientious manner. Congregations have been known not to include in reports major gifts to specific projects, like an organ. Knowing the total income to a congregation helps members to understand and be supportive of financial needs.

The opposite—too much information—also breeds mistrust. The expression "a snow job" refers to piling on layers of information to hide something. Page after page of financial data can be designed to ward off close scrutiny and thereby weaken the transparency of a system. Later some examples will be provided of ways to address and include the recipients of financial information in the process (see the material on budget development and reporting, below). Staff, co-workers, members who are treated as partners usually respond in kind; if treated as adversaries, they act accordingly. If there is nothing to hide, then attitude, attention to technical detail, and appropriate information shared in a collaborative fashion help to build a transparent financial system.

Build Budgets Better (Than Anyone)

The fourth admonition, about the development of budgets, includes three topics: the type of budget, the process for development, and the budget presentation or proposal.

Type of Budgets

There are three basic kinds of budgets.

1. The *line-item budget* is the most familiar and widely used in congregations. The expenses are listed with the estimated amount needed for the upcoming year:

Worship materials	$3,000
Education materials	2,000
Utilities	945
Cleaning the church	1,300
Benevolence to Diocese, National Church	4,000

Even congregations that stretch to cover the pastor's salary and building maintenance make some decisions about additional costs like benevolence and support of local projects. The line-item budget has an inherent logic that follows a certain pattern: last year's budget is the starting point for increases or decreases; certain incremental changes are made related to salaries and so-called fixed costs like utilities and materials; and any new spending on projects and ministries is usually added on to last year's budget in an incremental way.

The line-item budget can work when previous experience is reliable and a good predictor of the future, but it does not serve the congregation or organization well when, as the hymn says, "New occasions teach new duties." There is danger in missing new opportunities, as new initiatives have to prove themselves while old ones don't.

2. Beginning in the 1960s and over the next two decades, a new type of budgeting emerged—the *program budget.* Its origin was the United States Department of Defense (Office of Systems Analysis) and, as can be seen in these titles, its conceptual and operational parents were the application of scientific thinking and systems analysis (see chapter 1, thresholds 4 and 6, above). It seems the rational thing to do, that is, connect costs to program objectives. The questions were, "What are the total costs (materials, utilities, data processing, salaries and benefits) to achieve particular outcomes? During these decades, hundreds of church staff from congregations, middle judicatories, and national offices received training in Planning, Programming, and Budgeting Systems (PPBS). This type of budgeting makes use of and even develops new tools of analysis, such as cost benefit analysis

Types of Budgets

Connect costs to program objectives

and cost effectiveness analysis. Increased attention was given to the purpose of a program, not just carrying it out as an assumed valuable activity, and to the relationship of cost to outcome (benefit or effectiveness). But, like many offspring of the rational model, the analyses proved to be burdensome, often based on faulty assumptions, and contributed to accumulated fatigue over a given budgeting period. Many of the budgets of denominational national program units, while not following the complex steps of the earlier PPBS model, to this day show its residual effects in format, reports, and even process.

Do congregations ever try this? They do so, not with the same details, but in intent when the budget is presented to the congregation like this:

Worship	($31,000)	
	Bulletin	300
	Organist salary	3,750
	Music	450
	Pastor's compensation (30%)	18,000
	Building cost (35%)	8,500
		$31,000

This budget, the program budget, gives a clearer picture of what certain major ministries of the congregation actually cost. What may be missing is an analysis of the effectiveness of these ministries.

3. Toward the end of the 1970s, a third type of budgeting came on the scene, *zero-base budgeting* with its three features: the entire budget had to be justified from "scratch," the burden of proof shifted to each leader for every item, not just the new ones, and the "proof" of value was based on careful analysis (using some of the tools from PPBS and more) with programs ranked in order of importance.[4] Its use was short-lived, mainly because it took too much time, caused needless worry among staff and employees, and is based on the faulty assumption that there are no core *ongoing* programs of organizations. Zero-base budgeting can theoretically "clean out" outmoded programs, although it tends to intensify the "politics" of budgeting.

---

4. Logan M. Cheek, *Zero-Base Budgeting Comes of Age* (New York: American Management Association, 1977), 12.

It can be (and is) used occasionally as an evaluation exercise to determine as much as possible the present value of programs and their contribution to overall mission.

The Process for Budget Development

The process is shaped by clarifying the authority (who is involved, and what they do) and the time intervals (the date of the annual congregational meeting at which the proposal from the congregation council is presented for approval, etc.). Begin with listing the persons and groups involved and the dates of their regular meetings or when they will consider the budget. The following diagram shows "the who" and "how" in a national church organization for a two-year budgeting and spending cycle.

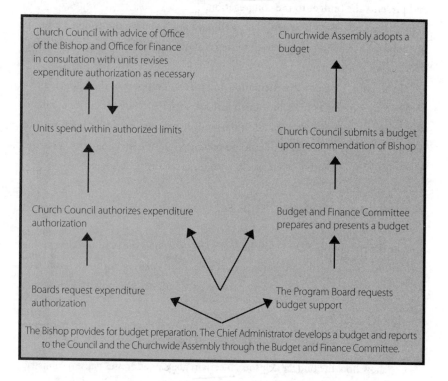

A second example, from the Treasurer's Office website of the Evangelical Lutheran Church in America, is a process for a congregation:

1. The council appoints a budget committee.

2. The various committees are made aware of their responsibility and of the timing they have to submit an estimate of their budget to the budget committee.

3. The committees determine their needs for the coming year.

4. The committees forward their budgets to the budget committee.

5. The financial secretary determines an estimate of the next year's income.

6. A representative from each committee meets with the budget committee to review the budget submitted by that committee. Rationale to keep or remove certain budget items is presented at this time.

7. The budget committee compares all the budgets submitted with the anticipated income and prepares a balanced budget, which it presents to the council.

8. The council reviews the budget, makes any adjustments it deems necessary and presents the budget to the congregation.

9. The budget is presented, discussed, and approved by the congregation. If not approved, the budget goes back to step 6 above for further evaluation and follows the remaining steps.

In an effort to expand participation and increase support of the budget, alternatives to this model may include open forums, which include the entire membership, prior to steps 2 and 3. In addition, budget hearings could be held prior to step 4, or in step 9 the budget could be presented in one meeting with a second meeting scheduled within a few weeks to take action on the budget.

Presenting a Budget Proposal

The third aspect of building better budgets, after selecting the type and developing the process, is presenting the budget to the decision-making authority group, be it a congregational meeting of forty persons or a national assembly of a thousand persons. Some guidelines are:

- Use written and oral narrative, be a teacher, treat the group as your partner in mission, relate the budget to mission, not just good finance procedures, and show how the budget helps reach certain goals or addresses gaps in ministry.

- Display figures in columns and in graphic form, for example, pie charts for income sources (pledges, offering plate, major gifts, income from investments and endowments) and expenses by program (worship, education, social ministry) and/or type (utilities, mortgage payments, salaries, building maintenance). Trends in attendance, giving, benevolence can be displayed on graphs over time. Staff compensation is better shown as a total. A smaller group, like a council or vestry, usually deals with individual staff salary decisions. Also it can be difficult to communicate total compensation in a larger meeting, for example, mistaking salary, benefits, and allowances as total "salary."

- Respect the different ways members understand and appreciate numbers related to finance matters. Experience shows that people pick up on budget numbers in one of three ways. Some want unit or program numbers. A national program budget, for example, can display the amounts for global mission or education or the moderator's office. This group of persons is usually satisfied when they know what "each unit is going to get." A second group, however, is very interested in types of expenses. Again for a national budget, this can be displayed in chart form for staff compensation, grants, new-church development, missionary compensation, health and pension benefits, office expenses, travel, special events, printing, depreciation, and interest. The third group, while smaller in number, is adamant about seeing total amounts and percentages related to broad purposes or areas of responsibility: vocation and leadership, $22,470,000 or 24.2% of the total budget; service and justice, $14,220,400 or 14.7%; governance, $1,100,500 or 1.6%. Arranged in this manner, one can scan the whole budget and gain a sense of proportion about "where the money goes."

- Develop the written report in a way that invites the reader in and tells the whole story. One report outline used to present a proposal was: process, issues, principles, and thanksgiving, followed by numerical reports and illustrative charts arranged by organizational unit, expense type, and purposes. Trends charted on graphs give a picture of the journey the congregation or organization is on. Remember, there is nothing to hide (transparency); therefore lay it all out in an understandable manner that honors the reader's needs and role as decision maker.

- Appropriate to time available and nature of the organization, ask the group receiving the budget proposal to answer some factual questions about it. The questions should be designed to illustrate what the money in the budget actually accomplishes. The questions can also be fun by providing some silly answers in a multiple-choice format, and almost always show in a very public way what the group really knows about the budget. Trick questions are inappropriate. Keep it simple, factual, and fun. A question for a churchwide budget could be:

The largest single amount in the budget proposal is designated for:

    a. Social ministry

    b. Global mission

    c. Health premium support for retired church workers

    d. The Bishop's yacht

The correct answer is (b), assuming that your bishop, president, or moderator doesn't have a church-purchased yacht! In explaining why (a) and (c) are not correct, you can make a comment about what the budget does grant to these areas and what the money accomplishes. Six questions, each with four multiple-choice answers, can cover a large portion of a budget. Whenever this approach has been tried in a church setting, it receives comments like, "That's the most exciting budget report I ever heard." "We got three wrong answers." "We don't know as much as we think we do." "I didn't realize budgets could be fun." "Keep up the good work."

The examples shared above have tried to show how the building of budgets can implement the first three admonitions: being mission connected, clarifying authority and checks and balances, and assuring transparency.

Report Accurately and Regularly, with Variety

Issue budget and finance reports accurately, regularly, and in a variety of formats. An accurate report contributes to the achievement of transparency and builds trust with people. The frequency of reports is partly determined by the times mandated in authority documents. "The Congregation Council shall prepare an annual budget for adoption. . . ." "The Congregation Council shall normally meet once a month. . . ." How often the reports are needed and expected also depends on culture and tradition. Recall that two ways to weaken transparency are to transmit too little or too much information. If information has been scarcely provided or held "close to the vest" by leaders (an act of power), then more is better. If, however, information has been sprayed on the recipients like a fire hose out of control, then less might help create new trust and outright gratitude.

There are four kinds of reports, each looking at financial systems from a distinctive perspective, which together cover most people's needs and meet most requirements.

The Budget Proposal

We discussed this report in the previous section (budget development). An additional idea is to present the current year's figures but also last year's (or even the last two years') actual experience, what was budgeted, and the percentage of change. It looks like this:

	Last Year		This Year		Next Year	
	Actual	Budget	Actual (10 mos.)	Budget	Proposed Increase	% Increase
Education	$2,434	$2,100	$2,651	$2,300	$2,900	+26

This kind of information helps in several ways. First, an appraisal can be made of last year's experience. At a glance, it can be determined what was underspent, overspent, or "on the money." The budget preparer might provide a written or oral commentary on last year's situation answering the question, Why? Second, this type of proposal is a source for determining the desirability of the proposed figure. The other source is the direction and goals set by the planning that has been done. Perhaps education is to play a larger role for the coming year in the congregation's plans. Then a twenty-six percent increase in budget amount makes sense. Third, a comparison can be made for each line item or program against the estimated amount of income. A twenty-six percent increase may fit the plans, but a three percent increase in income projections introduces a note of reality. What will be reduced so that an increase in education is possible? Or should education be budgeted at a reduced amount? We have seen budget proposals that simply raise each item the same percentage. For one year or even two, this might be appropriate because the items may finance mission at a level consistent with the

4 Kinds of Reports (handwritten)

congregation's present and future situation. If the practice continues, however, it probably signals a steady-as-you-go mentality. An invisible sign is placed on the lawn, "No risk taking allowed."

Revenue and Expense Statement (2)

These statements can be of two kinds: (1) a general fund monthly report that keeps a governance group like a Congregation Council informed and gives a basis for mid-course corrections, and (2) a comprehensive year-end report. The general fund monthly statement records all income and expense in budget categories in a vertical column and classifies them by the current month, year-to-date (YTD), budgeted amount, what remains in the budget, and percentage either of budget already spent or income received. (A sample report is found in Appendix B.) The comprehensive year-end report summarizes total income and expense for each fund, so that at one glance all funds in the organization can be seen. For a congregation this could be General Fund, Restricted Funds, Endowment Funds, Plant Funds, and a total of all funds. (Appendix C is an example of a year-to-date summary of income and expense by fund type.)

A Balance Sheet (3)

In addition to income and expense statements (monthly and year-end), another useful report shows the total financial situation at a point in time. The balances are displayed for funds in the organization according to assets and liabilities. (See Appendix D for a sample balance sheet.) The balance sheet is one of those checks-and-balances in a financial system. Trustees or Congregation Council members, for example, could be kept in the dark about "other funds" than current income and expense if only an updated budget report or even an income and expense statement is presented. When both balance sheet and income and expense statements are shared on a regular basis (monthly and end of year), everyone is "on the same page," in full possession of the information required for common understanding and action.

Cash Flow Report 4

A less used but important report is one that gives an accounting of revenues received against disbursements made for a specific period of time. This is a more complex report to prepare and understand but is helpful in answering questions like, "How much cash do we have?" "Do we have enough for expenses yet to come?" "Did we borrow money in the middle of the year to get by?" (An example is found in Appendix E).

Reports—the variety, the accuracy, and the timing—may seem inconsequential and not receive the careful care they deserve. They are, however, worth the energy, attention, and hard work they require. Without them, a budgeting and finance system could become the private, even secret domain of a few. That kind of administration is not what the community of faith desires or deserves. New software or database spreadsheets like Excel make these reports easier to prepare and enable the information to be shown in a variety of ways, including with accompanying charts and graphs.

6 Audit Accounts Authentically

Hare are two stories, one fiction and the other nonfiction:

> **Story 1.** The novel, *By Love Possessed*, published in 1957, depicts a series of memorable characters who struggle mightily with their human nature as bundles of emotion and reason. The author, James Gould Cozzens, seemingly wants to demonstrate that not only those driven by emotion make huge mistakes but those who follow reason's path also are sometimes victims as well. The worst (best) example of the latter comes in the final pages, as the senior partner in the law firm, the one considered by everyone to be a paragon of honesty and reason in the community, is discovered to have embezzled $200,000. There was no regular audit of the firm.[5]

---

5. James Gould Cozzens, *By Love Possessed* (New York: Carroll and Graf, 1957).

Story 2. The pastor resigned from the congregation and later from the ordained ministry. Embezzlement was not involved, but sloppy financial record keeping and an absence of checks and balances was. Check authorization commingled with other issues led to a destructive congregational fight. Things began to unravel when one member asked another, "When was the last time the books were audited?"

The constitution and/or bylaws or similar documents usually spell out the audit requirements. One congregational constitution establishes an audit committee of three voting members, elected by the Congregation Council, who are audit committee members for three-year terms, one elected each year to provide turnover. The frequency of audits or how they are to be conducted is not specified. It falls, therefore, to the leaders of the congregation to assure this essential matter does not "fall through the cracks."

There are four critical questions:

1. Who will oversee the audit? In the above example, the important principle is established that oversight is provided by congregational members, but not by designated leaders such as pastors, staff, or elected Congregation Council members. A semi-outsider perspective is thus established. In larger church-related organizations, audit committees are usually made up of a majority of members completely outside the organization such as the finance director of a local university or the CEO or CFO of a business firm.

2. How often will there be an audit? An annual audit is best; however, in some congregations, because of expense or other reasons, every two or three years may suffice. It is easy to forget, however, when it is not performed annually.

3. Who will do it? Our research uncovered three ways. The most obvious is obtaining a state authorized professional accountant. There is a fee involved and time is required to ready documents. A variation is that the professional may waive the fee. Our experience is that it is not wise to select an accountant just because the audit is done for free. The third way is to do it internally. Suggestions for how to do that are found on denominational websites such as those of the Evangelical Covenant Church and the Evangelical Lutheran Church in America.

One congregation discovered after several years of not acting on the audit's recommendations to find the source of the positive variance in income (more cash on hand than reported) that the previous treasurer had written Social Security payments checks for a part-time employee but not mailed them. The congregation had to pay the back taxes due and substantial interest, but the major penalties were waived (mercifully) by the Social Security Administration. Follow-up of audit recommendations is very important.

Treat Finance and Budgets as a Vicarious Ministry

> I appeal to you, therefore, brothers and sisters, by the mercies of
> God, to present your bodies as a living sacrifice, holy and accept-
> able to God, which is your spiritual worship. (Romans 12:1)

How, then, should financial affairs be treated as an activity of the community of faith? Answer: They are a vicarious ministry of response-ability. First, they are a *ministry*. Financial things should not be ill-treated as "necessary evils" brought on by the existence of the church in the world. This book has as its major motif that administration is a holy calling born of the practical responses which are "called for" by the intentions God has for the community God gathers and scatters. Likewise, when it comes to the handling of money, its gathering, storing, counting, and dispensing, that too, is a part of the pattern of response the community makes to God, to each other, and given the large role money plays in our society, to the wider human community as well. For eleven chapters in his letter to the Christian community in Rome, Paul described what God had done, was doing, and would do. Then in the first sentence of chapter 12, he performs one of his famous "therefores." God is trustworthy and gracious (first eleven chapters), therefore, I appeal to you, present your bodies (lay it all on the line) as your appropriate and holy response. In such an individualistic culture as ours, this verse is too easily applied only to the solitary person. Seen as applicable to the *response* of the community of faith, it follows that some disciples will be assigned caretaker roles of what the community is doing and accumulates (money, buildings, equipment, budgets, records, etc.). Following St. Paul, therefore, it is possible to stake the claim that tending to financial matters is a *ministry* of *response* to a loving and living God.

Why, then, is it a *vicarious* ministry? Two and even three (if you have a sense of humor) dictionary definitions are helpful.

vicarious 1. "Pertaining to a vicar, substitute, or deputy as in *vicarious* authority"

2. "Acting on behalf of or as representing another as in *vicarious* agent"

3. "Performed or suffered by one person with results occurring to the benefit or advantage of another as a *vicarious* sacrifice"

The third definition is included not only as attempted humor about the "suffering" role finance and budget people play (it may feel that way sometimes) but as a reminder that the responsible discharge of financial duties may draw little appreciation or even attention unless a "mistake" is made. The first two definitions, however, make the point: financial responsibilities are performed *on behalf of* others, even *representing* them as deputy or agent. Pastor and theologian Dietrich Bonhoeffer, referring to a parent as children's deputy, "standing in their place . . . working, providing, intervening, struggling and suffering for them," pushes the understanding further. The parent "is not an isolated individual but incorporates the selves of several people in [her or his] own self."[6] Those who are responsible for the ministry of finance in the community of faith should not only be regularly thanked for what they do but should be appreciated at a whole different level—"the standing in the place" of others as vicarious agent for the care of what must be considered a sacred trust. Faithful disciples of Jesus Christ actually give money to the church! Isn't that amazing! This giving should never be taken for granted or treated lightly. The money is given in order to be transformed into mission and ministry within the community and in the whole world. It cannot be misused or misplaced. Financial response-ability performed as vicarious ministry—is a high calling from the abundant God who gives more than we can ever use.

Postlude

Not all topics relevant to financial matters in the church have been covered in this chapter. For example, see the following websites for additional information.

---

6. Dietrich Bonhoeffer, *Ethics*; *Dietrich Bonhoeffer Works 6* (Minneapolis: Fortress Press, 2005), 257–8.

The United Methodist Church website (http://www.umc.org) for:

- church giving in an electronic age
- risk management
- clergy compensation and expense worksheet
- clergy housing allowance
- financial disclosure policy
- passenger van policy

The Evangelical Covenant website (http://www.covchurch.org) for:

- annual budget development (another model)
- real estate as charitable gift
- reasons the pastor ought to be involved in fiscal matters
- bulk mail permit
- church finance director job description
- audit guidelines
- annual balance sheet

The Evangelical Lutheran Church in America website (http://www.elca.org) for:

- responsibilities of the treasurer
- separation of financial responsibilities
- the handling of church income
- the accounting system
- fund-recording procedures
- a chart of accounts
- petty cash accounts
- clergy housing allowance
- payroll tax obligations
- audit procedure
- benevolence remittance to synods—churchwide

CHAPTER 6

Raising the Resources: Theology Talks and Money Matters!

*Now, if I had Wellington's cancelled checks, I would know what
kind of man he really was.*
—Philip Gaudella, biographer of the Duke of Wellington

*We want you to know, brothers and sisters, about the grace of
God that has been granted to the churches of Macedonia; for
during a severe ordeal of affliction, their abundant joy and their
extreme poverty have overflowed in a wealth of generosity on their
part. For, as I can testify, they voluntarily gave according to their
means, and even beyond their means, begging us earnestly for
the privilege of sharing in this ministry to the saints. . . . For if
the eagerness is there, the gift is acceptable according to what one
has—not according to what one does not have. I do not mean
that there should be relief for others and pressure on you, but it
is a question of a fair balance between your present abundance
and their need, so that their abundance may be for your need, in
order that there may be a fair balance.*
—2 Corinthians 8:1-4, 12-14

In any ministry setting—congregation, church agency or institution—God's mission can be carried out only if there are sufficient resources. As we have seen in the previous chapter, St. Paul says of spiritual gifts within the body of Christ that a great variety is given for the common good. In its people, with their energy and creativity, their commitment and desire to serve, a church or church-related organization has its key resources. Beyond its spiritual and human gifts, however, every ministry needs material resources—usually a building or physical space in which to worship and carry out programs or service activities; furniture, musical instruments, and other accoutrements for worship, education, and fellowship activities; office equipment; and perhaps one or more vehicles. Finally, to be effective in our time and culture, church institutions likewise need money—a goodly amount, and more each year as costs continue to increase. Money is needed not only for these local necessities but also for the wider work of the church as well. Outreach by a congregation in its local community, and mission and service carried out by wider church arms and agencies, all require generous monetary resources.

How to garner resources, including money, is the central focus of this chapter. Related to *how* is also *who*. Who bears responsibility for and will be engaged in raising funds and recruiting generous donors whose support is crucial for a ministry's success and faithfulness? If responsibility for resource development is not clearly assigned and accepted by key leaders, over time a ministry will flag and flounder as reduced resources lead to diminished capacity for carrying out plans and programs.

Each of the authors has served in a variety of ministries in leadership roles that required creative gathering of resources and careful stewardship in their deployment for mission. Both are currently engaged in governance or administration of institutions and projects that require millions of dollars in annual income. Both know that resource development and fund-raising activities are never-ending. More dollars must be raised every year just to maintain existing levels of program and outreach; any expansion into new arenas of service requires additional fund-raising. And both of us have grown ever more deeply convinced that raising resources need not be burdensome but can draw us into the unique joy—our own and that of others—that comes from responding to God's invitation to be generous stewards.

The intended scope of this chapter is rather modest: to share some fundamental theological convictions about stewardship, together with key issues and
some overarching principles for leadership in the area of resource development
and fund-raising. Specific *how to* programs or techniques are readily available from
a wide spectrum of other sources—books, journals and magazines, fund-raising
guides, and websites[1]—and accordingly will not be offered here.

Stewardship: Some Key Convictions

While all voluntary not-for-profit organizations depend on the generosity of their
donors, churches and other faith-based entities approach resource-raising from a
unique perspective. We do not simply ask people for money or other forms of needed
assets; we invite them to respond to God's great outpouring of gifts upon which we
all depend for our very lives! Another way of describing key differences would be that
while businesses say, "Give me your money in return for a product or experience,"
and most nonprofit service organizations say, "Share your wealth to serve others who
are more needy (and feel good yourself in return)," the church says, "Respond to
God's generosity as part of your discipleship!" In other words, our focus should be as
much on the donor's need and privilege to give as on our ministry's need to receive
support. Seen in this light, a donor-focused invitation for a person to share wealth is
an act of ministry with that person, as well as a cause-focused effort to raise funds.[2]

Often viewed as peripheral or even a necessary evil, the work of stewardship
education and motivation, including direct appeals for generous financial giving, is an important dimension of any church leader's ministry. It was for Jesus!

---

1. Searches under "stewardship" within most denominational websites will
lead to a host of context-specific resources which utilize that church's nomenclature and reflect appropriate underlying theological convictions. One of the most
comprehensive stewardship-related websites, which features a constantly changing
potpourri of ideas, tools, and resources, is http://www.stewardshipoflife.org.

2. For a comprehensive perspective on donor-centered stewardship ministry, see Thomas H. Jeavons and Rebekah Burch Basinger, *Growing Givers' Hearts:
Treating Fundraising as a Ministry* (San Francisco: Jossey-Bass, 2000).

Multiple scholars and teachers have noted the absolute centrality of *money talk* in Jesus' teaching, as well as his pastoral encounters with individuals. Several of the parables address matters of wealth and poverty, generosity versus stinginess, self-sacrificial giving instead of selfish hoarding.

A central tenet in a theology of stewardship is that everything comes from and belongs to God. As God's created ones given a special responsibility to name and be overseers of the other created beings (Gen 2:19), we humans are entrusted with caretaking. But those and that for which we care do not finally belong to us—they remain God's creatures and creations. Biblical examples of stewards show them to be servants given significant responsibility by a master; but they never become the owner-master. Our contemporary word *steward* is derived from two older English words, *stig*, probably referring to some part of a house (some have suggested even a sty, as in pigpen!), and *weard* (which later became ward or warden). The *stigweard* was entrusted by a master to tend, grow, and nurture treasured creatures or critters, and perhaps an entire household, whose well-being was central to that of the owner-master.[3]

As Charles Lane succinctly states, this understanding of the role of a steward renders inaccurate and insufficient the common notion of stewardship as "giving back to God a portion of what is mine." In the end, everything still belongs to God, the Master-Owner of the universe, so in our giving we are merely surrendering to its rightful owner what never has been ours.[4]

To be sure, this is a radical and shocking concept to materialistic individuals gestated in the amniotic fluid of American capitalism where private property is sacrosanct and almost synonymous with "life, liberty and the pursuit of happiness." Many in other cultures are equally addicted to the acquisition of possessions, the accumulation of wealth, and the self-aggrandizement that accompanies them.

Once the theological breakthrough occurs whereby we understand that everything remains God's possession and property, inviting individuals to relinquish a greater portion of wealth entrusted to them can be viewed as a deeply spiritual

3. Douglas John Hall, *The Steward: A Biblical Symbol Come of Age* (Grand Rapids: Eerdmans, 1990), 40.

4. Charles R. Lane, *Ask, Thank, Tell: Improving Stewardship Ministry in Your Congregation* (Minneapolis: Augsburg Fortress, 2006), see esp. chapter 2.

theol. of stewardship

I am against claim Jesus said - it is better to give than receive

ions is r ... courag ... es are t ... ng that ... ignifica ... ation o ... ... ng; it is ... Echo- ... t. Fran- ... eflected ... atter of

is Chri ... steward ... n that ... ence be

and gospel. The law of ste _____ true enough, insists that human beings must be faithful trustees of the life of the world. But it is one thing to know this and another to do it! The gospel of stewardship begins by overcoming that within us which prevents our being stewards—the pride of imagining ourselves owners; the sloth of irresponsibility, neglect, and apathy. And that gospel gives us the grace and courage that we need to exercise a love that is larger than our self-esteem or our anxiety about ourselves.[5]

overcoming apathy neglect

Within the framework of such an expansive understanding of the nature of creation and God's ongoing ownership of all that exists, stewardship is not a parish program or emphasis that rolls around once a year or when the bills are piling up on the treasurer's desk. Stewardship leadership is not the business of one committee or an item on the job description of one staff specialist. Stewardship, rather, is integral to and inseparable from other core dimensions of discipleship. In the words of Clarence Stoughton, utilized within the stewardship education materials and program of the authors' denomination, "stewardship is everything we do after we say 'I believe.'"[6] A

Stewardship integral to discipleship

5. Douglas John Hall, *The Steward*, 44.

6. See multiple stewardship education materials of the Evangelical Lutheran Church in America, especially those for the SALT emphasis, available from 8765 W. Higgins Road, Chicago, IL 60631 or at http://www.elca.org.

holistic approach to stewardship involves not just our dealings with money but recognizes also that we are stewards individually in every aspect of our lives and collectively in our care for the entire cosmos. It has been encouraging to see many churches and church-related agencies become deeply involved and even take the lead in environmental stewardship efforts (caring for creation) and in such global economic stewardship issues as debt relief for poor countries.

A biblical understanding of stewardship is intimately related to another key theological concept and pastoral concern, that of Christian vocation or calling. Among others through the ages, Martin Luther articulated a dynamic understanding of vocation when he asserted that not only the clergy or other religious professionals but also every Christian has a calling from God. One of the signal contributions of the Reformation was to radicalize the understanding of Christian calling. Not only are priests, bishops, and the pope called by God, said Luther. Through baptism every Christian is ordained into a particular ministry. This notion of the "priesthood of all believers"[7] goes hand-in-glove with a current emphasis on "ministry in daily life." Every Christian, be she pastor, physician, laborer, or homemaker; every believer, be he in business, education, or the military, is called by God. The very word commonly used to describe one's occupation—vocation—comes from a Latin verb vocare, "to call." In our daily paid occupations and/or

---

7. In a lecture at the 2005 Valparaiso University Liturgical Conference, "The Priesthood of All Believers and Other Pious Myths" (see http://www.valpo.edu/ils/documents/05_wengert.pdf), Timothy Wengert has asserted on the basis of extensive research that Martin Luther never actually used this phrase, which has been widely attributed to him. According to Wengert, the term was coined by Lutherans at some point in the eighteenth century. Nevertheless, it remains a central tenet in contemporary Lutheran understandings of Christian vocation, as articulated, for example, in the constitutions of the Evangelical Lutheran Church in America, wherein one of the church's key purposes is to "Nurture its members in the Word of God so as to grow in faith and hope and love, to see daily life as the primary setting for the exercise of their Christian calling, and to use the gifts of the Spirit for their life together and for their calling in the world" (*Constitution, Bylaws and Continuing Resolutions of the Evangelical Lutheran Church in America*, 2005, Statement of Purpose, chapter 4.02.e.).

volunteer activities, and in our callings in the home and community, we carry out our ministries. The living out in daily life of Christian vocation flows from a profound understanding that all we have, everything we do, and the totality of who we are belong to God.[8] This concept of vocation joins cheek-by-jowl with an understanding of Christian discipleship: the follower of Jesus Christ seeks to be a faithful servant living "the Jesus way" in every dimension of life, including the stewardship of material resources and money.

Just as an individual believer-disciple has a vocational calling, so do congregations or other forms of faith communities. Discerning a community's collective calling is part of developing a mission focus and engaging in both long- and short-range planning (see chapter 4 on planning). The careful articulation of this communal vocational calling is also a key component in work related to stewardship and resource development. Individual donors are confronted with innumerable invitations and opportunities to give, and they must choose carefully where to direct their time, talents, and monetary treasures. If a congregation's or organization's aims and purposes are so diffuse and vague as to cause a generous giver to wonder exactly how her or his gifts will be used in furthering God's mission in the world, that wise steward may well direct gifts elsewhere. Accordingly, as we asserted previously, having a ministry plan is not a luxury for a select few but rather an essential core for every congregation or faith-based organization.

Together with these concepts of stewardship and vocation already set forth, faithful resource-raising flows from a *theology of abundance.* In contemporary Christian discourse, this theological stance is frequently contrasted with both a *theology of scarcity* and a *theology of prosperity.* The theologian of scarcity asserts that resources are very limited and we must act aggressively against a plethora of other organizations and individuals vying for the same dollars from the same donors. In this view, "it's a dog-eat-dog world and we want to make sure we're the first, fastest, and biggest dogs in the fight for a meager portion of dog food!" The

---

8. For more extended treatments of the interrelationship of stewardship and vocation, see Douglas J. Schuurman, *Vocation: Discerning Our Callings in Life* (Grand Rapids: Eerdmans, 2004); also Michael Bennethum, *Listen! God Is Calling! Luther Speaks of Vocation, Faith, and Work* (Minneapolis: Augsburg Fortress, 2003).

theologian of prosperity holds a similar conviction that "there's not enough to go around for all, but God guarantees ample portions to those who are sufficiently good and who live according to certain rules and norms of piety and performance." By contrast, the theologian of abundance is convinced that the gracious and good creator God has blessed the creation with ample resources to meet the needs of all. Our role as stewards is to be engaged prophetically, and usually counter-culturally, in the distribution (and in some cases redistribution) of resources so as to allocate a just measure of God's abundance to all.

Resource-raising within a framework established by the theology of abundance approaches the task with confidence from a non-anxious stance. Our role is not to convince donors why they should give to us and withhold from other organizations; it is rather to simply tell our story of how we are trying to be faithful in our vocational calling, trusting that generous givers may support many worthy partners in God's mission.

Self-support Is Both Truth and Heresy!

In the course of our careers, both authors have had a hand in shaping and carrying out policies relative to what are commonly called "new church starts" or "mission congregations." Mission departments within most denominational structures, be they for domestic or foreign outreach, typically attempt to instill in missionaries and other personnel who will be leaders in developing new faith communities the importance of quickly moving to a stance of *self-support*. Typically, when a new congregation is under development, for the first few years a major portion of its budget is supplied by a national or regional mission board or outreach department. Such support or subsidy usually follows a plan of year-by-year reduction, in order to foster generous giving by new congregants and avoid developing financial dependency on the part of the newly birthed congregation. As a group of people are organized into a congregation, denominational mission executives, bishops, and others involved in supporting and shepherding them redundantly emphasize, "You need to become self-supporting in short order so that you in turn can offer your generous support to others." That seems to have been Paul's episcopal teaching in serving as the Corinthian church's bishop.

Particularly i [...] ons where churches have developed accordi [...] ns (by contrast with, for example, state-sup[...] in some European countries, including Sc[...] most congregations will be locally supplied- [...] the members. Likewise, most church-relate[...] ive the vast majority of their resources from [...] e relationship with the ministry, be they alu[...] college or seminary, or socially minded and [...] rm of social ministry.

While the idea of [...] te description and worthy goal for many if r[...] pective no community of God's faithful ever l[...]. As mentioned above, everything we have is a [...] ...ny notion of ever becoming "self-supporting" is a heresy that upholds a limited and false theology of who God is and how God acts! We are all always dependent on the sheer grace of God—for our lives as individuals, for all our possessions, and for the resources that enable any congregation or organization to fulfill its mission. In this recognition, we live humbly, always with open hands and open mouths asking others for their generous support. In words uttered by Martin Luther upon his deathbed, "We are beggars all!"

This recognition of our ultimate dependency may be particularly important for faith communities in affluent contexts or others blessed with extraordinarily abundant resources. A congregation of the very affluent can easily become smug and develop a sense of independence: "We have plenty of money to do anything we want; we don't need other churches or our denomination for any help whatsoever." Similarly, even a small congregation with a large endowment, or one that receives a windfall in the form of a major bequest or other huge gift, can isolate itself, become complacent, and lose a sense of mission ("We really don't need more members to meet our budget, so why should we do evangelism?"), denying members the opportunity to grow in their personal stewardship ("We have so much money we really have no need of members' gifts").

Ministry leaders in any context need to strive for a proper balance between a sense of dependence and self-support, neither expecting others outside the congregation or support network to provide the bulk of resources, nor falling into complacency and contentment with the current level of resources. There are always more opportunities for mission outreach, in one's own community or by generous benevolent giving to the work of partner ministries in one's diocese, synod, or presbytery, as well as globally through denominational or other missionary activities.

We Have Not If We Ask Not

In a typical congregational stewardship cycle, sometime in the summer or early fall, a stewardship committee or task force designs a program or process whereby every member will be invited to consider her or his giving, and ultimately to make a *pledge* of financial support for the following year. Increasingly, such stewardship emphases focus holistically in terms of asking members to consider their stewardship of not only money or treasure, but other *t's* as well—time and talents. An inventory of gifts is often part of the stewardship campaign; typically this involves a written survey instrument in which members can indicate areas of interest for serving within the congregation's ministries. In other words, members are asked to indicate how they might spend their time and talents in helping the ministry fulfill its mission.

As a stewardship education and emphasis endeavor proceeds, there may be a series of communications with members—through congregational newsletters and other written pieces, by means of temple talks at worship, along with perhaps a stirring stewardship sermon by the pastor. Many faith communities hold some form of discussion sessions, enabling members to offer their input for ongoing planning, share their concerns and even air any grievances that might impede developing a positive climate for congregational response. In some instances, a series of cottage meetings are held in members' homes, with motivational and educational intentions. An all-congregational stewardship dinner may be planned as still another way of fostering communication and reminding members of the rich fellowship they enjoy with one another. Along the way, materials are shared that highlight the ministry, demonstrate how people are being touched and lives changed as a result of the congregation's programs and support of outreach. While stewardship consultants differ in their advice on this matter, the authors recommend that the proposed budget for the following year be shared in order that members have opportunity for questions, and so that the need for increased giving might be demonstrated by the likely increase in expenditures (the "bottom line").

Finally, after weeks or months of education, sharing information, eliciting member responses to proposals for new programs as well as receiving their time and talent commitments, somebody, somehow, in some venue has to ask for money! In many congregations, what institutional development personnel describe as "the ask" is made by means of a letter to members that includes a pledge card to be returned at a worship service or by mail to the church office. The letter's author may vary from year to year, but typically will be the pastor, congregational president, stewardship committee chair, or another highly respected and widely known parish leader. Again, there is debate among stewardship experts as to whether or not such a stewardship packet should include the budget or other detailed financial information.

Another approach to making "the ask" is by means of personal contact by congregational stewardship workers and other leaders. This can range from telephone calls to all members or selectively to any who have failed to respond to written communication, to informal contacts during the coffee hour after worship, to more formal one-to-one or family visits in which one disciple talks candidly with another about their respective faith journeys, including monetary stewardship. Particularly in approaching persons for large gifts or pledges, such as those that might be solicited in a capital campaign for a major building program or staff expansion, experience has proved that the latter (the one-to-one visit or series of conversations) is most likely to result in a generous response. Development professionals cultivating major gifts for institutions such as universities or hospitals suggest that the minimum number of personal visits in an already committed individual's home or other setting will be governed by the number of "zeroes" in the hoped-for gift. In other words, a $1,000 gift will involve at least three personal visits, a $10,000 four, $100,000 five visits, and so on.

Who Makes "the Ask?" and for How Much?

In a modest fund-raising effort, such as a typical congregational annual stewardship campaign, a great deal of thought may not be given to who makes an appeal asking for response. The stewardship committee chair, congregational president, or pastor may seem the obvious choices. Even in such a low-key approach, however, considering carefully who will be solicitors of gifts may increase the likelihood of a generous response. The general principle that people give to people holds true in most contexts, so identifying the right person to approach an individual or family is important. Particularly when larger donations are being sought, who solicits a major gift can mean the difference between receiving and not getting the intended response. Many faith communities seeking support for a youth program, for example, have discovered that direct involvement by young persons in appealing for financial support is a key to adults' response. Likewise, if generous gifts are being sought for ministries beyond the congregation (for example, for World Hunger or a seminary), inviting representatives of those wider-church partners to "tell the story" or even make *the ask* may be most effective.

Credibility and generosity are key considerations in determining who will approach a congregation or individuals in a stewardship appeal. It goes without saying that anyone who is widely suspected of unethical or immoral behavior should not be in a leadership position, particularly one involving as sensitive a matter as faithful stewardship. Likewise, persons who exist in many if not most congregations within the category commonly called "persistent troublemakers" would not be good candidates for leadership in a stewardship effort. Strong, mature, wise persons of faith, regardless of their tenure of membership in a congregation, may be effective gift solicitors. The main consideration in inviting such persons to offer leadership is their personal understanding of stewardship, whether or not they are comfortable talking about sensitive matters like money, and if they can finally pose to another believer the question, "So, John and Jane, as part of your faith response to God's beneficence, how much can we count on from you in support of this vital ministry?"

The nature of the relationship between a prospective donor and the person inviting her or his response merits careful consideration. Close personal friends may be comfortable freely discussing anything—except money! Likewise, relatives may or may not be in the best position to approach a family member. Often, a certain degree of distance is helpful, so that if a donor cannot make as large a gift as requested, she or he will not feel embarrassed in front of a close personal friend or business associate. Or, in the other happy scenario when a giver says, "You've asked for $5,000 and I was really planning on $50,000 for our new building," she or he is not revealing to a friend or family member that the degree of wealth held far exceeds what was assumed.

the one who asks a generous giver

An effective *ask* can only be made by one who is already a generous giver and is unafraid to offer her or his witness to the extent of personal generosity. Once again, the wisdom of institutional development professionals as well as effective congregational stewardship leaders suggests that peer-to-peer invitations to give have the highest chance of a successful outcome. In this type of encounter, the congregational president, Bill, sits in a quiet corner of a restaurant with John and Mary. After a good meal during which many aspects of Trinity Church's ministry are discussed, over coffee Bill looks first Mary and then John in the eyes and says, "I'm wondering if you will join me in pledging $5,000 for our current ongoing ministries during the coming year, and also commit to a five-year gift of $25,000 to launch our new community evangelism effort." In circumstances where members with high-end giving potential are approached, there may be no or few peers. In such circumstances, the gift solicitor's testimony may need to shift to percentage rather than a dollar amount: "John and Mary, I'm grateful that God has enabled me to grow in my giving from 5% of my annual income last year to 6.5% for the coming one. I'm wondering if you can join me in a similar increase so that we can help Trinity respond to our exciting new outreach vision."

In recognition of the validity in the old adage, "We have not, because we ask not," specifically asking for growth in giving is important. A common way this occurs is by pegging a percentage to increases in expenditures: "Our budget bottom line for next year will be 4.5% higher than last, so we hope you all will consider at least that percentage of increase in your pledge." The inherent shortcoming in such an approach is that it may not lift sights enough for some donors who are capable of much more sizeable increases. An individual or couple who have just paid off their mortgage, or whose last child has graduated from college, may find themselves capable of a 25% increase in their charitable giving. Continually holding up the tithe as the basic biblical guideline for faithful giving is a general principle worth consideration. For those already tithing, there needs to be another message: "If you're already tithing, would you consider increasing by an additional percent in order to help us continue growing our ministry? Regardless of the benchmarks established for growth in giving—and the discussion here suggests there may be multiple goals tailored for the many individual circumstances that exist within every faith community—stewardship leaders should give very intentional planning attention in this area. Particularly in capital campaigns for building or program expansion, careful research and reflection on donor potential is an important component of preparing to make the *ask* for a large gift. There are a variety of ways to estimate an individual's giving potential, and one of the benefits of contracting for a consultant in a major campaign is the expertise that person will bring in this area of assessing donor capability.

There Are Many Ways to Give

If asked, "What comes to mind when you think of giving to your church?" most members would probably respond with something akin to, "Why, putting my offering envelope in the collection plate on Sunday morning or throwing in some cash out of my wallet when I forget the envelope." Indeed, regular weekly member giving in fulfillment of an annual pledge or as moved by the Spirit remains the bread-and-butter means by which most faith communities receive the bulk of their monetary resources. But, just as there are a variety of gifts from God in service to the mission, as we observed at this chapter's outset, so there are a multiplicity of means by which the faithful can offer their stewardship response. In this section, a few among the variety of giving venues will be explored.

Recognizing that "the spirit indeed is willing, but the flesh is weak" (Matt 26:41b) applies to personal stewardship as well as in many other areas of life, some congregations have found creative ways to help members cope with their fleshly weakness! Offering the option of automatic withdrawal from a checking or savings account can be helpful to some individuals, especially those who may travel a great  deal or otherwise find themselves unable to commit to a pattern of weekly church attendance. Just as many of us appreciate the convenience of paying mortgage, electric, telephone, and other bills directly from a bank account without our monthly attention, so are a growing number of folks finding this a good discipline to ensure the church and other charities receive our gifts on a regular and predictable schedule. In the case of Lutherans, such a direct withdrawal service is provided for congregations by a large fraternal benefit society, Thrivent Financial for Lutherans.[9] While

---

9. For information on Simply Giving, see the website of Thrivent Financial for Lutherans, http://www.thrivent.com.

it may be cumbersome for smaller congregations to establish this giving option for their members, a bit of research might unearth a local financial institution or other entity willing to provide it at a low-cost rate or on a pro bono basis.

"Nobody carries cash any more; we all live by plastic." That is, of course, an overstatement, but one that year by year comes closer to the truth. Compared to previous generations of consumers, who bought almost everything locally with cash or by check-writing, ours is a global economic context in which the vast preponderance of purchases in many arenas now are made by credit card. Increasingly, institutions, including church-related ones, are affording donors the opportunity to make their gifts by credit card; more and more such donations can be transacted online through an organization's Internet website. While it appears as though only a relatively small handful of large congregations have taken steps to enable credit card stewardship response, this is likely a trend that will continue to grow in the years ahead. At any rate, making it as easy as possible to make a gift is good stewardship practice, even if our operational theology teaches against "cheap grace" and comfort-seeking discipleship!

Just as there are different channels by which to give our gifts, so gifts may be offered in a growing variety of forms. Again, cash or a check in the offering plate is likely to remain the primary gift form for most church members for a long time to come. But, like educational and church-based institutions, some congregations can offer donors attractive options by which to contribute significant gifts in ways that may offer tax-related benefits (and thereby possibly further increase the size of the gift that otherwise would have been reduced by taxes). Direct contribution of stock or other matured investments to a charitable organization is often a legal option that will save the donor capital-gains taxation. Assets in other forms, such as real estate, can sometimes be transferred with similar mutually beneficial impact for both donor and recipient. Such potential gifts of property or material assets need to be weighed carefully by the receiving entity in terms of how much time may be required for disposition-related activity, and what strings may be attached, possibly without awareness on the part of the donor. Seeking professional counsel from accountants, attorneys, real estate appraisers, investment experts, or others is generally important prior to accepting a significant material asset or real estate gift.

When it comes to different ways of giving, another distinction is how people tend to respond to regular current needs versus their giving to large-scale opportunities that are often approached through what is commonly called a "capital campaign." Giving to the former is almost always from current income—a person's paycheck or pension or other retirement income. Percentage giving ("I strive to give 6% of my annual income to my church and 2% to other charitable causes") generally is based on current income apart from savings, accumulated pension, or other long-term assets. When it comes to a capital campaign, typically for land purchase, a building project, or major programmatic expansion effort, many generous donors are motivated to dip into savings, donate stock or other investments or convert them to cash, and thereby make a major gift that bears no direct relationship to their ongoing income stream.

There is one other decision that needs to be made fairly early in the planning process by any congregation or organization anticipating a capital campaign, namely, whether to seek and hire an outside consulting firm or individual to assist in the fund-raising. A mid-sized congregation in need of $50,000 for a new roof may well decide that parish stewardship leaders can carry out this modest campaign. The same congregation, faced five years later with the need for a new $1 million sanctuary to accommodate its growing membership would be well-advised to consider hiring a campaign consultant. In general, competent and effective consultation will result in sufficiently higher commitments that more than offset the costs. Most consultants are eager to arrange an initial meeting at no cost to describe their services, offer contacts with previous clients who can verify their credibility and effectiveness, and set forth costs for varying levels of involvement.

What about "Designated" Giving?

An ongoing debate in faith-based organizations' discussions about stewardship and member donations is whether or not to encourage designated gifts. These are distinguished from gifts or pledges that are committed for the regular and ongoing needs of a congregation or agency without specificity as to their use. Gifts to a capital campaign, as described in the previous paragraph, are almost always earmarked exclusively for a designated purpose, for example, "the organ fund" or "sanctuary renovation." Congregations or organizations must be scrupulous in utilizing designated

funds onl[...] [u]ses, permission may be granted (for example, [...] [t]o borrow against a designated fund for short- [...] [u]se of every dollar committed for a specific p[...] campaign.

All w[...] [phil]anthropy know of the strong trend toward de[...] [ce]ntury, more and more people want to know(v[...] [de]sire assurances that specific things will be ac[...] [...]h world in which we live, wherein individual[...] [da]ily basis with people who they will never mee[...] [...]h or charitable giving, many want "high tou[...] to the beneficiaries of their gifts. They may [...] [loc]al hunger-relief fund that benefits starving p[...] [...] to give to the local food pantry where they might even volunteer and help hand out food on occasion.

Faced with this reality, congregational leaders often struggle with the question of whether or not to allow and even encourage designated giving. Some denominations have debated whether the so-called unified budget in which benevolent causes are funded from the general treasury remains the standard for congregations, or if benevolence for mission beyond the local church should be the object of separate pledging and giving. Most major church-related institutions and agencies have followed their secular counterparts in taking a both/and approach to this matter, rather than either/or. That is, they encourage both undesignated regular giving to an annual fund for core budgetary needs while simultaneously constantly lifting up special causes where those who prefer to designate their gifts may do so. In the seminary stewarded by one of the authors, for example, opportunities are constantly offered to donors for general undesignated annual fund gifts and for an array of special funds that include student scholarships, faculty chairs, and particular programs. Under present circumstances, both types of gifts are essential.

A reality that faces organizations that decide to encourage designated giving is that it may become increasingly difficult to fund their core budgets or basic infrastructure needed to support the scaffolding upon which all their ministries are carried out. Both authors have served in the past with organizations that no longer exist, because their core funding eroded to the point that they could no longer survive. A sheer fact is that many if not most givers do not find it very attractive to make gifts that go to pay the light bill, hire a custodian to clean the bathrooms, or even contribute toward the salary of a pastor whose sermons occasionally make them uncomfortable! If offered too readily available alternative specific causes, such givers may designate a major portion or their entire contributions, thereby making it difficult to fund the more unglamorous core needs. Creative ways to strike an appropriate balance within a both/and paradigm will require careful planning and wise stewardship strategizing on the part of congregational or organizational leaders.

Dying to Give: Wills and Other Forms of "Planned Gifts"

A unique form of giving is exercised when an individual decides to include her or his church and other favored causes in planning for a final act of stewardship. Such donations fall into a broad category often called *planned gifts.* The simplest and most common means is a will. However simple or complex, an individual's will is a document in which she or he instructs: "One-quarter of the total net assets remaining at my death shall go to Trinity Church of Mytown, U.S.A." (It is important in coaching will-makers that they specify a beneficiary with its correct name and location; there are thousands of Trinity churches around the world!) In our current economic context, there are a host of other financial instruments that allow individuals and their families to benefit during their lifetime from funds set aside in, for example, an income-bearing annuity, with the remaining principal or corpus reverting partially or in full to a charitable organization at the donor's death.

Congregations that take a holistic approach to stewardship education will from time to time offer or sponsor workshops or seminars on estate planning. While they may attract members primarily, such events can be for the general public as part of the congregation's wider community ministry. Once in a while, stories are heard about a church that received a generous bequest from a neighbor who never darkened the door; enabling such anonymous supporters to fulfill their intent could be a surprise benefit of offering a public forum on estate planning. Such events normally may include a brief pastoral word about stewardship and the importance of planning for the ultimate disposition of one's assets. Normally, the bulk of the leadership will be provided by persons with expertise in estate planning, establishing annuities or trusts and the like—typically, attorneys, accountants, financial planners, or denominational staff with estate-planning know-how.

A growing number of ecclesiastical judicatories and national denominational offices make available to congregations and individuals staff persons who can offer assistance in the broad area of planned giving. Typically available at no cost to the church or individual donor, these experts can review all available options, inform the giver about tax implications, the impact on children and other beneficiaries of instruments like trusts, and assist in executing the legal documents that will ensure the individual's wishes are carried out upon her/his death. In the Evangelical Lutheran Church in America, for example, a network of ELCA Foundation staff is deployed around the country. These planned gift experts are widely available to congregations for seminars, and are at the ready for follow-up service with individuals motivated to complete their estate planning. Frequently, they offer advice and services at no cost to the donor, which include preparation of necessary financial instruments.

Stewarding Major Gifts: Endowments and Other Methods

Along with encouraging members to make plans for their final acts of stewardship and helping them to do so by offering wills and planned gift seminars, wise congregational or organizational stewardship leaders make plans for what will occur once such gifts come to fruition. We all probably have heard stories of congregations thrown into prolonged fierce conflict upon receiving an unexpected windfall from a deceased member. "Did you hear that Sister Sally left us a million dollars in her will? What in the world are we going to do with it?" is how conversations may begin on the part of members in a congregation that has not done advance planning regarding the stewardship of major gifts by bequest.

A congregation is wise to develop a simple gift-receipt policy in advance of receiving any major gifts by bequest or other manner. Such a policy spells out how such gifts will be received and deposited, and their disposition, or at least designation of a process by which allocation will be determined. As indicated above, if the gift is designated by the donor for a specific purpose, it must be used only for that ministry area. Major gift designations often also will specify whether the principal of a fund can be spent or only income or a fixed annual percentage of the corpus. A gift-utilization policy should indicate whether in the absence of any such donor designation the congregation or organization will limit expenditure to income received, an annual percentage, or a designated portion of the total fund. Major institutional endowment managers and other experts in the field of asset preservation advocate strongly for limiting annual expenditures to no more than 4–5% of the fund principal. Expenditure beyond that level reduces fund growth over time and erodes future income-generating capacity. Most colleges, universities, and other institutions with major endowments usually average the expenditure percentage over a 3 to 5 year period so as to avoid chasing the economy, and to guarantee a dependable income stream that is often a significant portion of current budget income.

In the absence of donor stipulation, whether or not a gift by bequest, trust, or annuity is set aside in an endowed fund or made available for spending in its entirety will depend on a variety of factors. The size of the gift itself is a consideration. While a wonderful gift, an amount of $10,000 spent at 5% annually would generate a modest $500. That could be a significant scholarship gift for a worthy congregational member, or a subsidy for a handful of summer campers. But if two or three particularly deserving congregational members could be college-bound only with more generous support, the congregation might decide to spend the entire $10,000 in scholarships awarded over a brief period. If an endowment already exists, adding such an amount to the overall corpus will increase the capacity for support of one or more ministries. A decision to simply spend at will and to use for current needs a major bequest of $500,000 or $1 million, on the other hand, if not very carefully managed, will tend to have a detrimental effect on congregational stewardship. In considering their commitment, many members will be tempted to say, "The church really doesn't need my money now that Sister Sally's gift has made us so flush."

Whether in the aftermath of receiving a major gift or in anticipation thereof, congregations do well to consider establishing an endowment fund. Depending on the specific state laws and other regulatory constraints, it may be wise to consider separate incorporation and the establishment of a fund management board. A growing number of congregations have developed such endowment funds and boards, and many are willing to share their experience and offer suggestions to others. In the

Episcopal communion, for example, there is an association of endowed congregations that maintains a website and holds periodic meetings.[10] National denominational offices may be able to offer guidance in this area as well as supply sample gift policies and other helpful resources.

Beyond the very important advantages of establishing a plan for good stewardship of major gifts intended for long-term purposes, setting up an endowment fund and publicizing it among members may encourage some to consider gifts that otherwise would not be made. Some persons of substantial means may even make gifts during their lifetime, in addition to a planned gift that will become effective upon their death. Most people who have inherited or accumulated substantial wealth are very concerned how and by whom it will be managed once it passes from their direct control. A congregation that establishes a gift policy, sets up an endowment fund to be managed by mature members with financial expertise, and guarantees prudent expenditure and absolute integrity in honoring a donor's wishes will be in the strongest possible position to attract the gifts of faithful members who themselves want to be good stewards of what God has entrusted to their care.

As in its regular annual "benevolence" or sharing of gifts for ministries beyond the congregation, so in stewardship of major gifts and endowments a church may give testimony to its faith by generously supporting others. Some congregational endowment policies stipulate a percentage (25% might be a minimum) of annual endowment-generated income that must be shared with wider church ministries. We have heard of some very generous congregations with policies stating simply that *any* endowment will be used only for benevolent purposes, either in the local community or by sharing with wider church ministries.

A final consideration relative to the receipt of major gifts from living donors or by bequest (which actually applies to gifts of all sizes) is how public a congregation or organization can be in sharing the good news of a faithful steward's generosity. Like most things, this too will depend on local context and customs as well as donor intent and permission. The identity of someone who makes an intentionally anonymous gift cannot, of course, be revealed. While rare, such a restriction may be included in a person's will. Celebrating large current gifts—for example, for a

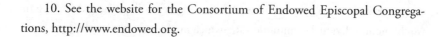

---

10. See the website for the Consortium of Endowed Episcopal Congregations, http://www.endowed.org.

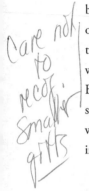

Care not to recog. smaller gifts

building program—may be a good way of saying thank you and can also motivate others to give more generously than they might otherwise. Giving public recognition to those capable of large gifts, however, should never be at the expense of those whose smaller gifts may actually represent greater sacrifice. Repeated recognition for Brother Bill's $100,000 gift to the new sanctuary campaign (which represents only a small portion of his multi-million dollar net worth) may fail to honor Sister Sandra, whose $5,000 gift will totally deplete her personal savings. Exercising wise judgment in this matter of donor recognition is a constant challenge to stewardship leaders.

The Most Important Word: Thanks!

Earlier in this chapter, the important matter of saying thanks already has been broached. Given the topic's importance, it merits a bit more extensive treatment. Nothing is more important for leaders in any organization or congregation who bear responsibility for resource development and financial stewardship than expressing gratitude to generous givers!

Generous giving is a measure (only one among many, to be sure) of faithful discipleship. Offering affirmation for such faithfulness is part of stewardship ministry to another member of the community of faith. While the truly generous give freely without expectation of recognition or credit, human nature being what it is, most of us also do expect at least a simple acknowledgment that the gift has been received and appreciated. From a practical standpoint, most donors to churches and other faith-based organizations regard their gifts as part of overall charitable giving and may be counting on a thank you receipt for income tax deduction purposes.

Prompt gift acknowledgment is the hallmark of a grateful recipient organization. In many institutional development offices, the goal is for a maximum two-day turnaround, meaning that within two days after receiving a donor's check, a thank you letter or note with a receipt for the specific amount will be in the return mail. Congregations obviously will not be able to issue such a thank you letter for every Sunday's offering, but a regular (at least quarterly) giving report should be sent or delivered to all contributors. Acknowledgment of special and larger gifts would merit individual communication, which might include a handwritten note,

Prompt gift acknowledge

telephone call, or even personal visit from the pastor, a key lay leader, or other member.

While acknowledging each gift on an individual basis is important, many donors also appreciate group fellowship events whose sole purpose is for the recipient organization to say a collective thank you. Many churches hold an annual recognition dinner during which members are recognized for their volunteer work as well as financial gifts. Such events need to be organized in such a way that everyone in attendance feels appreciated and no one is slighted, for, in one way or another, all have given something of themselves to the ministry. Small personal gifts in recognition of donations can be another means of saying thank you. Most people have heard ad infinitum the donor appeals on public television and radio stations, where a gift is always promised for various levels of donations. Particularly for major appeals in a congregation or other ministry, a symbolic gift or framed certificate can serve as a lasting keepsake that will remind donors of the appreciation expressed and what was accomplished as a result of their gifts.

Another common means of saying thank you and recognizing givers is by means of what is called a donor bulletin or special section in an organization's annual report. Most college and university alumni or communication offices publish a periodic magazine, and many include in one issue annually a listing of all those who have made financial contributions at various levels. While it does not appear to be a widespread practice in congregations with regard to annual giving for core budgets, such a donor recognition piece is commonly produced for special projects or capital campaigns. Again, as noted above, sensitivity needs to be exercised so that those capable of only modest gifts or perhaps no gift at all are not made to feel devalued. Any such publication, as any spoken tributes at donor recognition events and the like, does well to include the standard caveat: "If we have overlooked and failed to recognize your gift, we apologize and hope you'll remind us so that your generosity can be acknowledged in the future."

Resources beyond Member Giving

As suggested above, for most congregations the vast majority of resources will be generated from among the membership. Individual stewards placing a check or cash in the offering plate on Sunday morning continues to be the primary engine that drives and enables faith communities to move forward in their ministries. The bulk of stewardship-related work will generally be focused on sustaining and growing the member response. Nevertheless, many congregations deviate from this norm; perhaps a growing number will need to find alternative sources of income in the years ahead.

What are other sources of revenue that may be tapped by some congregations, as well as faith-based organizations? Depending on the nature of the latter, government grants may be available for community service programs and projects. Many church-related social ministry organizations, for example, receive multiple grants from federal, state, and local governments to support their work with the elderly or with homeless persons. Hospitals, clinics, and community health programs sponsored by religious-based agencies likewise frequently receive government funding. Church-affiliated colleges and universities are generally eligible to administer federally funded student loan programs.

In general, most local congregations will not be eligible for government funding in support of their ministries. Separation of church and state comes into play here, precluding consideration of applications from organizations whose primary purpose is religious. But some foundations, including those established and operated by for-profit corporations, will fund religious entities, including congregations. Investigation of possible funding sources is warranted, particularly if a church is seeking to develop a new outreach ministry that will serve the general public in its community. As an example, foundation grants or outright gifts from local businesses or service organizations may be available to assist in purchasing equipment for a new child-care center sponsored by a church.

In earlier times, discounts in good and services for charitable organizations, particularly churches, were widely made available by generous merchants. While that is less the case in our current context, in some communities it may still be fairly common. It is generally appropriate to accept or even negotiate reduced fees on the part of vendors, contractors, and others whose goods or services are purchased by a church-related entity.

Another source of revenue for some congregations, particularly those located in "high rent" urban commercial areas, can be rental income from church-owned properties. Churches in the heart of a downtown commercial district may realize substantial revenue from commercial use of their parking lots during weekday business hours, still leaving them available for member parking evenings and on weekends. Many congregations that once had a parish school or large educational wings find they no longer need all the space for their own programs; renting office space or making rooms available for commercial or non-profit agency activities can generate substantial revenue. Prior to entering into such arrangements, careful research should be conducted to determine possible implications on a church's real estate tax-exempt status. But even incurring real estate tax liability may be more than offset by substantial income realized from conversion of a portion of space to revenue-producing purposes. (See chapter 12 for more information regarding Unrelated Business Income Tax.)

There are many factors to weigh in approaching outside sources to fund a portion of a ministry's budget. In applying for and receiving grants, a congregation or church-related agency needs to exercise all due diligence to insure that its values and reputation will not be adversely affected by receiving funds from organizations with questionable products or practices. Similarly, while some governmental agency grants can be welcomed without fear of inappropriate intrusion by authorities into the conduct of a ministry, others may be rejected out of legitimate concern that strings are attached that could compromise a church's ministry and witness. Congregations may be eager to make available some space for rent to charitable organizations that serve the community and to reject out of hand requests from commercial outfits that exploit the public or deal in products and services that are harmful to individuals. Exercising good judgment in determining whether or not a prospective tenant's purposes are compatible with a congregation's is a critical responsibility of faithful leaders.

The Leadership Role of the Pastor/CEO

Left to last in this chapter is a topic that is by no means the least! In fact, it is one of the most important and often among the most neglected topics in publications regarding stewardship in congregations and other faith-based organizations. At issue is the question, What is the appropriate leadership role and stance for the pastor (or chief executive, in the case of an institutional ministry)?

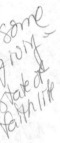

In formal seminary classroom discussions and in informal conversations over coffee with clergy colleagues, the authors have encountered a broad spectrum of opinions on the role of the minister when it comes to stewardship. "I've always said that I have nothing to do with money in my congregation; I won't even talk about stewardship in my sermon on the annual pledge Sunday." "I see it as my role to be the chief cheerleader for my stewardship committee and lend my support in every way possible as we give people opportunity to grow in their faith response through generous contributions to our ministry and the wider church." "I refuse to know what any of my members give so that my ministry isn't influenced and I can continue treating everyone the same, regardless of their contributions." "Since members' giving is one measure of the state of their faith life, I make it my business to know what people give; my response to those who criticize my stance is, 'Would you want to go to a doctor who refused to take your temperature and blood pressure because she might find out you're dead?!'"

As in most areas of ministry and leadership, the role expected of a pastor (or chief executive, in the case of a faith-based agency or institution) will vary greatly according to context, local tradition, as well as the leader's own gifts and convictions. A leader's role in a community of faith is also likely to change over time. In her or his first few years in a congregation that has been bereft of good stewardship for a long season, the pastor may have to take a strong hand in leadership. Then, as careful lay training and development take hold and members emerge into stronger leadership, the pastor may take a reduced role, working more behind the scenes, offering gentle coaching as needed.

Regardless of one's personal inclinations and level of comfort with matters of finance, some aspects of leading in a congregation's or agency's resource-raising probably cannot be fulfilled by anyone other than the chief spiritual leader. Articulating a biblical theology of stewardship is part and parcel of proclaiming and teaching the Word of God in its fullness. From an incarnational theological perspective, spiritual oversight of congregants' growth in prayer, Bible study habits, or relationships cannot be separated from overseeing such mundane matters as how money is collected and spent according to the highest ethical standards. While a spiritual leader will always heed Jesus' warning that one cannot serve both God and mammon, she or he will also recognize that all of life, including the material, is the arena in which God lives and moves among us.

CHAPTER 7

Oversight (Being CEO) Is a Worthy Calling

Whoever aspires to the office of bishop desires a noble task.
—1 Timothy 3:1

Who the president is personally and how he or she functions, even in small matters, deeply influence how others in the institution perceive what is possible for the organization. It is more than knowledge and skill. It is "persona"—the depth of a person, one's spirituality, one's interaction with others. It is saying the right words on critical occasions, being courageous and confident in the midst of crisis and conflict, conveying hope, and enabling others to become more than they thought they could be. There is no one pattern or prescription for how a president performs this mysterious dimension of leadership, but people in the community know when it is present or absent. A president can manage an institution with specific knowledge and skills, but without this more elusive dimension of leadership, success is unlikely.[1]

---

1. G. Douglass Lewis and Lovett H. Weems, Jr., eds., *A Handbook for Seminary Presidents* (Grand Rapids: Eerdmans, 2006), xii.

"What do you mean that I as your minister am the CEO of this church? I didn't sign on for that, and they surely didn't teach me how to be one in seminary! I just want to preach, teach, and care for the souls of my flock."

There was a time when the words *pastor* or *minister* and *executive* or *administrator* were seen by many as polar opposites. But, in many if not most of today's religious communities, the head shepherd is expected to be a strong if not the key administrative officer. Some larger congregations are blessed to have a parish administrator who manages the property, schedules the work of committees, the staff, and maybe even the minister(s). And, in small family-type congregations, a relatively light administrative workload may be carried out principally by lay volunteers. Nevertheless, in most faith communities the one called as minister is expected to carry out many roles and functions similar to those assumed by a lead administrator in a school or other public-service organization, or by the senior executive leader in a commercial enterprise.

For some religious leaders, overcoming long-held negative stereotypes about administration might be the first hurdle to cross. In another publication, one of the authors has explored this general antipathy toward administrative work on the part of many ecclesiastics, and offered biblical and theological exemplars of godly administrators.[2] To embrace enthusiastically the administrative tasks that fall to one's lot does not require abandoning a pastoral identity or shortchanging the many other aspects of one's ministry. While the title *bishop* today is generally reserved for a pastor with regional or even national responsibilities, its use in 1 Timothy probably referred to the local pastor in his (apparently all of them at the time were men) oversight of the local faith community. Such a ministry of oversight, whether as bishop of a diocese or pastor of a congregation, inevitably includes administrative dimensions.

The exact nature of administrative work one is called to assume will vary greatly, depending upon context, abilities of volunteer leaders and staff, technological adeptness, resources available, as well as other factors. But if the minister/pastor is understood to be the one in charge, as we believe is the case in most

---

2. Michael L. Cooper-White, "Administration as a Calling of the Spirit," in *Spirituality: Toward a 21st Century Lutheran Understanding*, ed. Brooks Schramm and Kirsi Stjerna (Minneapolis: Lutheran Univ. Press, 2004), 147–62.

places today, there are some common areas in which one has to develop some measure of competence and ability to exercise oversight. In this chapter, we explore basic principles and issues in the following areas: personnel matters, including hiring; supervision and termination of employees; staff compensation and benefits; volunteer coordination and support; planning and conducting meetings; office administration; and policy development and implementation. Some related issues are treated in the final chapter on legal issues in ministry.

Personnel Policies and Practices

Many of us in ministry grew up and began working in an era when employment arrangements, especially in the church and other voluntary sectors, were often rather informal. The first paid job one of the authors held was arranged like this: A neighboring farmer said, "You come to work for me and I'll pay you a dollar an hour." There were no contracts, no interview process, no personnel policies, benefits, or even withholding a portion of compensation for social security. Wages were paid in cash or by personal check on a daily or weekly basis. The employment was clearly at will and could be terminated any time by the employer for no stated reason. Supervision for the hired man often meant getting orders for the day on which field to plow or where to load hay bales.

While such informal arrangements still take place occasionally today, as a society we have moved into a time with highly regulated employment practices, many of which are mandated by federal, state, and local laws. Churches are not exempt from such laws, with the only exception being some First Amendment allowances to discriminate on the basis of religious convictions in key positions. A handshake and verbal promises may suffice for very limited occasional employment of a day laborer or independent contractor to cut the cemetery lawn. But most church workers will be regarded as part- or full-time employees, for whom all normal rights and privileges afforded in business, government, educational, and other institutions are applicable.

The employment by a church of any paid workers should occasion the development of basic personnel policies. These need not necessarily be extensive written documents maintained in a personnel manual of the scope to be found in a

major corporation or government agency. But, at a minimum, they should cover
such essential areas as

- Fair employment practices. Unless specific religious identity and adherence are required for a position (for example, Christian education director), there will be no discrimination in hiring, evaluating, or retaining
  employees.
- Pre-employment screening procedures. The personnel policies should
  specify conditions that may be required prior to finalizing an offer of
  employment. Increasingly, criminal, financial, and motor-vehicle background checks are advisable for any staff working with children or youth,
  handling money or financial records, and for those who may be driving
  church-owned or private vehicles on official business.
- Nature and categories of employees. A policy should spell out how full-
  time, part-time, occasional, and seasonal employees are defined and
  whether there are differentials in benefits provided. It should also delineate carefully those staff positions that may be considered exempt from the
  normal hourly work schedule (and thus, for example, generally ineligible
  for overtime).
- Work hours, holidays, and overtime provisions. The personnel policies
  should specify normal working hours, whether flex-time is allowed, and
  specific holidays (which in the church may or may not include liturgical or
  religious festivals) that are observed. New, stricter overtime legal requirements were recently established by federal legislation for those who work
  over a specified number of hours and must be adhered to by all employers.
- Supervision and evaluation. Both personnel policies and job descriptions
  should set forth by whom and how an employee will be supervised on an
  ongoing basis as well as make provision for periodic (at least annual) more
  thorough performance appraisals.
- Corrective action and termination. Probably no area is more important to
  address in personnel policies than how an employee whose work is deemed
  ineffective or unsatisfactory will be dealt with by the congregation or other
  employing organization. Some states define employment as at will, that
  is, an employer initiates and continues employment at his or her will,

and need offer no reason for terminating it. In general, however, prior to dismissing someone whose work is unsatisfactory, there must be a process of corrective action that includes identifying insufficiencies, coaching in an effort to remedy them, and allowing sufficient time for improvement. Only after such a remedial period and process may the employer dismiss an employee. In any such action, it is critical for the supervisor to document concerns and corrective actions in written form. The policies in this area should also specify whether there is a process for appealing a termination decision and whose decision is final.

- Workplace conditions and expectations. Included in the parish's or organization's personnel policies should be both standard conduct expectations and any that may be unique to a church or church-related entity. Declaring the workplace to be a safe place in which all forms of sexual harassment and abuse are forbidden is essential. Many, if not most, workplaces these days are declared smoke-free as well as off-limits for alcoholic beverages or inebriated workers.

- Record-keeping. The personnel policies should spell out what records are kept regarding employees, to whom they are accessible, and how an employee might challenge or respond to items in her or his personnel file.[3]

Some Suggestions on Search and Interview Processes

In the following discussion on processes whereby churches or church-related organizations bring persons into their employ, the term *hiring* will appear with some frequency. The writers are aware that, particularly for clergy but often more broadly, many traditions describe the process as one of calling rather than hiring.

---

3. For a thorough overview of church personnel matters, including sample policies downloadable from a CD-ROM, see Erwin Berry, *The Alban Personnel Handbook for Congregations* (Herndon, Va.: Alban Institute, 1999). Also, see chapter 12, below, on employment-related legal issues, especially note 5, which lists laws of particular relevance in employer-employee relationships.

That is the case in our own tradition, and we affirm the theological underpinnings behind it. Since many readers, however, will be working in settings where terms like *hiring* and *firing* are de rigueur, and since even those who are called are in an employment relationship, we will freely use the common terms.

One key to how well an organization conducts search and hiring processes may be the response from those not chosen for a position! Following a personal interview or at the end of a hiring process, do all candidates considered feel they were dealt with fairly and justly? Did the agents of the hiring agency communicate clearly and promptly following receipt of applications or nominations for a position? Was the focus on qualifications, experience, and abilities rather than on extraneous matters like place of birth, family size, and residence or skin color and accent? Were persons affirmed for their God-given gifts rather than disparaged or put down on the basis of perceived limitations?

From our faith convictions, the authors believe that an interview and hiring process should seek to establish what Martin Buber called an I-Thou relationship, in which the dignity of all persons is respected and honored. Cavalier attitudes or sloppy procedures in dealing with resumes and applications, interview scheduling, or questions asked of prospective employees betray a lack of commitment to the values of fairness and justice.

A search and employment process generally proceeds through several typical stages, such as the following:

- Development of a position description. As a result of a comprehensive and thorough planning process, a congregation determines to strengthen its outreach to and care for young persons, both members and youth in the broader community. Recognizing the minister's plate already is overfull and the volunteer pool overworked, the church decides to create a youth minister position. Some group or collection of individuals—perhaps a newly formed Youth Ministry Committee—begins to flesh out on paper the anticipated work areas, needed qualifications and experience, and desired personal traits and faith commitments of the youth minister who will be called. A challenge in developing a job or position description is to make it specific enough to provide a sense of direction and clear expectations while remaining open for gifts and directions that will emerge as candidates are considered and after a finalist is hired (see Appendix F for a sample position description).

• Posting or advertising the position. Depending upon the nature of the position, the organization's personnel policies and practices, and various contextual factors, the process of putting out the word about a position will vary considerably. For a part-time job, for example, maintaining the cemetery lawn, a congregation's leaders may determine to first search internally and determine whether a member may be interested and qualified. Some positions may require such in-depth knowledge of local conditions and context—for example, a Sunday school bus driver in a complicated urban area—that the search may be limited to those who receive a neighborhood newspaper's want ad section. In general, the more significant the position the wider the net is cast in a search process. In many if not most religious communities, the search for a senior clergy leader will involve a broad regional if not national search, often assisted or even conducted by judicatory officials. Once again, fairness and consistency are trademarks of an organization that seeks to convey its openness to many potential applicants. One matter to weigh carefully in posting a position is whether or not to establish a "closing date" by which all applications or nominations must be received. An obvious advantage is that it signals a precise deadline to all who may be considering submitting an application. Equally obvious is the primary pitfall that the day after closing, the perfect candidate's resume arrives in the mail, thereby excluding that applicant from consideration. In general, it is advisable to post a position with a statement like "the position remains open until filled by the church council."

• Reviewing applications and selecting interview candidates. Whether the decision-maker is one individual supervisor or a committee, careful and equitable review of all applications is the next step in a hiring process. If numerous candidates have surfaced, this may constitute the initial winnowing process whereby many are excluded and notified that they are no longer under consideration, with a small select group of applicants being invited to take the next steps. If additional pre-interview information is desired, it is appropriate to request an expanded resume or additional written statements that provide more details about prior employment and other factors. As in all stages of the hiring process, treating all candidates the same and requesting similar information of all applicants is a key to a values-driven and discrimination-free outcome. Exercising self-discipline is important at this stage of the process. A resume reviewer who finds herself or himself getting tired or bored after poring over dozens of applications should probably take a break and return to the process when refreshed. Insofar as it is feasible, working together with others is generally preferable to conducting a one-man or one-woman hiring process; others will hold in check one's often unconscious biases that can cloud fair and equitable consideration of candidates.

- Conducting interviews. If done well, a job interview should be a pleasant and affirming experience for all concerned. The objective is to put a candidate at ease so that she or he can display her or his qualifications and engage in a process of mutual discernment whether the position offered is a good fit for that individual's interests, experiences, and abilities. While each conversation with applicants will take its own twists and turns, asking the same basic questions of all candidates will help insure a bias-free and standard interview. There is ongoing debate whether or not to inform candidates ahead of time what questions will be asked or the general areas of conversation to anticipate. While there is undoubtedly value in observing how a candidate thinks spontaneously, in general we encourage sharing as much advance information as possible, including the kinds of questions that likely will be posed. So doing enables an applicant to do as much advance preparation as possible, thereby enhancing the probability that the interview will be of maximum value to both employer and prospective employee. If it becomes apparent that in spite of advance notice on areas to be covered the applicant has in fact done little preparation, that fact alone says a great deal about how she or he would approach a staff position. In a faith community context, it may certainly be appropriate to begin an interview process with prayer or even invite the applicant to pray if the interview is, for example, concerning the youth minister position.

- Posing experienced-based interviews. A common pitfall in many hiring processes occurs when interviewers ask candidates for a position to be highly speculative regarding areas where they have little or no opportunity to form opinions or make informed judgments. Asking, "If you come here to be our youth minister, how would you organize summer program activities?" invites candidates to proffer ill-informed opinions about matters where they are likely to be clueless. Having no knowledge about other summer programs in the parish, the availability of volunteers, and the interests and activities of young people, the candidate can only speculate and take a "shot in the dark" at this kind of question. Asking instead, "How have you conducted summer youth programs in your current ministry setting?" is a form of an experience-based question. Such a question draws out a candidate's experience and insights rather than asking her or him to be speculative. Of course, a certain degree of inviting candidates to envision themselves in the position offered is part and parcel of any interview and hiring process. Striving for a balance, with a tilt toward questions based upon candidates' prior experiences, educational background and interests, will serve well both candidates and an employer seeking the best qualified and most well-suited new staff person.

• Designing interviews as two-way conversations. Two hours after a very exciting interview began at 8:00 P.M., the chairperson of the Youth Ministry Committee turns to candidate Jane Smith and says, "Now that we've asked all our questions, Ms. Smith, do you have anything to ask about Last Lutheran Church or our youth minister position?" Pointing to what's wrong with this picture requires little genius! A good interview will be structured by its designers to be a two-way conversation from start to finish. Often a general question is posed to a candidate following self-introduction by an employer or by all members of an interviewing team: "Ms. Smith, would you be so kind as to share a bit more about yourself than you provided on your resume, and what interests you about our position?" After a brief or somewhat extended opening statement by the candidate, typically the interviewer(s) ask an uninterrupted series of prepared questions, some of which will likely prompt follow-up questions for further clarification on the part of the candidate. A better approach often is to intersperse the employer's questions with those of the prospective employee, with the interviewer pausing frequently to allow the candidate to seek clarification about the position, the organization, formal and infor-

Interview questions

mal working relationships, possible expectations for family members, and the like.

- Avoiding inappropriate (and possibly illegal) questions. As indicated above, resume review processes and interviews should seek to determine an applicant's job-related qualifications, avoiding questions that probe for extraneous information not directly related to a position. In normal conversation, even with a stranger, it may feel natural to ask about place of birth, family of origin, current residence, and marital status. Asking the same questions in a formal job interview setting makes the "don't do" list in most guidelines for hiring. Similarly, while it may be apparent, asking an applicant's age may be perceived as being age-discriminatory. Asking for a picture is generally taboo as well, inasmuch as it can be interpreted as pre-screening based upon physical appearance, race, or other characteristics that should have no bearing on the selection process.

- Note taking and other interview recording measures. Many of us, particularly as the years advance, may have learned the limitations of memory. From note taking in junior high school we learn the importance of writing down crucial information that needs to be retained. In an interview and hiring process, where a great deal is at stake for an organization as well as candidates, jotting down key points or rating candidates' responses to questions is normal and customary. It is important to be aware that if an ultimate decision is ever questioned or even challenged by complaint to a regulatory agency or filing of a lawsuit, notes on interviews become relevant information and fair game for discovery and evidentiary purposes. Summaries of interviews, email exchanges among members of a search committee, or anything else committed to writing likewise becomes part of the documentary paper trail that needs to be carefully stewarded. In some cases, for example when a search committee member must miss a candidate interview, it may be deemed useful to tape-record a conversation. That should only be done with the agreement of the candidate and all others in the room. As with notes or other documents, there should be careful understandings of how such material will be used, to whom it shall be made available, and for how long it will be retained.

• Discussing practical matters. Most of the numerous interview preparation guidebooks and similar resources counsel applicants that if their first question to a prospective employer is, "How much does this job pay?" they should not count on getting the position! Normally, the bulk of an initial interview will involve mutual conversation about a position, the organization, applicant background, education and interests, and other job- and candidate-related substantive matters. At a certain point in any process, however, including call processes for clergy and other church staff, practical matters such as salary and benefits, vacation, educational leave, and the like must be clarified. When to do so is typically left to the discretion of the employer, and the optimal timing may vary considerably depending upon circumstances. In some cases, if there is reason to believe that salary may be a "deal-breaker," it may be prudent to have some preliminary conversation even prior to an interview. If an applicant's current salary is known to be double that being offered for a new position, it may be wise for the employer to address this head-on in a telephone conversation by stating the available range. A great deal of time and energy may be expended in conversation with individuals who, had they known the salary or other employment specifics, would have withdrawn from consideration prior to an interview. On the other hand, an employer will do well to avoid making untested assumptions. Both of us have had experience hiring committed and highly competent staff members who in fact took major compensation reductions simply because they felt called to a position, or due to changed life conditions that enabled them to focus on personal and vocation fulfillment over compensation.

• Conducting reference checks and other final pre-employment steps. Following a series of interviews, a congregation, organization, or other employer may be centering around one finalist. Prior to offering the position, an interviewer or search committee members assume the responsibility for contacting individuals whose names were furnished by the applicant as personal or professional references. Depending upon policy and practice, such reference checks may have occurred earlier in the process, perhaps even prior to interviews. In conducting such reference check contacts, a few simple principles should be kept in mind. Be mindful that if the references are candidate-supplied, they are not likely to give much negative feedback, since most of us will choose individuals we believe likely to cast us in a favorable light. The ability to probe and ask deeper questions may be a key to penetrating a veneer and receiving useful information about a candidate's potential weaknesses as well as her or his strengths. If several individuals are involved in an interview and reference check process, it is important that similar information be sought regarding all finalist candidates. If some reference checkers ask about the youth ministry candidate's work style, and others focus in on personal attributes, hobbies, and other factors, lacking will be a common table of information to share with the full search committee. Increasingly in hiring processes, especially for certain positions, criminal background checks may be advisable or mandatory prior to employment. In this sensitive area, it is especially important to have clear policies (optimally in writing) that are followed to the letter with candidates. Many employers, including churches, have found it invaluable to contract for the services of third-party background check agencies. More and more such agencies offer services at modest cost. Utilizing their expertise can avoid awkward exchanges between an employer and someone it is about to hire. Additionally, such firms' expertise makes it unlikely an employer is subject to accusations of mismanaging or engaging in outright discriminatory activity in the process of conducting background checks (see Appendices I and J for sample background-check policy and guidelines).

• **Offering the position.** At last, the day has come. You are ready to offer the position to a well-qualified and exciting candidate! How that occurs and by whom the job is offered will vary depending upon past practice and the ethos of an organization. In many cases, the lead person in the organization wants to be the one to make a congratulatory phone call informing a candidate that she or he has been selected. Other organizations will have policy or practice that leaves such a happy communication to the person who will be direct supervisor of the new employee. Regardless of who gets the honor, verbal communication should be promptly followed by a written offer of the position. Such a letter will specify the position, salary, and other matters that may or may not already be detailed in a written position description and/or organizational personnel policies. The letter of offer should express a hoped-for starting date when the new employee is expected to begin work. It may also include an acceptance date by which the selected individual is expected to communicate a formal response, and indicate to whom the finalist candidate should communicate her or his acceptance or declination of the position.

Staff Supervision and Support

There is great rejoicing at First Church now that the youth minister has finally been called and hired after a lengthy search and interview process. At a special service, attended by more young people than anybody remembers being in church, the youth minister is installed and commissioned for the work ahead. Later that same week, at the regular staff meeting, the senior minister turns to the youth minister and says, "I'm so glad you're here to relieve me of all responsibility for the young people of the parish. Check in once in a while and don't surprise us with wild crazy programs. I'll run some interference for you with the church council, especially when it comes to budget, but for the most part, from now on you're on your own!"

In the church body in which we serve as ordained ministers, the Evangelical Lutheran Church in America, much attention has been given over the past two decades to the concept of mutual ministry. The operative philosophy or theology that underlies this emphasis is that no one ministers alone. Ministry occurs in relationships where we encounter one another and together seek to live in the presence of God. Many congregations list in their publications as ministers all the members of the congregation, with the pastor or ordained minister understood to be a leader among the saints who equips all members of the body for their Christian service in every aspect of daily life.

Applying this concept of mutual ministry to staff relationships suggests first that a climate of support for one another be fostered. But mutuality does not necessarily imply an egalitarian or totally non-hierarchical organizational pattern wherein no one is anyone else's boss or supervisor. In most organizations, even those staffed by highly educated and experienced professionals, someone or several persons need to be in charge or at least in a coordinating if not a directing role vis-à-vis supervisees.

While ela[...] re not de rigueur in most congregations or f[...] eporting (supervisory) relationships
should be [...] nd personnel manuals, if compiled),
if not esta[...]

Ther[...] upervisory styles and relationships
as there a[...] them. Each such relationship will
develop o[...] t the styles and personalities of the
coworker[...] tive supervision is a mutual commitment [...] cation. Depending upon the work
setting and work styles of staff members, this may range from daily face-to-face
interaction to infrequent in-person consultation supplemented by multiple times
of touching base by telephone, email, or other communication media. Many congregational or organizational staff teams accomplish multiple supervisory relationships in group settings, for example, when a senior minister, president, or CEO
has a cabinet or staff meeting in which each person provides progress reports on
her or his areas of responsibility and coordination of the whole team's efforts is
achieved simultaneously.

An important dimension of supervision is evaluation, often referred to as performance appraisal or review. Minimally, a somewhat formal annual review session
should be scheduled in which the employee's overall performance is assessed. A key
to effective performance appraisal is to evaluate in reference to established goals (ideally in writing) that have been mutually agreed on by the parties. Such an approach
helps avoid purely subjective evaluations by a supervisor that may be based on whim
or rather capricious views of what her or his subordinate should be doing.

Equally important as giving feedback and establishing goals for the next
period of a supervisee's work, a good supervisory session is marked by the supervisor's inquiring about and offering support. For the authors, the most important
question asked in annual performance appraisal sessions with those who report to
us has always been, "How can I better support you in your work?"

While many feedback moments and coordinating sessions are brief, informal,
and often accomplished "on the fly," an extended supervisory session or thorough
periodic performance appraisal is of a different nature. Ideally, such sessions are
preceded by some measure of preparation on the part of all parties. Prior to an
annual performance appraisal, it can be helpful if both the supervisee and supervisor

reflect in writing on goals and projects established previously, assess progress in all areas, and look ahead to establishing goals for the next work period. Following an annual performance review, a written summary should be prepared by the supervisor, shared with the supervisee (who may choose to offer some further written commentary to be placed in her/his personnel file) and entered into the employee's permanent work record (see Appendix G for a sample performance appraisal format and summary).

When Things Aren't Going Well

For many of us, perhaps especially those who work in religious contexts and view ourselves as kind and compassionate servant leaders, one of the most difficult tasks we face may be dealing with staff colleagues whose performance is ineffective or not up to par and whose work habits and attitudes are unsatisfactory or even destructive. Conducting regular supervisory sessions and annual performance reviews with highly effective and deeply committed colleagues can be one of the greatest joys in ministry. On the other hand, working with the occasional employee who is either unmotivated or unskilled for the job assigned may take enormous psychic and spiritual energy. Worst-case scenarios may involve incompetent or severely impaired staff members whose poor performance not only leaves important tasks undone but whose unhealthy attitudes may affect and infect an entire staff team and spread organization-wide.

Often times, ineffective job performance can be remedied with a bit of ongoing coaching, especially if detected and dealt with early when warning signs arise. Unfortunately, in all work settings, such early intervention often does not occur. The supervisor typically thinks, "Well, John doesn't seem to be living up to the high expectations established by his stellar resume and stunning interview, but he's probably still just making the adjustment to our congregation, so I won't say anything right now." Or the team leader who notices a member's performance slipping may rationalize, "I know Jane's had a tough time at home of late, so I'll cut her a bit of slack and shift some additional responsibilities to others."

Frequent interactions between a supervisor and those who report to her or him enable the former to monitor closely the work and well-being of the individual(s) supervised. When ineffective or substandard performance is noted, it is best to deal with it directly and forthrightly, again in a spirit of mutual commitment to improvement. Rather than ignoring or overlooking problem areas, a good supervisor finds means of gently but firmly inviting mutual strategizing about ways to enable or restore satisfactory work performance. Such coaching will be most helpful if set within a larger context where the supervisor can offer praise and affirmation as well as correction or constructive criticism.

If the problems are serious, and the supervisor begins to doubt an employee's ability to make needed changes in a reasonable time period, the possibility of termination may need to be faced. At the first sign that things may be going down this road, the supervisor will do well to begin documenting areas of concern, recording in notes the general substance or even verbatim summary of conversations. Such file notes should be dated, cite issues addressed, and document a plan of action whose aim is to enable the supervisee's improvement. This approach is commonly called corrective action. In many jurisdictions, employment law discourages or prohibits summary dismissal without a prior substantial and even prolonged period of corrective action by which an employee was given every opportunity to improve her or his effectiveness and meet basic performance standards.

For compassionate and caring leaders in faith communities, the most difficult employment-related task of all may be the dismissal, removal, or "firing" of a staff member. In our kinds of settings, working relationships typically take on broader dimensions of fellowship and friendship. Especially in smaller congregations in rural areas, part-time employees, like a secretary or custodian, may be relatives of some or many members; in many cases churches employ their own members. When such dual relationships exist, where a staff member is also a parishioner or otherwise closely allied with the community of faith, termination of employment frequently means loss of one or several or many supporters of the ministry. This may be the case even if eliminating a position is unrelated to performance, and is due to financial shortfalls or institutional restructuring. Even when termination is broadly disruptive, in the long run one can hope that the health and well-being of the congregation or organization is served. A supervisor who determines that terminating a staff member's employment is necessary is well-advised to engage in some post-firing assessment of whether or not broader systemic issues may have contributed to the situation.

Staff Compensation and Benefits

A basic biblical principle is that the laborer is worthy of her or his hire. Treating employees justly and as generously as possible will be a stance in most faith communities and church-related service organizations. This area can prove challenging, particularly for small congregations and ministries located in areas of high unemployment and low pay scales.

In setting ministerial compensation, many church councils, boards, or vestries will ask, in the spirit of Jesus' parables, "To what shall we compare our good shepherd?" Many judicatories have established helpful benchmarks, suggesting that a mid-sized congregation's sole or senior minister may have responsibilities akin to that of a local senior school administrator. Some denominations publish compensation guidelines or average clergy and other ministerial salaries in order to enable church leaders to determine whether or not they are in the ballpark with current levels elsewhere. Cost-of-living adjustments may be made depending upon local pay scales, housing and other living costs, and additional factors.

Another key principle in compensation matters has been increasingly mandated by law in many jurisdictions: similar pay for similar work. If two administrative assistant positions carry similar levels of responsibility and demands, paying one of the staff persons 50% more than the other raises questions of equity and fairness. Of course, compensation for similar positions may vary considerably if one is filled by a long-term employee and the other by a newly hired worker.

Compensation levels frequently are determined in part by the level of responsibilities, numbers of other staff or volunteers supervised, and the somewhat intangible assessment of a particular position's impact and influence. Frequently, in hiring a new employee, as well as occasionally in order to retain a valued staff member, prior or possible compensation also becomes a factor. In other words, a board or supervisor may say, "We really want Jane to come and work for us; we know her salary is above what we projected and, if we want her badly enough, we simply have to reconsider the compensation."

Beyond cash salary (which for ordained and other ministers often includes a tax-exempt housing allowance and/or SECA self-employment offset allowance), another compensation factor involves benefits offered. Conscientious employers are concerned for the total well-being of their employees (and dependents, if any), seeking to provide some form of a health plan as well as a retirement or pension benefit. In today's economic environment, it is not uncommon for such benefits to total 30% or more of cash salary.

Many church or agency salaried staff members will be regarded as exempt from some benefits offered to hourly employees at relatively low compensation levels. While strict daily or weekly work hours may not be specified, care should be taken so as not to exploit such exempt staff members by demanding unreasonably long hours, encroaching on days off or vacation time.

Recent federal legislation provides for mandatory overtime compensation with employees determined to be nonexempt (generally those who work regular office hours at positions not deemed senior executive or managerial level). As with other such provisions established by federal, state, or local legislation, churches and faith-based organizations generally are not excepted when it comes to strict compliance. One of us once consulted with a church whose parochial school went for years without sending in required employer and employee Social Security deductions. When the bills for overdue payments plus penalties arrived, it was not a pretty picture! (See chapter 12 for a more extended treatment of these matters.)

Who determines compensation levels, salary offers to new employees, benefits to be provided, raises to be granted, and the like? As we have suggested regarding most administrative matters, it depends. In small congregations, typically a governing board, vestry, or council will be the decision-making group. If such decisions are left in the hands of one or two individuals (for example, the treasurer), watch out! As discussed in chapter 5 on budgets and fiscal management, there should be appropriate checks and balances so that individuals in leadership are not vulnerable to accusations of unfair or capricious dealings in compensation-related matters. This becomes particularly true in some fairly common situations, such as a minister's family member being hired as church organist, part-time office assistant, or even for occasional summer hourly work. Even a hint of nepotism when it comes to employment and compensation matters can be detrimental to a leader's credibility and effectiveness.

In larger organizations, there may be highly structured approaches to personnel and compensation matters. As we mentioned earlier, both of us worked for years in a large national church organization with several hundred employees, dozens of outside contractors, and hundreds of grant recipients. In that "shop," a highly sophisticated approach to compensation, called the Hay system, established fifteen or more

Compensation

salary grade levels, with ranges depending on experience level, time of service, and other factors. The entire system was administered by a human resources department staffed with professionals whose background and training included compensation monitoring and management. Well-defined processes were in place when a staff member or her or his supervisor believed responsibilities had increased to the point at which a grade level increase (with corresponding compensation hike) was merited. Even without such a highly organized approach, all employers should periodically review position descriptions and determine whether or not revisions that may be accompanied by compensation alterations should be implemented.

The treasurer of many a congregation has spent a sleepless night before blurting out at the vestry meeting, "We're out of money and the pastor's monthly check is due tomorrow!" What to do? Many older members in smaller churches will recall the days when a significant part of the minister's pay was in donated vegetables, meat, used clothing, and other gifts contributed by caring faithful members. While such care packages may still be bestowed in some communities, the days are gone when they can be considered part of the compensation package. Congregations, like all employers, have at least quasi-contractual obligations with those they employ; such obligations include timely payment of salaries and other compensation. As is the case with businesses (and even governments!), in extreme cases a loan may have to be sought in order to meet salary obligations. If it appears that the inability to meet compensation commitments is likely to be of long-term duration, some difficult decisions—including temporary or permanent layoffs—may have to be made. Both of us have found ourselves in painful circumstances as leaders with primary responsibility for making budget reductions that could only be achieved by ending the employment of faithful, dedicated, and competent workers.

One topic within the broad scope of compensation that merits particular attention is the method of considering salary increases or raises. In many organizations, the process is as simple as determining how much overall budget is expected to be available next year compared to the current year. If it is anticipated that the employer can afford an aggregate 3% increase, all staff receive equal raises at that percentage. More complicated and challenging are efforts to reward outstanding work or signal the need for improvement by means of performance-based evaluations. In such a process, one employee might receive a 5% increment, another 3%, and one whose performance is weak no raise at all in a given year. Other employers, in an attempt to achieve greater equity and make adjustments where perceived injustice might be occurring, grant varying compensation increases. One of us served as an associate with a senior pastor who insisted that the junior partner's annual increases be a higher percentage in order to avoid further widening the gap between our respective salaries. Both served with a national bishop who also championed higher percentage raises for his senior staff than for himself. The important factor in approaching compensation increases (or the occasional decreases that may be required by budgetary constraints), so as to avoid formal or informal charges of inequitable treatment, is to have a carefully defined and articulated rationale setting forth the bases on which decisions will be made.

Supporting and Overseeing Unpaid Workers

It is probably safe to say that religious communities and most faith-based service organizations would not long exist if they depended solely on paid employees as their workforce. Volunteers constitute the bulk of workers in most congregations and in many faith-based agencies as well. At some point in our lives, most of us probably have experienced volunteerism at its worst. You show up at the appointed hour with only a vague notion of what is expected. No one is there to greet you, clarify the tasks to be accomplished, or provide the necessary tools and coworkers to complete the work. Or, being on the other side of the equation, many of us also may have experienced the trying task of attempting to supervise and coordinate the work of volunteers whose primary aim seems to be simply enjoying one another's company. Good fellowship may indeed be a worthy aim all in itself, but if the day's task includes painting the Sunday school classrooms or rehabilitating substandard housing in the community, one hopes that some hard work will accompany the lively camaraderie.

Recruiting, equipping, supporting, and overseeing the work of volunteers is one of the most important administrative tasks for leaders in many faith-based organizations. Such oversight is no less important than that which is provided for paid staff. Depending on the nature of volunteer work, a great deal may be at stake for the organization, and it will bear the same responsibility and liability for unpaid helpers as for those who are on the payroll. In many congregations, for example, volunteers staff the nursery, direct youth groups, visit and assist elderly and other vulnerable persons in their homes, and fulfill myriad other roles that are often broadly termed pastoral care. Conducting a responsible level of screening, offering adequate orientation and training, and establishing volunteer accountability and reporting back on activities are essential components of any program that fields unpaid workers who contribute to an organization's activity and help fulfill its mission. To simply send forth volunteers with no preparation, without careful background checks that verify the absence of prior criminal or other harmful behavior, is irresponsible.

While there are certainly significant differences, in general the same kind of preparation, oversight, and supervision needs to be provided for volunteers as for paid staff. While formal interviews are rarely held with volunteers who carry out simple tasks in the church office or who engage in group projects like painting the fellowship hall, fairly sophisticated screening does need to be conducted with any who offer to assist with child care or youth work, as well as those who volunteer to handle money and keep financial records. Just as an organization should expect high standards of conduct on the part of its volunteer workers, so they in turn should be assured of certain benefits and protections. If a congregation's umbrella insurance coverage, for example, does not afford protection to volunteers as well as those on the paid staff, is it fair to ask members to assume personal risk for such potentially dangerous tasks as lawn-mowing or steeple painting?

Those who have been involved in leading organizations that are highly dependent on volunteer workers readily recognize that significant differences characterize the contract between such individuals and the congregation or agency. As noted above, if a paid staff member's performance fails to meet reasonable expectations, such a person can be let go and another hired. A necessary removal of an incompetent or unsafe volunteer likely can be even more difficult than terminating the work of an ineffective employee. Depending on the nature of the volunteer work, it may be possible to fill the gaps by diplomatic assigning of responsibilities from one worker to someone else. But sometimes, painful and difficult as it may be, even the most influential volunteer must be removed from a role for the sake of the well-being of individuals and the community. It goes without saying that any form of abusive behavior that compromises the safety of persons within the organization or in the general public must be met with prompt removal of the offender from his or her volunteer capacity.

As with paid employees, careful preparation, planning, and providing support and supervision for volunteers are the key to their success. While it is unnecessary to craft written job descriptions for occasional volunteers completing rather self-evident tasks like lawn-mowing or a congregational mailing, such position descriptions may be developed for long-term major volunteer roles, like serving as financial secretary, supervising the educational program, or leading a major capital campaign. Written daily or weekly task lists and office protocol may be necessary and helpful for those who fill volunteer administrative roles or janitorial tasks. Such written job descriptions or task lists should spell out to whom the volunteer worker is expected to report, and whom she or he may contact if questions or unanticipated situations arise. Volunteers in any setting also should have readily available information regarding whom to contact in case of an emergency, like an accident or a threatening circumstance.

Organizations that benefit from a large volunteer cadre of individuals who engage in long-term sustained volunteer efforts have a characteristic in common: they find frequent ways of publicly expressing thanks and recognizing their unpaid workers! This can occur in a wide variety of venues, from written thank-you notes to public recognition in worship or volunteer appreciation banquets, by conferral of certificates or awards, or by means of publishing volunteer accomplishments in organizational newsletters or stories sent to local media.

Another important element of volunteer recruitment and retention in the twenty-first century involves the recognition of how expectations have changed on the part of unpaid workers. Just as broader cultural shifts have altered the way salaried workers approach their task, so have volunteer attitudes and hopes changed. A growing cadre of young retirees, for example, is reticent to be tied down with ongoing long-term responsibilities. Newly freed from having to report to work every Monday morning, these folks may be eager and willing to teach a class for a month or two but reticent if asked to serve for a full year. With more and more persons of all ages engaged in weekend work responsibilities and recreational pursuits, creative and flexible scheduling of volunteer activities may be essential if their involvement is desired. There appears to be a growing trend among churches to offer educational programs for children as well as adults on a midweek evening versus the traditional Sunday morning, thereby utilizing volunteer teachers' availability.

While most congregations and organizations probably lack the financial resources to hire a full- or part-time volunteer coordinator, there have been many such pioneering posts created in recent years. As opportunities to serve expand, any organization will do well to study carefully how it identifies, recruits, equips, deploys, supervises, and supports those who, while worthy of their hire, choose to offer their time, talents, and treasures as gifts.

Making Meetings Matter

Just as administration is viewed by many in church circles as a necessary but undesirable sideline that takes time away from the real ministry, so are meetings frequently seen as events to be endured rather than appreciated or even enjoyed. Myriad are the quips and jokes about church meetings, committees, and task forces. Ecclesiastical veterans like us have spent more hours in meetings than we can count. Our conviction is that well-prepared, organized, and purposeful meetings really do matter and make a positive difference in the life of a congregation or organization. We offered brief treatment of meeting preparation and leadership for governing boards in chapter 3. Here we engage in a more extended discussion to assist those responsible for leading committees, task forces, and meetings of other groups.

One key to effective meetings is careful planning or table-setting. Among the first decisions is determining whom to invite to the table. Many meetings fail to achieve their purpose because the right people with interest, expertise, commitment, and legitimate decision-making authority simply are not present. Meeting organizers, therefore, need to begin planning by clarifying the gathering's purpose and then determining who can best assist in fulfilling that purpose.

Many groups in churches and organizations are standing committees. Too often such groups meet simply because it is the regular monthly meeting time. If there is not real work to be done in a given month, it may be the best stewardship of everyone's time to cancel the meeting. While there is some value in groups gathering simply so that members can stay in touch with each other, frequent meetings that have no discernible purpose and end with nothing accomplished tend to have the effect of discouraging rather than exciting and empowering participants. Another common pitfall is to restrict meeting participants purely on the basis that only certain individuals' names appear on a committee roster. If the primary agenda item for the finance committee is to strategize how additional funds may be identified for a much-needed emergency furnace repair, inviting outsiders with HVAC expertise as well as members of the stewardship committee may be prudent.

Once it is determined who should be invited to a particular meeting, attention needs to be directed to planning the agenda. Who should be involved in such planning? A group's chair and one or more key staff persons relating to its areas of responsibility usually are involved in meeting planning. A worship committee meeting agenda, for example, would typically be planned by its chair together with the pastor and perhaps the music director. Rather than simply listing all the discussion items seriatim, prioritizing and categorizing them can contribute to meeting efficiency and effectiveness. So that areas where decisions must be made receive adequate discussion time, it can be prudent to deal with those items first while a group is fresh and unhurried, leaving purely discussion or informational items to a later point. Many groups find it helpful to assign an estimated timeframe to each item in order to keep the agenda moving and enable the chair to exercise discipline and corral meandering discussion (see Appendix H for a sample timed agenda).

As already noted, leadership is always shaped by and needs to be appropriate to the context and organizational culture in which a leader serves. The degree of formality with which meetings are conducted will vary greatly depending upon a group's makeup, size, and ethos. In a small, family-oriented rural church, for example, the very notion of formally adopting a timed agenda at the outset of a meeting may seem strange and alien. Correspondingly, not doing so in a large suburban congregational context may violate members' sense of propriety and create mistrust that someone is attempting to manipulate the agenda. In general, giving all members of a group even a brief time to review and buy into the stated agenda usually fosters a climate of mutuality and conveys the sense that every person has a stake in the agenda and can influence the meeting's outcomes. Establishing a pattern of allowing too many items to be added last-minute to the agenda can make it difficult for the chair to conduct the meeting within the allotted time, and it often frustrates the group as matters are discussed without proper preparation, including dissemination of background information.

Another question that will be governed by local custom and culture is whether a proposed agenda (not finalized until the group adopts it at the outset of the meeting) and the accompanying background materials should be distributed prior to the meeting. In general, such pre-meeting distribution is to be encouraged, because it has both practical and symbolic value, enabling members to give forethought to important matters and simultaneously signaling the seriousness with which meeting preparation is undertaken in order to make the most of participants' time. In some cases, where documents are of a sensitive nature, for example, involving delicate personnel matters, pre-meeting distribution may be unwise. Such documents could inadvertently fall into hands other than those entrusted with such sensitive matters. In the contemporary context, meeting agenda and materials distribution may be expedited by electronic transmission. Once again, given the nonsecure nature of such communication media, appropriate care must be exercised with sensitive materials.

Depending on the nature of an organization and the size, context, and dynamics of a particular group or task force, its chosen leader(s) will need to determine the extent of preparation necessary and helpful to the group's accomplishment of desired outcomes. If a group's purpose is to be a think tank that generates programmatic ideas for a Christmas pageant or annual community fair, very little advance preparation may be required on the part of its leader. Coming to the meeting with one or more pre-packaged ideas may squelch a group's creativity and engage them in debating the leader's proposed program rather than in wide-ranging generation of several possibilities. Near the other end of a spectrum of gathering types will be a finance committee's annual session to plan the following year's budget. For the treasurer and financial secretary to have done no preparation and bring with them no figures on current-year finances, trends over several years, and estimates of future income and expenses will frustrate the committee and cause members to spend unnecessary time gathering and interpreting such data.

Chairpersons and staff who relate to a group or committee must walk a fine line in exerting an appropriate degree of leadership. Too much preparation on the leader's part may detract from group commitment, involvement, and engagement, with members concluding that decisions already have been made and that their role is relegated to rubber-stamping a set of pre-packaged conclusions and actions. On the other hand, nothing can more frustrate every member of a group than to spend hours wrangling over the wording of a brief resolution, bylaw amendment, or other formal action that needs to be carefully crafted. In such cases, most groups will appreciate having placed before them the enabling actions prepared in advance by staff and others involved in meeting preparation. Whenever official action involves entering into legally binding contracts, establishing or severing formal relationships with external partners or vendors, or adopting major policies with organization-wide implications, careful pre-meeting preparation of motions and resolutions will both save a group's time and also help ensure against mistakes or missteps resulting from hasty or imprecise actions.

Over the several years that we worked together as senior executives of a churchwide (national) organization, we were involved in planning, preparing, and leading meetings of many types, sizes, and for multiple purposes—from small 2–3 member staff task-forces to semiannual meetings of the denomination's thirty-four-member governing council to the biennial churchwide assemblies that involved thousands of people. In the case of the latter two groups, each meeting involved preparing hundreds of pages of background information and action items. For these large governing bodies to conduct all the business on their agenda, hundreds of recommended motions and resolutions were prepared by dozens of staff, committee members, and legal counsel. In the course of a churchwide assembly, action items were frequently grouped together in so-called en bloc motions similar to congressional omnibus legislation, whereby in one motion the body dispatches a host of matters.

As noted, a group's or organization's purpose, context, and culture will suggest how meetings are prepared and conducted. These same factors will govern the degree of formality with which leaders and participants carry out their work. In the type of large national or international meeting described in the previous paragraph, most sessions will require strict adherence to parliamentary procedure in a very formal setting. At the other end of a spectrum, imposing Robert's Rules of Order on a small parish mutual ministry committee established by a church council to offer occasional support and feedback to the pastor may work against the group's purpose, which can better be served in the context of a supportive informal conversational setting. The nature, purpose, and modus operandi of some standing groups and entities may be set forth in governing documents or policy manuals, whereas how a group operates, who leads it, and in what manner may be left to the group itself in the case of temporary task forces or informal working committees.

Setting the Table and Hosting the Meeting "Meal"

Just as the outcome of an informal family picnic or formal state dinner in a grand ballroom will hinge in major measure on pre-meal preparation and table-setting, so the way the table is set for a meeting will have a significant impact on its ultimate results. Many fine resources are available on group dynamics, the typical stages a group experiences (for example, Bruce Tuckman's classic "forming, storming, norming, and performing"),[4] and how a leader may read the tea leaves in order to best serve a group's purposes and enable its effective work. We will not seek to replicate such widely available resources. But since the focus of this book is on ecclesiastical administration and leadership within congregations and church-related organizations, we offer a few context-specific suggestions on leading groups and conducting meetings.

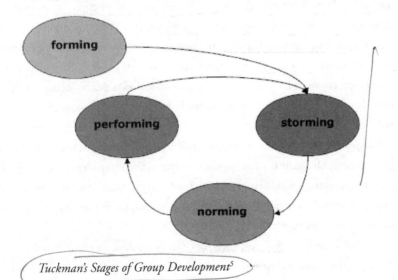

Tuckman's Stages of Group Development[5]

---

4. Bruce W. Tuckman, "Developmental sequence in small groups," *Psychological Bulletin* 63 (1965), 384–99. The article was reprinted in *Group Facilitation: A Research and Applications Journal* 3 (Spring 2001), and is available as a Word document on the website http://dennislearningcenter.osu.edu/references/GROUP%20DEV%20ARTICLE.doc.

5. Diagram found at: http://www.infed.org/thinkers/tuckman.htm.

While the authors' conviction is that not every church meeting needs to begin with prayer, doing so frequently is a good practice—both to invoke God's blessing upon a gathering and also as a reminder of the congregation's or organization's overarching mission and purpose. Leaders will do well to avoid manipulative prayers or devotions which express the pray-er's biases or even seek to prejudge outcomes by implying that one or another course of action surely is God's will for the group! A brief devotional time led by a group member is common practice in many churches' ethos for most or all groups and committees.

A further conviction on the part of the authors is that every group and deliberative body should strive to become what is widely described as a learning organization, that is, an entity that continues growing, embracing and incorporating new knowledge, and learns from both its successes and failures or disappointments. Setting aside even a small portion of most meeting agenda for a time of study and reflection will begin to develop such a self-identity whether or not explicitly articulated and will enable the group as a whole, as well as individual members, to continue learning and growing. In congregational settings, brief Bible studies or group reflection on a short article treating some topic of particular relevance to a given group's task can be a good educational experience incorporated frequently on the agenda. More in-depth study and sustained theological reflection is required when a congregation or ecclesiastical body is attempting to discern God's will regarding its corporate stance on complex and controversial social, ethically laden issues. A frequently used approach to enhance a group's learning and growth involves providing each member with a book or collection of essays and over the period of several meetings discussing chapter-by-chapter or focusing on a particular theme or topic each time the group gathers.

While in many bodies, task forces, or committees there are group members capable of preparing and leading such study and discussion sessions, on occasion it may be helpful to bring in an outside resource person to stimulate creative thinking and provide expertise not represented within the membership. A planning task force involved in gathering information on the local community or mission context, for example, could be well-served by inviting a series of outside experts—local officials, city planners, area college professors—who have their fingers on the pulse beat of that locale.

Just as a wise host or hostess and banquet planner needs to know who and how many will be at the table, their tastes (and food allergies!), the hour and mood of the desired dining experience, etc., so an effective meeting planner/leader needs to ask a series of questions before each gathering of a group or task force: Who needs to be at the table? What information is needed for the group to conduct its business at this meeting? Shall the menu, an agenda with accompanying background information, be distributed in advance to whet their appetites and anticipate the experience, or should they be surprised and hopefully delighted by something unexpected this time? Is it prudent to solicit members' input and agenda suggestions in advance, or might that result in an uncoordinated potluck that will overwhelm us all? If prolonged discussion and even conflicted debate is anticipated, and particularly if I as chair or leader have my own strong feelings, might we consider bringing in a neutral outside facilitator to guide or even conduct the meeting?

A wise and gracious meeting host also will give some advance thought to the needs and desires of each member who will be at the table. If a new member is joining the group for the first time, she or he should receive some pre-meeting orientation (in chapter 3 we discussed the matter of new-member orientation). The effective chair will envision in her or his mind's eye the group as a whole and each participant. Who are the extroverts prone to talk frequently and even occasionally dominate the group with their strong opinions? Are there ways to firmly but graciously rein them in so that the more introverted or inexperienced newer members can voice their feelings and share their insights?

In conducting a meeting, an effective chair may also provide occasional summations of discussion, pointing out where there appears to be consensus and which aspects under discussion need further clarification or refinement prior to a decision. Whether or not a timed agenda has been prepared and adopted (see Appendix H for a sample timed agenda), a good chair will keep an eye on the clock, neither rushing the group to premature decision making that may leave at least some feeling unresolved or unheard in discussion, nor allowing rambling and irrelevant remarks to go on and on for hours. If a standing recorder or secretary is not appointed or elected by the group, the chair also will want to give attention to the matter of minute-taking. In some groups it can work to have a revolving door of meeting recorders while in others, particularly with important official actions which may have major long-term impact and/or require legally binding resolutions, financial matters and the like, it's generally best to have a designated secretary who is held accountable for maintaining thorough and accurate records of the proceedings. If not dictated by policy, practice, or protocol, a committee's chair and secretary, together with collaborating staff members, will determine who should receive meeting minutes. As discussed above, particular care needs to be taken with minutes of groups at which sensitive personnel and other delicate matters are discussed.

While it may appear awkward or even impolite for the host or hostess to ask, "So how did you like the meal?" at the conclusion of a dining experience, soliciting feedback from and self-assessment by a group at the conclusion of a meeting is a final important step in a learning organizational culture. This may be preceded by a brief summation on the part of the chair, recorder, or other designated member in which highlights and major points of discussion and decision are rehearsed for the entire group. As with other factors discussed above that are shaped by a group's culture and context, meeting evaluation and group self-assessment may be formal or informal, achieved through discussion or by means of a brief written instrument. Going around the circle asking each member to offer one new insight gained or sense of accomplishment can help a group recognize its achievement and end a meeting with a positive sense of progress and accomplishment. Such a process of assessment may also include noting unresolved issues and unfinished business to be slated for a future agenda. While individual and collective self-assessment is a challenge for most groups, it may be fostered in non-threatening ways by simple questions such as, "Can you suggest how we might improve future meetings?" "Are there ways the chair or staff can better assist you to accomplish what you hope to achieve as a member of this group?" "Are we as a group moving in the right direction and fulfilling our overall purposes?"

Office Administration: Another Aspect of Oversight

In almost all denominations and religious communities these days, candidates who aspire to serve in official public ministry are required to undergo a battery of psychological tests. A test-taker confronted with a yes/no question, "I like administering an office," may puzzle about its implications as being akin to one's answer to common personality test questions like, "I like repairing door latches." Will they think I'm crazy if I answer yes to the office administration question?

While some who serve as ordained or lay servants have extensive backgrounds in managerial positions through prior work in arenas like business, government, or the military, many aspiring or practicing clergy have little experience and even less interest in running an office and tending to day-to-day tasks that will ensure its smooth operation in support of the church's or organization's ultimate purposes. Some creative re-imagining might help one see beyond the mundane aspects of office routine to envision such administrative work as yet another dimension of a ministry of oversight.

In most contexts, unless a church is a new mission or one is heading up the formation of a new organization, a well-established office already staffed by competent personnel is likely to be in place when a leader arrives on the scene. Once again, of course, this will vary greatly by ministry context. In small rural or urban churches, for example, there may be no paid office staff. Necessary tasks are accomplished by a cadre of volunteers whose functioning may have either flourished or languished during a season of ministerial transition. The offices of larger congregations or ecclesiastical organizations may be well-oiled machines whose operators at best require a bit of occasional encouragement and affirmation from the senior minister or chief executive. These latter kinds of offices can pose an even greater challenge if they are malfunctioning or working at cross-purposes with a faith community's overall mission.

Particularly in larger organizational contexts, at the outset of a new leader's tenure, the conduct of some form of an administrative audit can be very helpful in assessing the state of affairs and where changes may be suggested. Both of us have been involved on both sides of such endeavors—serving as outside auditors seeking to assess an organization's effectiveness, including office procedures, and serving as leaders whose organizations and offices were being evaluated. From our experience on both sides of such processes, we commend them! There can be great value in having a small team of persons, perhaps a combination of insiders and outsiders, review the operation of a church or organizational office. Are policies in place to guide staff members and ensure that the workplace is a hospitable and safe environment? (Learn more about this in chapter 12, on legal issues.) Is the office properly equipped to perform expected functions, or should some new items be budgeted in the future? Are calendars of church events as well as individual staff members' schedules available to those who receive phone calls or walk-in inquiries? Do the

locked doors

right people have the right keys to enable their access to facilities and to allow others to gain entrance? Have protocols been developed to guide volunteers who may be faced with gentle or disruptive walk-in visitors, persons seeking assistance, or the occasional emergency situation?

Under the broad umbrella of office oversight is the whole matter of property and facility management and maintenance. A periodic facilities walk-through by key staff, volunteer leaders like property committee members, and outside experts such as fire marshals or building engineers can identify routine maintenance areas and serve notice of problems or hazards that may be alleviated or must be remedied.

The tasks carried out by administrative offices are as varied and diverse as are congregations and organizations. No two will work exactly in the same way or fulfill the same list of tasks in a week's or month's time. But there is a fairly common set of roles and functions fulfilled by most administrators or staff teams: generating, preparing, and disseminating bulletins, newsletters, correspondence, and other documents; setting up and maintaining files and records concerning members, organizations, programs, and finances; discerning the need for and developing policies and written procedural documents; answering telephones, emails, and performing general office receptionist duties; preparing and providing reports to both internal groups and committees as well as external regulatory agencies; and a myriad of other tasks included in one or more administrative job descriptions under the catch-all, "Other duties as assigned."

Unless a small organization truly is a one-person shop, most office administrative work will involve several individuals. Even if office workers are volunteers, holding regularly scheduled or at least occasional staff meetings is generally an important arena in which coordination of efforts, problem-solving, and planning upcoming events can be accomplished. Unless otherwise assigned, it will be the role of the minister or lead staff person to call, prepare agenda for, and conduct such meetings. Including some aspect of team-building in such meetings from time to time can help enhance the group's camaraderie and foster the encouragement and building up of office workers' practical skills and self-esteem.

Just as emergency room personnel facing multiple victims from a serious accident or catastrophic incident must establish priorities, or airline pilots encountering unexpected stormy conditions or equipment malfunctions must determine which of many matters require their most urgent attention, so prioritizing among

What not to do

the multiplicity of tasks in most office environments is crucial. An efficient secretary who maintains every file in the cabinet in meticulous fashion, weekly shipping out duplicates for off-site storage in case of fire, can be a wonderful asset in a busy church office. But if she or he fails to produce the Sunday bulletin and thereby an entire congregation stumbles through its weekly worship service, some corrective supervisory action may need to be taken! Periodic reviews of the work of volunteers and staff (see above in this chapter) can help establish priorities and ensure they guide the workflow.

As we go through life, we learn both from our own successes and failures, as well as those of others. So it is with congregations and organizations. In addition to sharing our perspectives on important "what to do" items, we believe we can be helpful by sharing a few "what not to do" anecdotes from our experiences:

- Avoid forgetting to send important documents to appropriate government agencies. Things like annual tax-exempt filings and payments of employee social security obligations should not be overlooked. In conducting an abbreviated administrative audit of a congregation some years ago, one of us discovered that a decades-old congregation still had in its files the original documents that would establish it as a not-for-profit corporate entity in its state! This congregation had been operating without proper legal corporate standing for decades, likely thereby subjecting congregational council members and others to personal liability for actions taken in name of the congregation. In another situation, it was discovered that a particular minister was lackadaisical in sending marriage licenses to the county recorder after he performed weddings. One couple seeking a certified copy of their marriage certificate from the county were informed no record existed to show that they had in fact ever been married! Beyond the obvious perilous circumstances in which such irresponsibility on the part of parish leaders placed themselves and parishioners, the failure to perform relatively painless and brief administrative tasks erodes overall confidence in the pastor's and congregation's ministry.

- Do not fail to maintain proper financial records and make broadly available reports generated by the treasurer and other fiscal officers. The board of an educational institution of a church body met for several years, and at least some members perennially raised their eyebrows as the chief financial officer reported verbally, saying he had been too busy to prepare a written report. In the absence of insistence on the part of either the board or chief executive, this practice persisted until such time as the institution's true fiscal position was brought to light, forcing it to enter a prolonged period of financial exigency whose dire measures included releasing tenured faculty members and taking other extraordinary steps to avoid bankruptcy. In another case, a denominational staff member was asked to visit a small church that "needed a little help" in its financial record-keeping. Upon arriving for the meeting, the consultant was handed a box containing two years' worth of unopened bank statements! "I knew in that moment they needed more than a little help," quipped the denominational official. Nothing outside immoral behavior on the part of a church's minister or other key leaders can cast a gloomier cloud around its integrity and reputation than cavalier conduct with regard to financial record-keeping and reporting. (See chapter 5 for detailed information on budgets and financial reports.)

- Be sure to verify that critical payments are rendered in a timely fashion, especially in cases where nonpayment may not be readily noticed. For some years, one of the authors administered an emergency assistance fund created by our denomination to assist retired clergy and spouses whose pensions were grossly inadequate to provide for their financial needs. In reviewing applications, occasionally the source of the problem was traced to an employing congregation that had been negligent in making regular payments to the pension fund. If the minister failed to review her or his regular statements from the pension fund, such nonpayment could go on for years undetected, finally leaving that faithful laborer without financial assets sufficient to meet life's basic necessities when no longer earning a salary. As a result of this sad state of affairs, some additional steps have been implemented to increase the likelihood that such irresponsible behavior on the part of a congregation would be detected and remedied. In other cases, where congregational officers have failed to review carefully periodic denominational statements verifying contributions to the wider church's mission, crooked church treasurers have absconded with such benevolent funds for months or years without being detected.

- Give priority to prompt and precise entries in parish records (as well as denominational reports) of all pastoral acts such as baptisms, marriages, and funerals. Beyond the courtesy to members of exercising all due diligence to preserve their spiritual life histories, such records often serve as important back-up to legally recognized documents in the event that civilly recorded birth or marriage certificates are destroyed by fire or natural disasters. With more and more record-keeping, including parish register information, now being accomplished through electronic data entry, it is critical to establish protocol for regular transfer to off-site storage of back-up files. Whatever information used to be kept in a fireproof safe, which is now on an office computer, should have a back-up duplicate file at another location.

- Be scrupulous about maintaining in permanent files critical documents like insurance policies. A common misunderstanding that would make sense on the surface is that an insurance policy can be tossed after the coverage period indicated. In some cases, however, the ability to verify that liability coverage was in place may be important documentation years after the policy period expired (this has become particularly crucial in litigation involving clergy sexual misconduct in the distant past). Some documents, such as fire insurance policies, are probably best kept in a bank safe-deposit box or other off-site secure location. At a minimum, if maintained on the premises, crucial legal documents, as well as key archival materials that capture and preserve a church's or organization's history, should be kept in a fireproof and waterproof safe.

It is impossible in a book of this nature to provide in-depth and detailed guidelines for all manner of administrative matters related to the smooth operation and oversight of a busy church or organizational office. Other publications offer a broad array of sample administrative checklists, procedural guidelines, and practical suggestions.[6] As indicated previously, most denominational websites now field an ever-growing body of church-specific guidelines, sample policies, and other valuable resources.

---

6. See especially Otto F. Crumroy, Jr., Stan Kukawka, and Frank M. Witman, *Church Administration and Finance Manual: Resources for Leading the Local Church* (Harrisburg, Penn.: Morehouse, 1998).

CHAPTER 8

Communication:
Ministry Means Messaging

Speak out for those who cannot speak, for the rights of all the destitute. Speak out, judge righteously, defend the rights of the poor and needy.
—*Proverbs 31:8*

It was impossible to get a conversation going; everybody was talking too much.
—*Yogi Berra*

Martin Luther declared in one of his sermons that the church is a "mouth house." Its fundamental purpose, he asserted, is to spread the Word of God by human word of mouth. In this recognition, Luther pointed to the centrality of communication for congregations and faith-based organizations. The process of sending and receiving messages is called communication. Thus, for faith communities, communication is not just peripheral, one among many matters on a laundry list of topics to be considered; rather, it stands at the heart and center of the church's mission—indeed, effectively communicating a message and gathering people around it is *the* mission of any faith community!

Our English word *communication* is derived from the Latin *communicatio* (from *communicare*), and means to share or, literally, to make common. As sharing a message occurs, people come together, and *communitas* or community is

179

formed as a group holds things in common (*communis* means shared by all or many, from *com*, "with," and *munia*, "public duties related to an office").[1] "Community" therefore literally means being together in shared duties or a shared office as a result of hearing and believing a common message.

The master communicator of the early Christian church in its infancy was one Paul of Tarsus. It has been suggested that without his skilled communication of the gospel—through powerful and persuasive preaching, personal one-to-one sharing, and particularly through his letters to fledgling, far-flung, small emerging Christian communities, letters that have endured through the centuries and form a substantial portion of the New Testament—the church may never have been born and likely would not have survived. In his longest, and many say most important letter, Romans, Paul revealed his awareness of the centrality of communication for the Christian church: "But how are they to call on one in whom they have not believed? And how are they to believe in one of whom they have never heard? And how are they to hear without someone to proclaim him?" (Rom 10:14). It is in the proclaiming and hearing, the sending and receiving of a message, the process of communication, that the gospel spreads and the faith community is formed.

In its earliest days, the church's communication occurred primarily in two media, the spoken word and writing. Enhanced communication through the visual arts, particularly iconography, would emerge a bit later; today the arts remain another important form of communication and proclamation. While early religious believers would marvel at the communication tools available to us today—television, video, radio, computers, email, the Internet, mobile phones, and others—all these remain variations of the same two media available since ancient times. The human senses and capacities available for communication remain the same today as they have always been. We hear, see, speak, touch, and taste, and thereby we either succeed or fail in our attempts to hold things in common, that is, to communicate.

In this chapter we explore some rudimentary elements of communication theory and then focus on some guiding principles, particularly for those who bear responsibility for developing communication media and messages in faith communities.

---

1. Online Etymology Dictionary (http://www.etymonline.com).

Communication Theory: How Do We Listen and Learn?

At its core, communication theory is about the learning process—about how human beings send and receive messages and, as a result of message transmission and reception, gain greater knowledge and common understandings. In any communication transaction, there are two or more parties seeking to exchange information. Ideally, information is flowing in both directions. Message sender (S) conveys some piece of information; the receiver (R) takes it in and offers feedback, in essence reflecting back to the sender another message, "I got it."

Communication failures often occur when S makes the assumption that message sent is message received. The receiver, R, may or may not have registered the message. If the feedback arrow pointing from R back to S is left to chance, with S simply assuming the message was received, and not awaiting or seeking

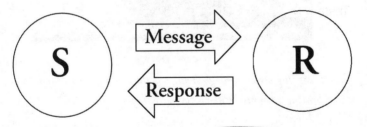

R's response, there is no guarantee that communication actually has occurred. It is this breakdown in communication that frequently causes frustrations in our human encounters and in our churches and organizations. "But I told the confirmation class three times that we were to meet here at the church at 6:00 P.M. this evening," complains the pastor who finds himself alone with his youth minister at 7 o'clock. Message sent apparently was not message received—or at least not message heeded!

Another common element in communication failures is based on an assumption that all media are created equal, and that all recipients receive and process messages in the same way. Educational psychologists and other experts in pedagogy and communication theory have helped us immensely by recognizing that some persons tend to be more visual in how they process information, whereas others take in and grasp information better through listening to the spoken word.

Scientific studies utilizing extensive research have arrived at some general conclusions about the effectiveness of various communication media in effectively
transmitting information. The Federal Aviation Administration cites the following
statistics regarding how student pilot learning (defined by the FAA as "a change in
behavior as a result of experience") occurs:[2]

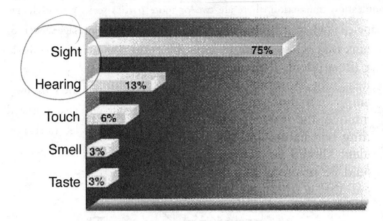

*Most learning occurs through sight, but the combination of sight
and hearing accounts for about 88 percent of all perceptions.*

    Given the reality that most humans learn and change their behaviors as a result
of experiences that engage them in receiving messages by sight, the method of
delivering sermons and so much else that is done in communities described as
"mouth houses" may merit reexamination. Indeed, many preachers and other communicators in various arenas have moved to supplement their verbal proclamations
with visually enhanced messaging, utilizing such readily available media as Pow-
erPoint presentations or printed outlines. Many churches throughout the global
community, particularly in places life Africa and Latin America, as well as African
American congregations in the United States, have long understood the importance
of seeking to become "full-person houses" in which the gospel is conveyed and

2. Reprinted from *The Aviation Instructor's Handbook* (Washington, DC: Federal Aviation Administration publication H-8083-9, 1999), 1–6.

received with all the senses rather than exclusively by the ears or primarily through the disembodied spoken word. Innovative usage of artistic expression, including liturgical dance, enhances many faith communities' messaging.

The challenge of communication expands as degrees of difference between the would-be communicators increase. As people travel in other countries, it is fascinating to watch how communication patterns change. Faced with an impenetrable language barrier of different tongues, some will speak more loudly, as though more forceful delivery will overcome the communication gap! Or we may shift to signals and a kind of primitive, self-designed sign language in the attempt to convey meaning. Cross-cultural communication can be challenging even when the same language is spoken. While they use the same words, persons of different cultures and backgrounds may see the world differently. Subtleties of nonverbal cues may be equally or more important than actual words used. In her ground-breaking work, Deborah Tannen has explored how there may be signifi-cant nuances embedded within gender communication patterns, which can make male-female working relationships challenging.[3]

Clarifying the Message and Choosing the Media

Prior to determining the medium by which one will communicate, the content and intended impact or outcome of the message must be decided by the sender. In everyday conversation we often give little advance thought to topics or what we are attempting to communicate. Talk among family members and friends simply flows freely back and forth. As a conversation may grow tense or conflicted, how-ever, we may unconsciously begin to slow it down (or speed it up!); if the former, a reason might be that we are choosing words more carefully, pausing to make sure we understand the other person and crafting responses a bit more precisely. In more formal communication settings, such as delivering a speech or sermon, or

---

3. Deborah Tannen, *You Just Don't Understand: Women and Men in Conversa-tion* (New York: HarperCollins, 1990), and *Talking from 9 to 5: Women and Men at Work* (New York: HarperCollins, 1994). A video of the latter is available from ChartHouse International Learning Corporation (800-328-3789).

in a business meeting, job interview or giving testimony in a court case, we may give a great deal of thought and preparation to a presentation, as well as to our responses to questions or assertions by others. If an exchange is adversarial or even hostile, words may be chosen very precisely so as to defend oneself or attempt to avoid escalating a conflict—or in the extreme to prevail in a debate or contest.

One of the delights and challenges of being human is that we are all different. No two persons understand a word, sentence, or longer communication in precisely the same way. As the message sender, I may understand perfectly what I seek to convey, but you the receiver may understand some parts or even the entire message in a slightly or completely different manner. Message-testing is therefore important prior to delivering a significant communication piece to a broad audience. We are grateful that in our professional lives we have always served in team-ministry settings, surrounded by coworkers and colleagues who were good sounding boards for our ideas and proposed communications. On occasion, such advance message-testing of a speech, sermon idea, letter, or report has saved us public embarrassment when a colleague asked, "Are you sure you really want to say that or put it quite that way?" More often, even some minor editorial suggestions have helped sharpen a message, increasing the chances that it will convey the message we desire to the intended receiving audience.

Even ministers and other church leaders who work alone much of the time have access to message-testers who can review drafts of important documents, serve as sounding-boards for new ideas, and otherwise assist in clarifying messages or occasionally dissuading one from sending it at all. Trusted lay leaders in congregations, nearby colleagues, or even distant friends readily available by email or telephone can provide initial feedback, help one walk around a message and look at it from several vantage points, and thereby enhance the likelihood of a positive outcome in conveying it to a broader audience. In the case of written communication pieces, a writer may intentionally seek out message-testers who also have a good sense of grammar and style and who can thereby help avoid awkward syntax, misspellings, and other common errors that detract from a document and speak poorly of its author.

In the case of major communication events—the Sunday sermon, a newsletter article, devotional writing, or a local newspaper column—it can be helpful to follow the counsel of many who teach college speech or seminary homiletics courses.

Prior to crafting a spoken or written message, attempt to summarize in one or at most just a handful of sentences the essence of what you are attempting to communicate: In this sermon I am attempting to. . . . By means of this article I want to say clearly that. . . . A related exercise in sharpening one's focus for spoken communications, particularly in difficult situations, like a challenging pastoral conversation, is to clarify the hoped-for outcome. Such a simple exercise has been called an "impact profile" in which a communicator self-queries, "What is the impact or desired outcome I hope will be achieved by means of my message(s) in this conversation or meeting?" When it comes to actual message delivery, offering succinct introductory and/or concluding summaries of key points can underscore them. Among professional communicators and teachers, there is a familiar mantra: "Tell them what you are going to say; say it; and tell them what you just said!"

Once a message or series of messages has been selected and tested, ideally with several hearers who will give honest feedback, the medium or media by which to convey it need to be selected. In many, if not most, cases, this may be readily apparent. The monthly informative and inspirational column goes in the parish newsletter, of course. But it might also be sent via email to some who so request or are more likely to read electronic communications at work than paper ones received along with mountains of junk mail at home. Frequently these days, communicators in all arenas may ask themselves, "Telephone or email?" A short email dashed off can be a time-saver as compared with a phone call that inevitably will involve a certain amount of extraneous chitchat about matters beyond the topic at hand. On the other hand, some receivers may be not be connected electronically or adept at this still relatively new medium, or may expect and appreciate a warm pastoral voice on the telephone or even in person. If a communiqué is directed to several individuals or a mass audience, email distribution may be the clear choice, assuming that those not reachable by this medium will otherwise be notified.

Permit us by way of digression to offer a bit of advice regarding email communication. Both we ourselves and colleagues we know have on occasion regretted succumbing to this medium's apparent informality. The ethos created by the electronic community can lull one into regarding emails as virtually identical to spoken conversations with a friend in the same room. The key difference, of course, is that in casual conversation we not only hear the words spoken to us, but also observe and register the message sender's body language. An apparently somewhat sharp exchange is softened by seeing the smile or wink across the room. In email conversation devoid of the subtle visual cues, misunderstandings are much more likely to occur, and offense can be given quite inadvertently and unnecessarily. The electronic community of message senders has attempted to cope with this reality by introducing written cues (such as <grin>), whereby the sender gives the receiver a clue as to the feeling tone behind the message. Even such emotion-indicators, however, like <XXXOOO> "hugs and kisses" to a spouse or child in a letter or email, do not have the same impact on the receiver as the real thing! Given our fast-paced lives and growing societal expectations for quick response, we may often feel compelled to respond at once to a troublesome or challenging email. A late-night e-mailer does well to ask, "Will my response survive the test of daylight?" In other words, giving oneself time to reflect more carefully and review a draft before sending can be an important discipline when it comes to email communication. Finally, as noted below in chapter 12, some communicators have felt burned to discover that e-messages they regarded as similar to casual cavalier conversations created a paper trail and ended up as evidence in court proceedings.[4]

In choosing one's media, a communicator does well to consider the possibility of seeking to convey messages redundantly via multiple channels. As noted above, in any small group or mass audience there will be receivers who process information differently. While the spoken word may get through to some, others will get it when presented in writing or through pictures or diagrams. The more critical the message, that is, the more that hinges on its being received and understood, the greater the importance of considering delivery through multiple media. Just as hospitals have backup generators for life-sustaining equipment, and airliners have multiple built-in redundancies, including at least two fully qualified pilots, so communicators should consider sending highly important communications redundantly and through more than one medium. Communication research indicates that most solicitations or invitations issued by relative strangers must be transmitted six to nine times before an average recipient makes any response. Even when a message is acknowledged by the recipient, further follow-up is often required. In good business practice, agreements or verbal contracts arrived at

4. An excellent online email etiquette guide can be found at http://www.library.yale.edu/training/netiquette.

through personal visits or telephone conversations are followed up in confirming written correspondence and/or other documents.

Follow ups w/ Confirmation

Utilizing Public Media: Reporters Can Be Your Friends

Politicians and pundits in our society often speak disparagingly of "the media," generally meaning television and newspaper reporters, editors and producers of papers, magazines, and radio and television news. While not as many reporter jokes have surfaced as those about lawyers, they tend to be of the same genre. Both from personal experience and that of other colleagues, we want to assure you, the reader, that many persons who work in the media are outstanding public servants living out their vocations as communicators with the highest standards of integrity. Many are interesting, delightful people and might even become your friends!

The point of the preceding paragraph is to demythologize those who work in the public media, and serve as a reminder that they are just people too. By education and experience, news reporters and editors have learned a craft. To be sure, just as is the case in any profession, there are a few unscrupulous ones out there who are always in search of the sensational story and will bend the truth as much as necessary to get their scoop. But the vast majority of media personnel want to convey the truth with accuracy and straightforwardness. And, as in any human exchange, things generally go better once a positive relationship is established. Leaders in churches and faith-based organizations will serve their own purposes by being proactive and getting acquainted with key individuals working in local media outlets. Initiating and cultivating a positive relationship with the reporter who covers religion news (only in the largest metropolitan newspapers will this be such a reporter's only beat) may serve well your hope to make the local news on occasion, and in a positive light.

Believe it or not, there really are many slow news days when reporters are not hot on the trail of dramatic late-breaking stories. Some actually sit around wondering what they will cover and write about tomorrow or next week. Getting a call from a local minister one knows, who suggests covering her congregation's new ministry that will uniquely help a group of folks previously unnoticed in the local community, may capture such a reporter's attention. Despite the reality that clergy may not be as high profile in many communities today as in bygone eras, news media often do go in search of the perspective of religious leaders on a contemporary issue or local event. While one may not wish to be the go-to person for local or even national media newspersons, if such a status is desired it may well be within the realm of possibility with just a modicum of cultivation. Your chances for such favored status are enhanced greatly by giving attention to a few simple factors:

- A reporter on an important story is always on deadline; she or he has to produce a story by a time (usually within hours) established by an editor or the news cycles. The 6 o'clock news always airs at 6:00 p.m.! If an interviewee is not immediately available when the reporter calls, getting back to her or him promptly increases the likelihood of being quoted on a current issue as well as the probability that the reporter will call again, having discovered that the contact is reliable and responsive.

- Clarity of expression makes for good quotes or sound bites. If a reporter interviewing for a story discovers that the person contacted rambles on and on about all manner of irrelevant issues, fails to even stay in the same ballpark when tossed specific questions, or is nonresponsive or even mildly belligerent, that will probably be the last time she or he calls. If an interviewee or subject of a story knows why the reporter is calling and there is time to do a bit of preparation, including jotting down some notes or key points and even specific statements to be made in the conversation, chances are enhanced for a positive exchange and repeat contacts from the reporter.

- One does not need to respond immediately. This may seem to contradict the first point about prompt response. The key word here is *immediately*. Getting back to reporters within an hour or two usually will suffice for their deadline purposes. Particularly if one wishes or is asked to address a controversial and highly sensitive matter, taking a bit of time to craft ideas and even a written statement can avoid awkward top-of-the-head responses. "Let me fax or email you our statement" is a perfectly appropriate response to a reporter. Recognize, however, that without some form of brief contact in person or by telephone, it is less likely that the reporter will quote a source on the basis of a written statement. But in such an interview, one can readily respond, "As I said in my written statement. . . ."

- Know the context and culture of the particular medium's target audience. Even a casual and unsophisticated reader will readily discern the difference between *The New Yorker* and *Reader's Digest*. A local talk-radio show probably has a significantly different feel from "All Things Considered" on National Public Radio. Using technical philosophical or theological language when speaking to a current local issue might play well if the audience members are primarily well-educated listeners to a broadcast from a university-sponsored lecture series. But the first time one speaks of the "eschatological implications of global warming" on a typical community radio program may well be the last time the speaker is invited!

- Even if a reporter is involved in the church, she or he probably will not know much about your congregation or religious organization. Both the reporter and interviewee will be well served if the latter regards a telephone or in-person conversation as a teaching moment. Be prepared to give fairly extensive background on a complex issue that may be controversial in your denomination. Offer a bit of history and set in a larger context the reason why the innovative program at your church is newsworthy. Recognize that, at the same time the reporter is attempting to make a story understandable by the typical person on the street, she or he is one too and may be as uninformed at the outset in considering a subject as everyone else is.

- Make it easy for the reporter to establish contact and follow-up. Just as a minister working on Sunday's sermon may need to go back to the library because she or he forgot to research some part of a biblical text while there yesterday, so reporters discover as they begin writing a story that there are some gaps or missing pieces. An interviewee who has taken pains to encourage follow-up may soon become one of that reporter's favorites. At the conclusion of a conversation, hand the reporter a business card. If you'll be available during certain hours at a given number, specify what they are. Inform a secretary or administrative assistant that, if reporter Smith calls, you are available, even if in a meeting.

- Be presentable and remember that you represent yourself, your church or organization, and your profession. Another myth about public media is that they only go for the glamorous guests and subjects who are perfectly coiffed and dressed to the nines in designer clothing. Most stories are about average people, and reporters and editors know they will rarely have the opportunity to interview subjects who are household names and need no introduction to a viewing, listening, or reading audience. But, again, reporters are like everyone else and generally prefer to be in the presence of well-groomed and appropriately dressed individuals. While the use of slang and poor grammar may be endearing in some circumstances, speaking poorly and in an overly casual manner in an interview may result in a product that will publicly embarrass the interviewee and community that she or he represents.

- Help the reporter ask the right questions, and make important points you want communicated even if you are not responding to specific questions. A busy reporter often simply does not have enough time to conduct extensive background research and learn enough about a situation to ask the important questions. A savvy subject will prepare for an interview and note the points she wants to make, finding ways to "tack on" additional responses to posed questions. "Yes, I am excited about the proposed new senior citizens center here in Our Town. And let me tell you about how we at Great Church have developed an intergenerational Sunday school where seniors and preschoolers find they have a lot in common."

We hope that you are now convinced that on the "to visit" list as you begin serving in a new community will be local news reporters and perhaps editors or publishers. Having already established personal relationships and a measure of trust will be especially helpful to a church or organization and its leaders, should they endure the unfortunate experience of a crisis or scandal. While serving in large institutional settings, both of us have undergone times when an incident or event captured the attention of public media. In these circumstances, we have been grateful that our communication staff persons had the wisdom and foresight to have already developed strong connections and positive relationships with local and even national reporters and other media contacts.

Communication in Times of Crisis

"Pastor, it's almost gone!" shrieks the shrill and shaky voice on the other end of the phone. "What's almost gone?" replies the befuddled minister who has just arrived home late from a rare enjoyable evening out dining with her husband and a handful of close friends from their days at the seminary. "Our church, it's on fire, and it was so far gone by the time the firefighters arrived that all they can do is stand and watch it burn."

"Mr. Nieland, I understand you are the president of St. Philip Church, is that correct?" queries the police officer standing at Nieland's front door on a Saturday morning just as the president is about to leave for an early golf game. "Yes, that's right. Is there something wrong?" "I'm afraid so," replies the woman in uniform. "We have just arrested a gentleman who teaches in your Sunday school; he's been accused by several parents of molesting their young children, and our preliminary investigation has determined the complaints are credible."

On an ordinary Tuesday morning, the parish administrator at a large suburban congregation receives a call from the church's local bank vice president. "I'm sorry to bother you, and debated whether to call," explains the banker, "but we noticed some unusual large withdrawals from the church's account and are wondering if you've had some big bills or perhaps made a very generous contribution to the Red Cross following the several natural disasters of late." Attempting to reach the church treasurer for several days following the phone call from the bank, the parish administrator gets only the treasurer's answering machine. The following week it is verified that the treasurer has left town, and maybe the country, with a very large sum of the parish's current funds and some endowment monies in tow.

Leaders in each of the three fictional churches whose fabricated stories are related above find themselves in a time of crisis. While the stories are made up, they mirror crisis situations that, sadly, do occur in congregations and church-related organizations. While not all who serve as leaders in such churches and organizations will encounter such a crisis, in the course of a career many will. Less dramatic but nevertheless painful and public crises come along with a fair degree of regularity in most faith communities. It is rare when a crisis occurs that it does not draw the attention of local and regional media. In the case of particularly egregious behavior on the part of a minister, church leader, or parishioner, national media may get wind and send their camera crews and reporters.

Wise are the church leaders who anticipate that crises, like conflicts, are part and parcel of the life of a faith community as it lives through time. Such leaders prepare in advance; they have a plan for crisis management and such a plan includes steps to be taken in managing information flow and media contacts. While it is impossible to anticipate every possible crisis situation, and inasmuch as differing circumstances will require varied responses, some general principles for crisis communication will apply in most circumstances, and can help shape a crisis communication plan that is developed and reviewed on occasion by an organization's leaders.

- Asking yourself the question, "Who needs to know immediately?" develop a short list of those to be informed at first hint that a critical situation is brewing and about to break. In a congregation, the list likely would include the pastor, president or board chair, and other key officers, as well as the bishop or other ecclesiastical authority. Obviously, if the crisis involves individuals or families (as in the case of a tragic death or accident), attempting to reach those most directly affected before the news breaks in wider circles is crucial. Depending upon the nature of the crisis, the police, one's insurer or attorney may also be on the "to be called first" list. Measures may need to be taken to protect victims or others from being barraged by reporters. Removing affected persons' or church council members' contact information from a website may be a wise precautionary step in this regard.
- Have a plan in place ahead of a crisis regarding rapid communication to the entire membership (of a congregation) or most important constituencies

(for agencies and institutions). Even if most have email capability, they cannot be relied upon to check it regularly; so activating a telephone chain or issuing a first-class mailing to the entire membership/constituency is critical once it's possible to go public. In spite of such efforts, do not be surprised if some hear first from public media or word of mouth; a few may feel blindsided despite your best efforts, and it's helpful to respond non-defensively, simply expressing regret they heard it first from others.

- As noted above, having already-established relationships with key media personnel will serve well in a time of crisis. If reporters have even rudimentary knowledge of your church or organization it will assist in their fair and accurate description of events and surrounding circumstances. Trusting the church's or organization's leaders because of prior connections, such media staff members are likely to exert extra effort to report the news but avoid sensationalizing or overstating the facts. Obviously, this will not be possible in every circumstance, particularly if a crisis occurs shortly after a new leader takes office. A widely circulated story of some years ago tells the sad tale of a minister driving from his former home to begin a new call; as he neared his new community and tuned in the local radio station, he heard the news bulletin that his new charge's venerable and stately old building had just been totally destroyed by fire!

- Be responsive and possibly even preemptive in fielding media inquiries. As a general rule, refusing to return phone calls or issuing terse "no comment" statements will be received by the media and general public as stonewalling, conveying an implicit acknowledgment and confirmation of whatever is being alleged. Double damage to an organization's reputation can be done by such a stance. Honest, straightforward answers to reporters' questions, while preserving appropriate confidentiality for individuals who should not be exposed to the public eye, will engender confidence in the organization's leaders. Persons in the media and broader public will tend to respond, "Well, they have a problem and something tragic has happened, but they're dealing with it, and they seem like responsible folks."

- Develop a press release or written statement. Particularly if a crisis involves something of a scandalous nature, like the last two vignettes posed above, a church does well to craft a carefully worded statement for release to the press and other inquiring parties. It is important to note that in both cases above, at the time of the police officer's appearance and query from the bank officer, the church's leaders were dealing with accusations or possible allegations of wrongdoing. No one had been found guilty of criminal and unethical behavior in a court of law or ecclesiastical proceeding. Under such circumstances it is important to avoid stating verbally or in writing presumptive conclusions about guilt or innocence. At the same time, if victims of the alleged behavior have come forward, their needs and feelings should be uppermost in crafting a statement. All attempts should be made to avoid sounding defensive or calling into doubt the veracity of persons who have told gut-wrenching stories about wrongs suffered. Particularly in situations such as those described, a draft written statement should be reviewed by several persons, including ideally the church's or organization's legal counsel.

- *Seek outside help immediately.* In the throes of a crisis, the most level-headed and otherwise non-anxious cool heads among us will be reeling from devastating news that generally comes out of the blue. Under such circumstances, it is wise for even seasoned communication-savvy veterans to call for the help of outside expertise. In many denominations, a diocesan, synodical, or other judicatory office has communication professionals who can offer good coaching, review press releases and draft statements, and perhaps be an alternative source of comment to news media. Giving one's bishop or other ecclesiastical leader an immediate heads-up when a crisis breaks also enables her or him to prepare for possible media contacts as word spreads in ever-widening circles. A key element of crisis communication planning would be the identification of such outside communication coaches and contacts to be called on for help in the event of a crisis.

- *Designate one primary, and at most one or two backup spokespersons.* While again we stress that the vast majority of news media reporters and editors are trustworthy and scrupulous individuals, there are some who do go for the sensational headline-grabbing story and who may have a tendency to manipulate a crisis for their own purposes. Recognizing that conflict and controversy sell, some in the media are constantly in search of people at odds with each other. If they can interview a number of individuals in a community in crisis and get varying or contradictory comments, a controversy has been discovered if not created. Casual uninformed or inaccurate comments by members who are not in the inner circle of leadership may create complications and legal liability as well. While it's generally unwise to issue a gag order or muzzle free speech on the part of all members and staff of a church or organization, designating a spokesperson and widely disseminating his or her name usually will have the effect of channeling most inquiries to that person. The names, telephone numbers, and emails of key contact persons should also be cited on a press release or public statement.

Internal or In-house Communication

Much of the preceding discussion centered on relations with and shaping communications for the external public media. In any congregation or organization, however, there are also multiple messages directed primarily if not entirely to the membership or internal constituency. Such communication vehicles in churches typically include print media like Sunday bulletins, parish newsletters, and occasional circulars or memoranda to committees or program and interest groups. Increasingly, many churches can contact most congregational members by email. While a website has a dual readership of external "visitors" and members, most hits for a typical congregational website likely come from members. Some communication pieces, like brochures, picture postcards, or bookmarks may be designed for distribution both to current members and prospects as a church or organization engages in outreach and seeks to expand its membership or constituency.

It is unfortunate that organizations often take little time and effort to make communication pieces designed primarily for an internal audience interesting! The sad truth is that too many entities damage their own self-image and how members feel about the organization by a lackadaisical attitude toward internal communication pieces. Sure, everyone will understand an internal memorandum with a few misspelled words and grammatical errors. But what does it say about the author and organizational ethos that not enough care is given to take a few extra moments and clean up a draft? With regard to parish newsletters, these too can and should have a *feel* of being interesting and inviting, rather than boring and always the same, issue after issue. It is not necessary to spend huge sums of money on graphic design and a glossy final product. Even simple photocopied materials can have an inviting format and feel by using a variety of fonts and graphics that are now widely available for free on websites and with word processing programs.

Periodic communication audits or surveys can be helpful in getting feedback from message receivers. Every good communicator is constantly asking the question, "Are we getting through? Is the message being received and acted on?" With tools such as newsletters and flyers, it can be difficult to assess impact and effectiveness. Conducting a survey by means of a written questionnaire or series of focus groups in which straightforward inquiries are made as to the effectiveness of various communication tools and strategies will help communicators and leaders assess and utilize the discoveries as an aid to planning, revising or perhaps eliminating altogether some ineffective message bearers.[5]

Websites Can Be Wonderful or Woeful

More and more organizations, including congregations, have developed websites whereby a great deal of information is made available to a worldwide audience via the Internet. A website can be a wonderful low-cost tool to serve members and close constituencies, as well as spiritual seekers and the general public. Like any other medium, they also can be used poorly and even work against conveying a positive image of the ministry. If poorly designed, unattended to the point that a great deal of outdated material remains posted long after events, or missing key information (like the church's address and directions how to find it!), the website may convey a message: "We're really not interested in making ourselves available, helpful, or hospitable."

Increasingly, congregations or organizations will have within their membership technically skilled persons who can perhaps design and maintain a website at little or no cost. As with all volunteers, careful selection as well as monitoring

---

5. For a good congregational communication audit outline, see the website of the Communication Service Unit of the Evangelical Lutheran Church in America, http://www.elca.org.

and providing support are important. A webmaster who has his or her personal agenda may post items and information that parish leaders deem inappropriate or irrelevant. If the volunteer's schedule gets busy, the site may go untended for an extended season, resulting in some of the problems noted above. Developing careful guidelines to govern content, timeliness, and other factors will help minimize tensions and foster good understandings between parish or agency leaders and all involved in stewarding its website.

Beyond telling the story of the congregation's or organization's own ministry, a website can be a wonderful tool for expanding horizons and communicating partnership with the wider church. Offering easy links to the synod/diocese/presbytery or other judicatory, as well as national church offices, and church-affiliated agencies and institutions invites site users to connect with broader church ministries and avail themselves of a growing richness of resources being made available. Increasing *Webfeeds* are being made available by denominational offices; these can bring voices and images from the wider church to members' home computers.

Communicators who utilize websites do well to remember the worldwide audience to whom items posted are made available. In routinely posting sermons, a preacher needs to be mindful that messages intended for her or his flock may be interpreted quite differently by the general public or even international readers who happen upon the homily while doing a Google search. And, as noted above on crisis communication, caution should be exercised about making broadly available personal information about members, staff persons, and others who may become targets for the growing inappropriate, unethical, and illegal activity occurring on the Internet.[6]

---

6. Excellent guidelines, "Designing Congregational Websites," are available from the Hartford Institute for Religion Research: http://hirr.hartsem.edu/cong/cong_designing_church_sites.html. Also, a growing number of denominational websites offer helpful website-related guidance and resources.

Consistency and Cohesion

A common critique of both external and internal messaging on the part of organizations is that their multiple vehicles and communication pieces lack coherence and result in conveying confusing or perhaps even conflicting images of the entity's mission and identity. A consultant to educational institutions began a presentation on communication strategies by tossing on the table a dozen or more admissions, alumni, and other brochures and magazines. The consultant then asked, "What do these pieces have in common?" Workshop participants, assuming that these several pieces emanated from a variety of institutions, responded instantaneously, "Nothing at all beyond being printed on paper." To their surprise, the consultant went on to reveal that each of these widely disparate communication tools was in fact published and distributed by the same institution. According to the consultant, it was not the case that this major university had intentionally chosen to field a widely disparate and diffuse set of publications. The lack of any coherence just evolved over time as various offices and departments each did their own thing and designed and distributed materials without reference to a university-wide communication plan.

The opposite of boring sameness is overwhelming and confusing diffusion. An organization's communication strategists may well decide to have several different *looks* in their materials and images projected, particularly if logos, slogans, and color schemes become identified with discrete and high visibility programs. But projecting too many disparate images can cause identity diffusion, particularly if a church or organization is seeking to make itself known among groups and constituencies where it is unfamiliar. In terms of communication strategies and their effectiveness, we can learn from large corporate entities with huge marketing, public relations, and advertising budgets. All MacDonald's everywhere are marked by the golden arches and have been for decades. While menus and other communication media and messages may change to avoid become boring, the golden arches are the principal message-bearer known throughout the world.

As coherence of various communication pieces is important, so is a measure of continuity. Organizations blessed with an abundance of creative innovators may have to find ways to restrain a tide caused by too much desire for constant change and newness. While ministries may stagnate and decline due to lack of adaptability to change in the environment, organizational effectiveness also can be hindered by a lack of coherence, commonly held identity, and overall sense of mission. Finding the balance between these two extremes in its messaging is a never-ending quest for every organization.

CHAPTER 9

Ministry Teams: Teeming with Talent

Alone we can do so little; together we can do so much.
—*Helen Keller*

A team with a star player is a good team, but a team without one is a great team.
—*Unknown*

Snowflakes are one of nature's most fragile things, but just look at what they can do when they stick together.
—*Vesta Kelly*

"Team" is not a church word. There is a community of faith that gathers for worship and edification and scatters into the world for witness and service, but a community is not a team. When we grew up (some time ago) the only teams around were playing sports, and that phenomenon not only continues but has exploded into our everyday lives to such a degree we cannot escape its effects. That is not all bad, because sports teams (at their best) can teach what it means to depend on someone else to achieve a goal; for that is what a team is and how it differs from a group or random collection of persons.

Coach Mike Krzyzewski of Duke University in Durham, North Carolina, has achieved fantastic success in men's basketball. He teaches things like, "You develop a team to achieve what one person cannot accomplish alone. All of us alone are weaker, by far, than if all of us are together. . . . There are also five fundamental qualities that make every team great: communication, trust, collective responsibility, caring, and pride. I like to think of each as a separate finger on the fist. Anyone individually is important. But all of them together are unbeatable." Coach K believes there is such a thing as team identity. It happens when "any combination of five players can play as one."[1]

Teams in the Church

Though not a church word, there are teams in the church, the presence of which helps (or hinders) its work. Think of these five examples. The governance function in the church (see chapters 2 and 3) is executed by groups of persons (elected or appointed) who take on some of the characteristics of teams even though they may not spend much time with each other. In some congregations multiple staff members work together as a team even as they carry out their individual responsibilities alone or with others. Larger church-related institutions, such as universities, hospitals, and social service agencies, are packed with a wide variety of teams for administration, coordination, planning, budgeting, personnel, and task force work. Within these organizations, the language about teams resembles that of a business corporation or government agency, sectors where the use of teams has expanded almost without limit.

Most United States–based denominations have something in the middle, that is, an agency or office between congregations and whatever the national or international structure is called. Wrongly labeled "middle judicatories," as if adjudication was their main or sole reason for being, in recent years these collections of staff, volunteers, and their governance units have taken on even more important roles with greatly expanded responsibilities. As they grow in scope they also grow in numbers, and increasingly they work together as a team. Likewise in national and international church offices, the work would simply not get done without

1. Mike Krzyzewski, with Donald T. Phillips, *Leading with the Heart* (New York: Warner Books, 2000), 67, 71.

the formation of teams, especially to cross the boundaries of organizational units. We were members of the same team for six years, a team made up of people who supported the presiding bishop and the churchwide organization in a variety of ways—planning, budgeting, synod services, personnel, research, administration, communication—an experience described later in this chapter.

A Society of Teams

Thirty-five years ago, newspapers and television coverage heaped praise on Astronaut Mike Collins for waiting patiently in the circling space capsule while the eyes, ears, and glory of the whole earth focused on his two teammates getting moon dust on their shoes. It was widely recognized that Collins's contribution was part of a total team effort. That is high praise in such an individualistic "Lone Ranger" society.

Awareness of teams and their importance to society is supported by a whole industry of research, training, degree programs, workshops, articles, and books. Two of the best and most complete studies are *The Wisdom of Teams*, by Jan R. Katzenbach and Douglas K. Smith,[2] and chapter 12, "Team Learning," in Peter Senge, *The Fifth Discipline*.[3] From these two works we learn that: (1) Teamwork is not based on friendship. Friendship in fact may get in the way of confronting obstacles, truth telling, and making hard decisions. (2) Teams in the workplace may fail because of the absence of top management support. (3) Types of teams include those that recommend things (for example, task forces), make or do things (for example, worker teams, sales teams), and run things (management teams at various levels). (4) Effective teams attend to basics: appropriate size, clear purpose and goals, sufficient interpersonal and group skills, a shared approach, and individual and mutual accountability. (5) Team learning is correlated with effective

---

2. Jon R. Katzenbach and Douglas K. Smith, *The Wisdom of Teams: Creating the High-Performance Organization* (Boston: Harvard Business School Press, 1993).

3. Peter M. Senge, "Team Learning," in *The Fifth Discipline: The Art and Practice of The Learning Organization* (New York: Doubleday/Currency, 1990), 238–49.

handling of conflict. (6) Three conditions for dialogue (as opposed to discussion likened to "batting a Ping-Pong ball back and forth") are suspension of assumptions, acting as colleagues, and having a spirit of inquiry. (7) Good interpersonal relationships are secondary explanations of why some teams perform well and others do not; the primary reason is having accountability for group performance, not only individual performance.

The complaint that teams are slow, though they may eventually produce results, has led to the development of "hot teams," who exhibit a "communal state of mind." Such attitudes and high commitment to performance "flow" around the workplace. New solutions are found to sticky problems, innovations abound, and higher and higher performance goals are reached in record time. "Hot teams" are speedy and meet the new demands of the workplace.

There was a short fling with self-directed work teams in the business organization. The theory was that with decreased restraints, including reporting to someone else, self-direction would meet new demands for speed, flexibility, and creativity. After some initial success in highly selective environments like research laboratories, most were shut down amid stories of "runaway" teams doing their own thing, resulting in a highly uncoordinated effort and the pursuit of multiple missions.

Building a Team in a Church Setting

Eight members of the team in a national office had in common the delivery of services and fulfilling functions that provided major support for the presiding bishop's role and the entire churchwide organization. This was not a decision group but a group whose work needed coordination and, as it turned out, became a learning team; that is, we taught each other how to do our jobs more effectively and efficiently. We also anticipated major events, issues, and challenges that called for a coordinated and early response lest they catch the churchwide organization by surprise.

A worksheet was prepared for the first meeting. It included what seem to be the important dimensions of effective team development drawn from experience with previous teams and the available research on teams:

1. Engagement. What would it take for you to become engaged in a team effort? How should our spiritual life as a team be nurtured? How should we spend our time? How often and for how long each time?

2. Expectations. What are your expectations, hopes, and fears for and of this team?

3. Contributions. Name two strengths you bring to this team. Name one "not-so" strength (limit, weakness, area for improvement).

4. Purpose. Describe the purpose of this team in twenty-five words or less.

5. Agenda building. What are the most important tasks, issues, or topics for this team to address?

6. Learning. What will this team need to learn to be effective? I could teach this team about _____. What should be the name of this team?

Please share anything else not covered above that is pertinent to this team.

Also included were some guidelines about organization, authority, membership, "eight strong individuals who value a radical service orientation and exhibit a willingness to develop an equally strong team, not another cabinet" (decision group), agendas, anticipating the future, and listening.

The team met for a full day twice to listen to each person as they responded to each question. From that point on the group normally met once a month for three to four hours for ten years. Members came and went as jobs changed, but the group became, as one member put it, "the meeting I don't want to miss."

Each meeting started with prayer and often with Bible study. There would be a one- to two-hour block on "learning": a review of a relevant book or article, reflection on a work experience, sharing of a continuing education event, and an occasional "outside" speaker. The content of this learning period focused on theology, biblical studies, personal learning, and organizational issues. The remainder of the time included a "round robin," brief updates from each person. We learned over time how to do this with an economy of time by focusing on the most relevant matters. Also there was at least one agenda item that cut across our individual responsibilities, like preparing for a churchwide assembly or a report on an ecumenical matter.

There was a certain discipline that developed over time that had to do with improving effectiveness (we did periodic evaluation on ourselves) and efficiency (we all improved the ability to focus rather than engage in general platitudes). Yet the maturity the team reached encouraged a relaxed and enjoyable style. The name of the team did not emerge immediately. Over time it was called the "No Name" group, an expression of pride in its value without being on the organization chart.

Two assumptions underlay the ongoing life of this team, and they can be generalized to all teams. First, both individuality and teamwork were affirmed and encouraged. Being an individual and having specific individual responsibility are not cancelled in an effective team. In fact, it can be claimed that in the example of the team being described here, individual competence and responsibility were enhanced, not diminished. American society tends to trumpet the value and role of the individual until it becomes individualism. The message is "Beware of others, especially groups. They will rob you of your personhood." Good teams are "both-and" projects; both personhood and group solidarity are honored and respected.

The second assumption is that an effective team need not be destructive to the larger organization in which it exists. It can be, of course, and that danger needs to be watched. A multiple-staff team in a large congregation can enjoy its internal relationships and "being a team" to the point that it shuts out the many volunteers who are needed to carry out the congregation's ministries. Team leaders can be reliable role models in the way they operate in the larger organization and function in the team to assure that an insularity and even an "over-againstness" do not materialize. Some pastors have been reluctant to begin care groups or fellowship groups within the congregation, having heard "war stories" from other pastors about destructive small groups who work against the grain of the whole congregation's life and mission. This is not inevitable. Vital teams can strengthen the congregation or organization in which they exist.

The weakness in the use of sports teams as models and drawing guidance from their development (like the reference with which this chapter began) is that sports teams by purpose are developed to defeat a competitor. They do not, therefore, contribute to the larger environment, except perhaps as others (those defeated) learn from them.

Code of Collegiality

In the example described above and in other teams as well, the need arises to have a few "ground rules" or guidelines to follow, such as:

- respect for one another
- keeping confidentiality (specify what this means)
- non-pairing (refrain from an exclusive partnership with another over against the rest of the team, either when the team is together or outside the team)
- commitment to accomplishing significant things together (as opposed to a trivial sharing of nonessential matters)
- trust of each other
- use of appropriate authority (the team may operate in an egalitarian manner, but the authority of team members in the larger organization is rarely equal. In the example above, one team member did the performance appraisals of most of the team members and was responsible for the administration of the whole churchwide organization)
- meeting attendance (rare exceptions for being absent)
- pray for each other in and outside the team

Vocation and Team Membership

One of the questions used in starting and developing the team described above was, "Name two strengths you bring to this team." This is a deceptively simple inquiry. It is possible to answer the question from several different orientations. One study of public service workers (government employees) shows that persons tend to approach their work as job, career, or vocation.[4] The concept of vocation links a person to a larger community in which a calling is a contribution to the good of all. The ideas of job and career are based on the powerful tradition of American individualism. A job is a way to make money and support a self-determined idea of economic success and security. A career is not so defined by money as rooted in notions of competing, power, social standing, and self-esteem. A career is portable work.

Martin Luther applied vocation to all Christians. God's call to serve is answered in the structures of everyday life as worker, volunteer, family member, citizen, and even what we stake out as "free time."

The prayer for Labor Day in the Episcopal Book of Common Prayer reads, "So guide us in the work we do, that we may do it not for self alone, but for the common good." If "work" here is understood as all the pursuits we undertake, including but not restricted to work-for-pay, then this prayer expresses a sense of vocation: God's call is singular ("I," "me") but also plural ("we" and "us" are involved).

"Right where they happen to be, human beings ought to hear the call [of Jesus Christ] and allow themselves to be claimed by it. . . . It is Christ's address and claim at the place at which this call encounters me; vocation inspires work with things and issues as well as personal reflections. Vocation is the place at which one responds to the call of Christ and thus lives responsibly. The task given to me by my vocation is thus limited; but my responsibility to the call of Jesus Christ knows no bounds." So wrote Dietrich Bonhoeffer in his *Ethics* three years before his death at the hands of the Nazis.[5]

A team is an intersection of individual vocations and the common good for which the team exists. "Name two strengths you bring to this team." The question can provoke a dismissive answer, "I'm great with people and like to get the

---

4. Robert N. Bacher and James F. Wolf, "The Public Administrator and Public Service Occupations," in *Refounding Public Administration* (Newbury Park: Sage, 1990), 167–77.

5. Dietrich Bonhoeffer, *Ethics;* Dietrich Bonhoeffer Works 6 (Minneapolis: Fortress Press, 2005), 290–2.

job done quickly." A more reflective response, coming from the deep well of one's experiences with the God who calls "at the precise place" where we are, will speak loudly to team members and to oneself.

There should be times in the life of a church team when these answers coming from deeper places in the heart and soul can be shared, not as intrusions into team members' lives but as reports of what God is doing with each member, that is, what kinds of vocation are present and developing.

A suggestion for how to provide an opportunity for the intersection of vocation and team purpose to be lifted up and celebrated follows. Developed for seminary board members, it can easily be converted for other uses by inserting the purpose or ministry of the team where "theological education" appears. For example, "Describe the intersection of [social justice] as a calling with your gifts, values, passions, faith." After the responses to the four questions are shared by each person, God should be thanked in prayer for the presence of the many examples of vocation that have been expressed:

1. In what ways is the call of Jesus Christ coming to you in "your place"?
2. Describe the intersection of theological education as a calling with your
   a. Gifts
   b. Values
   c. Passions
   d. Faith
3. What do you find attractive, exciting, and challenging in theological education today?
4. When you think about the future of theological education, what engenders hope and causes fear?

All for One and One for . . .

Most teams do not ride off into the sunset holding hands and singing camp songs! Problems crop up from time to time and, as noted about conflict in chapter 11 below, the successful handling of problems, not their absence, is a strong key to being an effective team.

According to two experienced team trainers, there seem to be four kinds of problems:[6]

1. Individuals abdicate responsibility. Teams who either have a designated leader (selected or by virtue of position) or one chosen tacitly by the team, often without recognition, can develop a "let her do it" style. Team effectiveness is diminished because the talents and contributions of team members are not utilized while they wait for "the leader" to solve all problems, make all the suggestions, set the agenda, and just "follow."

2. Teams jump to conclusions when faced with ambiguity. While individuals don't usually seek shortcuts to solutions or determining next steps in an unclear situation, groups do. This leap to the seemingly easiest way through a decision often provides an inferior result than if more time had been taken to pool the insights and wisdom of the team into a better response.

3. Members judge themselves and others. From those who teach "the inner game" of tennis or golf comes this observation: There are two selves in a learning situation. Self Two is that part of the brain that actually learns by watching how a tennis stroke or golf swing is made. Self One does the negative feedback, "You're stupid. How could you miss the ball entirely?" The coaches seek to distract Self One so that Self Two can competently master the game.

In a team this dynamic is even more complex, because team members are not only judging themselves but each other, and perhaps positioning themselves to appear the "smartest." This jockeying for position can easily drain energy away from goals, tasks, and challenges as it is used up on self-protection and self-promotion. A frequently observed experience in teams, namely, the continuation of a discussion or debate past the point of resolution, may be explained by this desire to prove that certain team members are worthy of respect and admiration.

4. The hardest lesson to learn in teams may be that my personal opinion need not be held by everyone on the team. Does anyone ever really give up their strongly held view because they are convinced that the team has actually come to a better decision or solution? Yes, definitely yes, in mature teams; otherwise the strength of the team does not rise above that of the strongest member. The next

6. Timothy Gallway and Valerio Pascotto, "All for One," *Context*, October–November 2000, 68–69.

section contains an exercise for practicing the improvement of the decision by team interaction.

Practice Makes Perfect

A little practice helps. Since most team decisions or problem solving cannot be measured quantitatively, it is difficult to know how well the team has done. Practice sessions that introduce a measurement that can actually be compared to the "correct answers" can paint for the team a realistic picture of its interaction. There are several ways to proceed. Excellent resources can be found in publications. Or a consultant/trainer can be retained to provide the framework for these experiences, perhaps in a retreat setting.

A third approach is to develop your own exercise. Choose an interesting and relevant topic and describe it in writing (six to ten pages). Prepare ten questions, the answers to which have a factual basis, that is, they can be answered correctly from the information in the text. The answers are not opinion but fact-based. Each member of the team reads the material and answers the questions without conversation with others. Then the team answers the questions by making choices that must be unanimous. Ten points are awarded for each correct answer. Individual and team scores are posted on a chalkboard or newsprint. The following questions are discussed:

- Is the team score higher than any individual score? If so, team interaction has produced results greater than individual talent. If the team score is lower than any individual score, then the best use was not made of individual talent. Discuss why not.
- Did the team score higher than the average of individual scores? If so, then good use was made of more than one member of the group. If not, then better results could have been obtained by averaging individual scores and never trying to reach team answers.

Why do this? There are three reasons: (1) The team is forced to decide what "unanimous" means. Do we take a vote? Should objections be solicited? (Have you ever heard a chair say, "Well, I guess we all agree, as I don't hear any objections"?) (2) The evaluation after such an exercise can make the team more aware of how they really operate as opposed to their ideal image of themselves. (3) Individuals are given data for reflection and learning about the strength and weakness of how they are functioning in the team. What do I do when my view is not that of the majority—withdraw into my shell? Attack with a fierceness designed to intimidate others into my way of thinking? Offer reasons for my view? Go with the majority? Create a new coalition from those who agree with me? Support the decision even though I disagree? Pout if I don't get my way? Because these practice exercises have factual answers, a team member with the correct answer could say, "I told you so," when the team answers wrongly. There are an infinite number of responses and defenses (the psychologists tell us). Finding the healthy and productive ones makes for personal well-being and team effectiveness.

A tip in preparing the ten questions: Questions that can be answered true or false or by multiple-choice answers (a, b, c, d) are easier to score and help to avoid debates.

Gender and Multicultural Issues in Teams

Several times in this chapter, the phrases "research shows" or "studies indicate" have been used to present some finding or guideline that would be helpful to you, the reader. The problem with such language is that almost all of these inquiries report the experiences of white males. Within organizational studies as a field, including the work on teams, there is a recent (last 5 to 7 years) attempt to point out the limits of such research and to develop both conceptually and operationally more inclusive models of human behavior. Such statements as, "We need a group development model that is more inclusive and can be more helpful for the development of mixed gender and multicultural groups in organization" are finally becoming more frequent.[7]

---

7. Judith White, M. Ceclia McMillen, and Ann C. Baker, "Challenging Traditional Models: Toward an Inclusive Model of Group Development," *Journal of Management Inquiry* 10/l (March 2001), 50.

This is not the place to describe the various attempts to correct the imbalance in the study of organizational life. Suffice it to say that nearly every basic set of theoretical assumptions about group behavior used in research and that form the basis of manuals, training, or workshops on team building are built on the white male as the norm. While there is a long way to go in addressing the situation, some statements can be made that help to examine our assumptions and thus guide our behavior about:

- Human behavior. Human beings have the capacity to be cooperative and collaborative as well as competitive, seeking win-win solutions as well as win-lose situations.
- Leadership has feminine, masculine, and multicultural forms. It can be shared, rotated, and spontaneous as well as subtle, gentle, and/or emotional. Mid-wife is an appropriate metaphor for leader.
- Power. Traditional definitions and connotations of power need to be expanded. Power involves the expression of one's voice and allowing others the same. Power can be seen as a resource for the common good rather than for domination, control, or mastery.
- Emotion. Groups are an appropriate place for the expression of emotion both positive and negative. Storming, pairing, and dependence on the leader (all classic stages of group development theory) need not be assumed. Emotions are not the conceptual opposite of rationality; emotion can inform.
- Diversity. Differences are a resource and opportunity for learning, not a problem to be solved. Differences can be valued, not feared, equaled with the unknown, and problematic. Acknowledgement needs to be given to those who have suffered exclusion, oppression, and being marginalized in groups. Differences can be honored.
- Conflict and its effective handling can be sources of growth and energy. Learning can come from experiencing different points of view, even those accompanied with emotion. Conflict brings new ideas, experiences, and contributes to group maturity.[8]

---

8. These assumptions are found in ibid., 50–52.

These assumptions present a way to think about and live out team relationships. They encompass the issues that almost always develop in teams. Recognizing and handling these issues will make teams stronger.

A second set of issues has to do with sexual harassment in teams. Both the
workplace and the church have made recent strides in developing policies and
training leaders to confront this issue with strong resolve and a non-tolerance
stance. Back in 1985, Barbara A. Gutek presented a set of recommendations for
organizational leaders based on a thorough study of business corporations: (1)
establish a policy on sexual harassment (or review the current policy) and establish
a set of procedures for implementation; (2) vigorously pursue allegations of harassment and act on the basis of evidence discovered; (3) include assessing dynamics
related to sexual harassment in performance appraisals, and act on the results;
and (4) promote professional behavior and professional ambience throughout the
organization.[9]

What is your congregation's or church-related organization's policy? The
Evangelical Lutheran Church in America, of which we are members and rostered
clergy, has pursued this matter with vigor, going beyond words and promises to
action. The ELCA's personnel policies regarding sexual harassment state in part:

> The ELCA is committed to maintaining a work environment
> that is free from harassment. Harassment consists of unwel-
> come conduct, whether verbal, physical, or visual, that is based
> on a person's protected status, such as sex, color, race, religion,
> national origin, age, physical or mental disability, or other pro-
> tected group status.[10]

In addition to stating the expectations and standards, a sexual harassment policy should spell out the process whereby anyone who feels they have experienced

---

9. Barbara A. Gutek, *Sex and the Workplace* (San Francisco: Jossey-Bass,
1985), 174–84.

10. "Policy on Sexual Harassment," available from Evangelical Lutheran
Church in America, 8765 W. Higgins Road, Chicago, IL 60631 (http://www
.elca.org).

offensive conduct can file a complaint and seek redress. Potential consequences for violators of the policy, which should include the possibility of employment termination, likewise need to be spelled out clearly.

The Future of Teams

D. Quinn Mills predicts that the wave of the future is the cluster organization. By that he means an organization that is peopled with clusters of every kind and shape doing the work in smaller units, operating as teams. These clusters will arrange themselves in a variety of ways for a variety of purposes. There will be clusters for problem solving, the introduction of change, international business, technology, research, planning, new product development, and evaluation. They need not appear in uniform vertical or horizontal patterns on an organizational chart, especially a pyramidal one. They can be seen by taking up a position directly above the organization. The look down into the organization takes on the appearance of a "pizza," with clusters related to each other and to some central authority in a somewhat loose arrangement, but one that works because of the invisible ties through leadership, common data, shared purpose, and high commitment.

A cluster does not mean "chaos, anarchy, or lack of central direction. It does not mean the end of management."[11] It does mean a new style of leadership and a common vision of strategic goals. Microsoft has done most of its software development through an interlocking set of teams, each with a high degree of autonomy and freedom to create. They are all held together by a few rules related to project completion, not to individual behavior (employees come to and leave the workplace as they wish), and to good communications within and across functions and teams. This replacement of departments, divisions, or any such nomenclature denoting permanency, "siloism," or "chiefdoms," gives way to a more free-flowing pattern of highly performing clusters whose continued existence is not assured past their usefulness.

---

11. D. Quinn Mills, *Rebirth of the Corporation* (Hoboken, N.J.: Wiley, 1991), 3.

An entire new industry of books, articles, and consultants has arisen to help organizations who rely on semi-autonomous teams to develop linkages, common purpose, and appropriate leadership styles.[12]

One trend in congregations is the use of ministry teams in place of the old committees. While sometimes this initiative seems designed to "shake up the troops" with new language and little more, this approach can be fruitful if three conditions are met. First, the ministry teams need to function as teams. They need to exhibit the characteristics described in this chapter and require nurturing in the ways described. Second, an integration of volunteers and professional staff needs to occur at a very high level. Who does what? It can be done but calls for careful and competent attention. The third condition is that someone (the pastor?) needs to keep it all going in the same direction. Some congregations develop a leadership team made up of professional staff and the convener of each ministry team. This leadership team also operates as a true team and provides the glue that holds it all together. Another trend is that the conveners can become part-time staff compensated for their work.

"Team" is not a church word. Teams, however, not only have a future in church life but it is likely that their presence and contributions will increase. In this chapter we have considered definitions, teams in the church, teams in society, a model for building a team in a church setting, a code for collegiality, the interplay of vocation and team membership, four problems that teams face, some practical ideas, gender and multicultural issues in teams, and the future of teams. "Gung ho" is Chinese for "work in harmony." The authors are gung ho for teams. We hope you are too.

---

12. For example, see Peggy Holman and Tom Devane, eds., *The Change Handbook: Group Methods for Shaping the Future* (San Francisco: Berrett-Koehler, 1999). Methods include future search, open space technology, the conference model, participative design workshop, the whole system approach, appreciative inquiry, real time study change, and others.

CHAPTER 10

External Relationships: Loving Thy Institutional Neighbor

The second is this: "You shall love your neighbor as yourself."
—Mark 12:31a

But wanting to justify himself, he [the lawyer] asked Jesus, "And
who is my neighbor?"
—Luke 10:29

Does responsibility place me into an unlimited field of activity,
or does it tie me firmly to the limits given with my concrete daily
tasks?
—Dietrich Bonhoeffer[1]

This chapter is about the importance and role of external relationships. Church administration, at least in an older image, was seen as keeping the internal workings humming. As history shows (see chapter 1, above), this older machine-like image has given way to more dynamic ones: organism, system, flow, change, "psychic prisons," cultures, "constructed realities," and power dominions. With the increased use of multiple images to grasp what

---

1. Dietrich Bonhoeffer, *Ethics*; Dietrich Bonhoeffer Works 6 (Minneapolis: Fortress Press, 2005), 288.

organizations really are and do has come the appreciation for the critical role played by the environment in which the organization exists. How organizations, including ecclesiastical ones, relate to these "externalities" becomes a major factor not just in how efficient they are but also how effective the organizations become over time.

As is the case with all the administrative topics addressed in this book, more is at work (and at stake) than the organizational trappings. Therefore, we begin with some theological perspectives.

The Place of Responsibility: Loving My (Our) Institutional Neighbor

We call on two sources: the discourse of Jesus about "the neighbor" (Jesus is quoting Lev 19:18 and Deut 6:5) and Dietrich Bonhoeffer's elaboration of the same theme.

External relationships take on a face (or faces): "'You shall love the Lord your God with all your heart, and with all your soul, and with all your mind.' This is the greatest and first commandment. And a second is like it: 'You shall love your neighbor as yourself'" (Matt 22:37–39). The impact of this response apparently makes the one who prompted it uncomfortable enough to counter-respond with another question, perhaps designed to escape the clarity and directness of Jesus' first answer: "But wanting to justify himself, he [the lawyer] asked Jesus, 'And who is my neighbor?'" (Luke 10:29). In Luke's version of this critical encounter, the lawyer receives some storytelling as the answer to his second question, namely, the parable of the Good Samaritan (10:30–37). This parable concludes with another question from Jesus to his interrogator, "Which of these three [priest, Levite, Samaritan], do you think, was a neighbor to the man who fell into the hands of the robbers?" The lawyer, now fully caught in Jesus' web, answers, "The one who showed him mercy." The story ends with an imperative, "Go and do the same."

Four assertions are engendered from this exchange:

• Christian responsibility includes a relationship with "the neighbor"; it is not optional.

• That relationship is not passive, that is, it is not enough to have neighbors; we are to act positively toward them.

• We cannot escape responsibility by asking questions about who is the neighbor. The neighbor is at hand and far away. The neighbor's presence (and need) breaks through our preoccupation with internal matters.

• A change from "you" to "we," "my" to "our," and, in the quote from Bonhoeffer, from "me" to "us" produces the concept of *institutional neighbors* in addition to individual ones. Thus the title of this chapter: "External Relationships: Loving Thy Institutional Neighbor."

Dietrich Bonhoeffer is helpful at this juncture. In an extended discussion in what later was to be published as his *Ethics*, he reflects on both the content and location of Christian responsibility.[2] This section is titled "The Place of Responsibility."

Bonhoeffer makes three claims: (a) the call of Jesus Christ comes to each person (and institution) right where they are; (b) two "disastrous misunderstandings" are to be avoided—fleeing the world or becoming too much a part of it (he protested against what he calls "cultural Protestantism" going on around him as the church's program was absorbed into Nazi ideology and practice); and (c) while the call of Jesus Christ has no limits, each person (institution), given the particulars of history, geography, and culture, does have a "field of activity" that comprises the specifics of a response to the call. Thus there is a *place* of responsibility that has content, breadth, and depth. What is the *size* of your congregation or church-related organization's place of responsibility? It should be added that Bonhoeffer had considerable interest in enlarging the sense of "place" by going "behind the neighbor."

> Behind the neighbor, whom the call of Jesus commends to us,
> also stands, according to Jesus, the one who is farthest from

---

2. Bonhoeffer never completed his work on ethics. The thirteen surviving manuscripts have been arranged in several different ways by editors over the years. The most recent is volume 6 of the Dietrich Bonhoeffer Works (Minneapolis: Fortress Press, 2005). The material used here is found on pages 289–97 of this edition.

us, namely, Jesus Christ himself, who is indeed God. Whoever does not know this "farthest" behind the "nearest," and at the same time this "farthest" as this "nearest," does not serve the neighbor but themselves, and shuns the free and open air of responsibility to hide in the more comfortable narrowness of fulfilling a duty. Even the commandment to love the neighbor therefore does not mean a legalistic restriction of my responsibility to the neighbor whom I encounter while sharing the same place, citizenship, profession, or family. The neighbor can be met precisely in the one who is farthest away, and vice versa.[3]

Bonhoeffer offered an example of restriction of place. He was in the United States doing postdoctoral studies at Union Seminary in New York City when nine young black men were sentenced to death with no evidence presented in the trials. A church official in Germany refused to "become involved" in what would now be called advocacy, because (and this is what burned Bonhoeffer) it would be contrary to his Lutheran understanding of the scope of his responsibility. In other words, the incident was too "far away." Bonhoeffer adds, "We need to keep the boundaries open."

Following Bonhoeffer's analysis, four claims can be made:

• The call of Jesus Christ to love the neighbor will run over into corporate or institutional responsibility, given the complex nature of society and the recalcitrance of social issues to being "solved" by individual action alone.

• As each person has a "place" of responsibility so each collection of persons also has a "place," the dimensions of which are to be explored, tested, and readjusted based on experience, always with a bias toward enlargement.

• Selective expansion of the place of responsibility is in order. This is necessary, given the tendency to either "take on the whole world and its problems," leading often to disillusionment and fatigue as in the contemporary phrase donor

---

3. Ibid., 294–95.

fatigue or toward a self-protection that takes on such a small portion of responsibility that the world is not fully served.[4]

• Distance is a key variable: Do not limit responsibility to the local. Behind
the term "local" lurks not only many assumptions about the call of Jesus but a
tendency to limit that call and the resulting place of responsibility.

Some Help from Organizational Theory

Thinking about organizations and their external environments has gone through
several phases of development. *Systems thinking* (see chapter 1) encourages the
inclusion of the environment in the attempt to understand and improve organizations. Soon there was interest in describing the variety of environments as
benign or hostile, simple or complex, stable or changing. Two new terms were
introduced to capture the dynamic nature of an organization's interaction with
its environment: *integration* and *differentiation*. A series of studies observed that
organizations that were effective developed the ability to (a) arrange and allow
their internal parts to differentiate, that is, be different from each other in order
to respond to the relevant parts of their environment, and (b) have the means to
hold it all together, that is, integrate in ways that neither suppressed differences

---

4. Bonhoeffer's criteria for self-examination in considering the size of one's
place of responsibility shows that he knew the twin dangers of taking on too much
or too little: "Neither the limitation nor the expansion of my field of responsibility must be based on principles, but rather on the concrete call of Jesus alone; if,
according to my character traits, I knew that I tend to be a reformer, a know-it-all,
a fanatic, one who does not heed any limits, there I run the risk of expanding my
responsibility arbitrarily, and confusing my natural desire with the call of Jesus;
if I knew myself to be cautious, anxious, insecure, and legalistic, there I must be
careful not to equate the call of Jesus Christ with my limiting responsibility to a
narrow domain; and finally, I am never set free to act in genuine responsibility by
looking at myself, but only by attending to Christ's call" (p. 294). We believe that
these criteria work for congregations or church-related institutions as well, since
organizations as well as individuals have character traits.

into uniformity nor cut loose the parts so excessively that *one* organization ceased to be.[5]

Perhaps the most helpful development for the contemporary church administrator was the move beyond classifying the texture of the environment to discover practical ways of identifying the various groups who are in some important relationship to the organization, for example, suppliers, government agencies, competitors, and customers. Environments were broken down into groups with immediate, intermediary, secondary, or future impact. Previously noted was the rise of these analytic tools in marketing, including for religious organizations. The famous mega-church in Saddleback Valley, California, developed its strategies around an initial understanding of their environment as having "five constituencies—core ministry, committed, congregation, crowd, and community."[6]

Soon in nonreligious and religious organizations the term "stakeholders" was used to identify those who cared, that is, held some "stake" in the organization. For example, the key external relationships (stakeholders or neighbors) of a Lutheran vocational training center operating on both sides of "the wall" separating Jerusalem and the West Bank are:

- Palestinian young people (male and female)
- the Palestinian Authority
- the local church: The Evangelical Lutheran Church in Jordan and the Holy Land
- non-governmental organizations (NGOs)
- local businesses in Jerusalem and the West Bank
- Chamber of Commerce
- Ministry of Labor (Palestinian)
- Ministry of Labor (Israeli)

---

5. Paul Lawrence and Jay Lorsch, *The Organization and Its Environment: Managing Differentiation and Integration* (Boston: Harvard Graduate School, 1967).

6. Norman Shawchuck, Philip Kotler, Bruce Wrenn, and Gustave Rath, *Marketing for Congregations* (Nashville: Abingdon, 1992), 84.

- donors: local and international
- labor unions
- Lutheran World Federation
- ecumenical partners
- the United States Aid for Development program
- the Israeli checkpoints
- the changing role of women in Palestinian society
- other training centers
- United States Policy in the Middle East
- a future Palestinian State

Each neighbor plays a vital and different role in the Vocational Training Center's life and mission. Each presents a specific set of challenges and opportunities and calls for careful shepherding and attention. To ignore or neglect these relationships would be to place the Center's present and future in jeopardy. Together they comprise a *place* of responsibility. Notice that some neighbors are near and some are far away. Distance is more a matter of attitude and a function of imagination than physical miles. Key questions are, Who are your neighbors? How far away or near are they? What is the span and depth of your responsibility?

The above theological and organizational insights lay the foundation for exploring the issues associated with external relationships: patterns, styles, tasks, and futures. We turn to these now.

Patterns of Ecclesiastical Relationships

Among the many variations and combinations, there seem to be five basic patterns of church life in the United States. These patterns come close to what the sociologist Max Weber called "ideal types," meaning a construct designed to gain understanding rather than a pattern that actually exists in that pure form.

These patterns are not presented in any historical order, that is, one pattern did not necessarily morph into another over time, although each pattern could be traced that way. The purpose of naming these patterns here is to recognize the differences among U.S.–based church organizations and therefore the various strategies that emerge for getting closer to or father away from other ecclesiastical structures.[7]

Pattern 1: The independent congregation. From a theological point of view, as noted in chapter 6, there is no such thing as an independent or autonomous congregation. Wherever people gather in Christ's name, there is a bond among them that Christ creates, not human arrangements. In the United States, however, there are those congregations who from their start-ups or at some time in their histories have for a variety of reasons declared their independence from a denomination. There are still congregations who see themselves continuing an ethnic or cultural heritage, which, if connected to others, would run the risk of dilution or extinction. More likely the independent stance is fortified by particular biblical and theological emphases. These congregations still have neighbors in the sense described in our earlier theological and organizational perspectives, and like all ecclesiastical organizations they relate well or not so well to such neighbors. Being independent is not a release from having a place of responsibility; it means, however, that other church relationships may be highly selective or nonexistent. Contrary to popular perception, the Crystal Cathedral in California is not such a congregation, being a member of the Reformed Church in America (RCA), but the Chicago area Willow Creek Community Church is not formally affiliated with any denomination.

Pattern 2: Congregational authority. This pattern comes about when congregations are participants in larger church systems but, by definition, primary or final authority rests with the congregation, not the system or any of its parts in which the congregation exists. The United Church of Christ (UCC) is an example of this pattern, although it could be included in the next pattern as well. "No power vested in the General Synod shall invade the autonomy of Conferences, Associations, and Local Churches, or impair their right to acquire, own, manage, and dispose of property and funds" (Constitution of the United Church of Christ, 2001, Paragraph 54).

---

7. The five patterns described are formed partly because of the distinctive character of church-state relationships in the United States, namely, organizational separation and functional interaction. Patterns for churches in other lands would reflect the historic fusion of church and state, although more degrees of separation are emerging in the last decade, for example, in Sweden, Norway, and Germany.

Like the independent congregation, these congregations relate to their neighbors and have places of responsibility. They are, however, more interactive with other
church-related structures, both denominational and ecumenical, but when "push
comes to shove," they are the final arbitrators of their destiny. In addition to the
UCC, the American Baptist Churches (ABC) is another example of this pattern.

Pattern 3: "Middle" authority. There probably is no such U.S. church, but
the United Methodist Church comes close in that the Methodists have no central
policy body like a general board or church council and no one designated leader
like a president, moderator, general secretary, or bishop. They have many leaders and they all relate to each other, helped by a variety of coordinating bodies
and mechanisms. Actually they have invested some final authority in the General
Conference, but it meets only once every four years. It is the General Conference,
however, that turns away the attempts (many over the last three decades) to "cen-
tralize" or "coordinate" or "integrate."

Methodists put stock in the power and authority of Christ's people meeting
together to work things out for the sake of mission and ministry. Thus they conference (verb) together and also call their structures conferences—annual, general,
jurisdictional. This pattern is characterized by increased contact with others in the
denomination compared to the previous two patterns, precisely because no one
entity has sole or final authority. The sharing of authority in this case promotes a
high degree of interaction and at times frustrations over making a common decision
that sticks. The Presbyterian Church (U.S.A.) could also be included as an example because of the degree of authority lodged in the entity from which their name
comes—the presbytery. The glue to tie together 172 presbyteries has been a judicial
process and constitutional authority. Some deliberate loosening has been occurring
more recently. The Roman Catholic Church may come closest to this pattern within
a single country, given the strong authority bishops and archbishops have in individual dioceses. There is no national bishop. The pope oversees it all from Rome.

Pattern 4: Churchwide authority (national). Here too there probably is no
pure example of this pattern. The Episcopal Church (ECUSA) and the Evangelical Lutheran Church in America (ELCA) are probably seen as functioning with
strong churchwide or national authority. This is to be expected in churches that
have episcopal structure, that is, bishops. This authority, however, is exercised
in a very particular way: major policy and constitutional decisions are made by

deliberative bodies, not individuals, including bishops. Both churches meet in
two-year (ELCA) or three-year (ECUSA) cycles of assemblies made up of voting
members elected by middle judicatories' assemblies (who in turn were elected by
congregational voting members).[8] The national assemblies call the shots, not in
details but on major policies and program directions. Roles are defined and the
whole system is highly interactive. Both also function within larger global communions (the Lutheran World Federation and Anglican Communion), whose
decisions are advisory and non-binding upon national member churches.

Pattern 5: All three (congregation, middle, national) interacting. This pattern is
included because it captures the way most denominations really work, even given
the differences in where authority is located. The Evangelical Lutheran Church in
America has declared itself to be such a church.

> The congregations, synods, and churchwide organization of
> this church are interdependent partners sharing responsibly
> in God's mission. In an interdependent relationship primary
> responsibility for particular functions will vary between the
> partners. Whenever possible, the entity most directly affected
> by a decision shall be the principal party responsible for deci-
> sion and implementation, with the other entities facilitating
> and assisting. Each congregation, synod, and separately incor-
> porated unit of the churchwide organization, as well as the
> churchwide organization itself, is a separate legal entity and is
> responsible for exercising its powers and authorities.[9]

---

8. A variation of the assemblies described here is that the Episcopal Church
has a bicameral assembly made up of bishops in one house and laity and priests
in the other.

9. *Constitution, Bylaws, and Continuing Resolutions, Evangelical Lutheran
Church in America*, 2005, 5.01.c., 23. The theological basis for this statement of
interdependence is found in chapter 3 of the same document, Section 3.02:

> The Church exists both as an inclusive fellowship and as local congrega-
> tions gathered for worship and Christian service. Congregations find their

Participants in the ELCA differ from time to time about how well the authority is distributed and whether in the right amounts, as the two authors can attest. The point is that churches in patterns 3, 4, and 5, and some in 2 all sense that the complete mission with which God has entrusted them cannot be carried out by one expression, be it congregation, the "middle" or national. By means of differentiating roles, sharing resources (facilitating geographical redistribution, including internationally according to mission needs), and reinforcing non-oppressive methods of integration (especially leadership), the odds of faithful effectiveness are greatly increased.

How the Evangelical Lutheran Church Is Not Organized

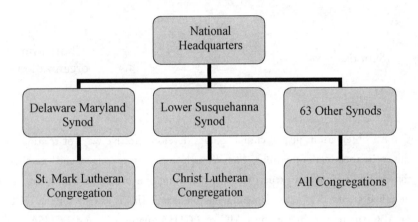

fulfillment in the universal community of the Church, and the universal Church exists in and through congregations. This church, therefore, derives its character and powers both from the sanction and representation of its congregations and from its inherent nature as an expression of the broader fellowship of the faithful. In length, it acknowledges itself to be in the historic continuity of the communion of saints; in breadth, it expresses the fellowship of believers and congregations in our day.

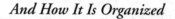

And How It Is Organized

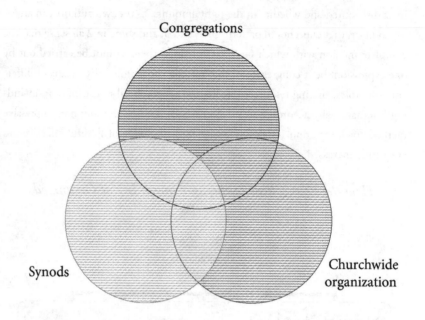

An observation: just as church bodies develop effective ways of relating to others in their denominations, even though authority is lodged and exercised differently, it seems also true that each denomination functions with what can be called a "practical, everyday congregationalism." This is as true for the UCC or ABC (pattern 2) as for the UMC or PCUSA (pattern 3) and ECUSA and ELCA (pattern 4). The late Tip O'Neill's phrase "all politics is local" is sometimes (unconsciously) applied to the church as well. "Keeping it at home" or "our needs first" can prevail when it comes to pitting buildings, worship, "our children," etc., over against community needs near or far. We ask again, "Who is my (our) neighbor? Where is our place of responsibility? How wide is it? How deep is it?"

Forces at Work in Relating to Others

There are at least three formative factors in the development of relational attitudes and practices.

Theological and Ecclesiastical

As suggested in the preceding section, different conclusions can be reached regarding ecclesiastical patterns, and theological reflections on the concept of neighbor can vary, not least because distinctive life experiences shape external relationships. A National Public Radio program describes recent attempts of the Internal Revenue Service to revoke (or at least bring to trial) the tax-exempt status of specific congregations because of their alleged political activity. One congregation cited was of the Episcopal Church (ECUSA). A listener called in not to defend or accuse the congregation but to ask the question, "Since the Episcopal Church is one church, is this accusation made against all congregations of the ECUSA?" The interesting (funny!) development was that neither the invited expert on state-church relationships nor the show's moderator exhibited any understanding of what the caller meant by "one church." They understood what a congregation was but not the Pattern 4 or 5 *church* the caller assumed. The conversation went nowhere. All three—moderator, expert, and caller—gave up in utter frustration. Theological and ecclesiastical underpinnings make a difference not only in how relations are formed, but which ones are deemed important.

Missional

A second formative factor is the nature and extent of the mission pursued. Several decades ago, J. B. Phillips wrote a little book entitled *Your God Is Too Small*. Someone ought to write a book called *Your Mission Is Too Small* or *Your Church Is Too Small*. The mission God assigns is a full sense of mission. It is here and there. It includes evangelism and social ministry. It is domestic and international. It is local and global. The contemporary phrase "mission starts at the door of the church" has served well to remind missionary-sending churches that they have become the mission field. It can, however, truncate—or in Bonhoeffer's term, "narrow"—the field of mission activity. Then the *there* suffers, as exclusive attention is given only to the *here*. Congregations (and denominations) that are the most intensively involved in a wide-ranging set of relationships—local, regional, national, international, denominational—are often the ones who enjoy a healthy *interior* life, including administratively. Fresh experiences are imported from relating to neighbors far and wide. New visions are engendered. New insights are gained that inform, and in some cases correct, present practices. New encouragement and hope are experienced as the loving ways of God that are shared by someone *external* to "my place." As the leaders depicted in Acts learned (Acts 10–15), Yahweh proved not to be a tribal deity but Lord of all.

Modeling

In addition to theology (ecclesiology) and mission providing the motivation for and content of external relationships, a third force has to do with being a good example to members and colleagues. If the corporate message is, "Keep it at home; tend to our needs first" (that is, "We should only engage in a select set of safe external relationships"), then the members of the congregation or employees of the church-related organization will over time almost inevitably treat the congregation or organization in exactly the same way. Stewardship of members' time, talent, and money follows the example set by the way the congregation or organization deals with its environment. Selfishness begets selfishness; but it also is true that a positive, active, generous set of external relationship models for the members creates an attitude that is infectious. To wit:

Styles of Relating to Others

1. *Go it alone.* We don't need anyone else. In fact, closer contact is dangerous. Our identity may be threatened. We may from time to time relate to others but on a selective basis. We will, however, initiate the contact and terminate it when no longer useful.

2. *Dealing with "evil partners."* We are participants in various networks, but some of those groups or organizations are not helpful to or compatible with our mission. We may choose to sever our relationships or remain in relationship through active programs of criticism, evaluation, and protest. We may form or participate in an alternative group to gain support, and carry out education and strategy building. This alternative group may become our "home" from which we receive energy, perspective, encouragement, and a platform from which to operate.

3. *We are not alone.* The first two styles have in common an *over againstness* toward others in the environment. The third exhibits a salutary difference: others

are friends, helpers, co-learners, co-strategists, partners-in-mission. Just as a person does not surrender personal identity in healthy relationships with others, neither does the congregation nor organization lose itself. Its identity is actually strengthened and recharged by including others. Psychologists have a term, identity diffusion, that points to the danger of individuals and organizations losing themselves in the interaction with others. The "we are not alone" style recognizes that risk, but develops strong external relationships in order to "love the neighbor" or engage the place of responsibility with vigor, wisdom, and faithfulness.

4. *Identity diffusion.* This fourth style occurs when there is total identification with the other. Organizational unity may not be present, but through similar theology, common experience, or admiration, a oneness is assumed that can be very powerful and real.

Tasks in Building External Relationships

What can be done to help build strong external relationships? We see four essential tasks: attitude development, mapping the environment, interpreting to *insiders* about *outsiders*; and multiple involvements.

1. *Attitude development.* Perhaps not much more needs to be said about the role of attitude. The theological and organizational perspectives with which this chapter began provide a base from which to operate; "loving the institutional neighbor" and determining a "place of responsibility" are concepts for locating external relationships at the heart of organizational mission, not on the periphery. Which of the four styles is characteristic of your congregation or church-related institution?

- Go It Alone?
- Dealing with Evil Partners?
- We Are Not Alone?
- Identity Diffusion?

Attitudes don't just happen; they are modeled and molded through information, advocacy, and interpretation.

2. *Mapping the environment.* Anniversaries, milestone achievements, strategic planning, and similar occasions provide the opportunity to increase understanding of and relationship to those groups who indeed have a stake in what happens to your congregation or institution. The book *Marketing for Congregations*, cited above, illustrates many examples of such analysis. It can be done simply or in a complex way depending on how well the external groups are known. Who are they and what do they want, or better, what do they contribute, and what do they need? These groups give and receive. If that transaction is well understood, then more research and analysis is not needed. If, however, these relationships cannot be readily and accurately described, then more work should be done until they are clarified.

Environmental mapping can utilize a three-step process: First, appoint a group of members/employees to map the environment. This begins by drawing a circle (your organization) on a newsprint or chalkboard and identifying the stakeholders as spokes emanating from the center circle. The second step is to describe each "spoke" in terms of what it contributes and what it needs. Relationships not active, which perhaps should be, can also be identified at this time. If the group concludes that the amount and quality of knowledge about stakeholders is thin, then sub-groups or individuals can be requested to bring some "homework" to a future meeting. The third step is to make decisions about the most fundamental relationships, secondary ones, and ones to be developed. Appropriate action to strengthen these relationships follows.

There is an illusion created in this exercise, namely, that your organization being symbolized as the center circle *creates* spokes growing out of the "center." This diagram, however, is not reality. Your congregation or organization is not the center of the universe. It is, rather, a node in a web of relationships. The design of center/spokes is what it is, a tool to identify, think about, and improve external relationships.[10]

3. *Interpretation.* A third task in building strong external relationships is a positive, active program of interpretation. Include ministries of the church body

---

10. Most manuals or books on strategic planning have a section on environmental scanning. Note the references in chapter 4, "Planning with Passion." For a more sophisticated approach called "visual thinking," see T. Irene Sanders, *Strategic Thinking and the New Science* (New York: Free Press, 1998).

in the prayers and budget of the congregation alongside various local and regional groups, and you might be surprised at the increase in support from members.

The groups who are represented by the spokes around the center in the exercise mentioned above are usually quite ready to assist in interpreting themselves to your organization. If they are broad *cohorts* like "youth," they may not be another organization, but much can be learned about them and, more importantly, from them. Interpret, interpret, interpret is one of the four keys to strong external relationships.

4. *Involvement.* Task four is straightforward. Get involved with the groups in your environment. A warning: they will change your organization.

The two of us have benefited from many examples of productive external relationships over the years. To name a few: resettling refugees, faith-based community organizing efforts, mission trips to Central America, teaching adult education classes on trips to Palestine-Israel, community literacy programs, HIV-AIDS education, civil rights and peace demonstrations, and description of the participation of members and pastors in denominational ministries and governance.

Actions do speak louder than words. It is rewarding to hear from persons attending national assemblies such comments as, "I never realized our church (denomination) did so much good stuff. I'm proud to be a member."

The Future as Network

What might the future look like for external relationships? Clearly, *network* has become the organizational image of choice, supposedly driving out the pyramid (△) and even the hub (▢) or center-periphery model, as it is sometimes called. Many observers and theorists of administrative practice believe that organizations, including religious ones, will participate in networks of various kinds and even trans-denominational arrangements. If this view of the future is accurate, it makes sense to learn as much as we can about networks and how they operate. There are also several myths about networks, and these need to be addressed. Some preliminary observations:

1. The term network is not brand new; it first appeared (as far as we can determine) in administration materials in 1971. Donald Schon (*Beyond the*

Stable State),[11] described the diminishment of the hub model whereby a central authority "runs things" and the "spokes" emanating from "the hub" carry out its "orders" or at least implement its policies and procedures. Schon predicted a network of mutually beneficial relationships that would spring up to replace the "hub" and that would be characterized by exchanges among individuals, groups, and institutions, which will be temporary and practical. New networks will form around interests, needs, and aspirations to be replaced by still newer networks. As various denominational restructuring projects have taken place over the last decade, a few proposals have been floated but never adopted to structure relationships according to ethnicity, theology, ecclesiology, various social issues, or interests. Geography, however, remains the primary organizing principle.

2. A claim can be made that networks do not make obsolete the three previous dominant organizational forms—team, hierarchy, bureaucracy—but incorporate them into a web. This claim addresses one of the myths about networks—that they are without roles, rules, and expertise. Networks are apparently not free-floating super-democratic systems, although they do promote initiative, fluidity, and flexibility. Networks try to avoid the worst aspects of hierarchy and bureaucracy without jettisoning them entirely.[12]

3. Networks seem to have five essential features: (a) unifying purpose, (b) independent members, (c) voluntary links, (d) multiple leaders, and (e) integrated levels. This last feature is a reference to the necessity of some sense of hierarchy in function and role, although it is not a continuation of "command and control."[13]

4. Networks create new communities for their participants, some direct, others indirect. "The constitution of the 'network society' is such that nearly all of us are connected in some way or another. We all coexist in the ecosystem of the natural world and the social spheres and through our actions on the social and natural environments. Although we are all connected, we are not necessarily connected directly. Communities form around interests, values, principles,

---

11. Donald A. Schon, *Beyond the Stable State* (New York: Norton, 1971).

12. Jessica Lipnack and Jeffrey Stamps, *The Age of the Network: Organizing Principles for the 21ˢᵗ Century* (Essex Junction, Vt.: Oliver Wight, 1994).

13. Ibid., 82–96.

aims, viewpoints. . . ."[14] These "imaginal communities" call forth different skills and attitudes than previous kinds of community participation to which we have been accustomed.

5. Three competencies that may come into their own along a network are connective leadership, connective technology, and connective justice. Connective leadership is not a special kind of leadership but one that reflects the increasing reality for all leaders as they are called upon to build bridges among constituent groups and organizational members. Connective justice and the values surrounding it are called forth by the tendency of networks, given their pragmatic and self-seeking orientation, to remain in relationship until the "benefit" runs out. This exchange dynamic can over time help "the rich get richer" and foster a "survival of the fittest" climate.

6. A sixth observation is about another myth: "The net will remake the world." Two "techies" from Silicon Valley caution that the expectation of networks, especially the technical aspect, is over the top and out of touch with reality. From two people who ought to know, they advocate increased attention to the social dimension of information flow. Attention to technology is only half right; identity, relationships, and roles are equally, if not more, important than the technology involved.[15]

7. A concluding observation is that church organizations, including congregations, would benefit from thinking and acting more in a network fashion than as a pyramid ($\triangle$) or hub ($\square$). Such thinking would include trans-denominational arrangements—local, regional, national, and international. Many denominations in the United States, as expressions of who they are, have engaged in theological dialogues that have in some cases resulted in formal agreements on clergy exchange, mutual recognition of ministry, cooperative projects, and broad information sharing. Again, these new kinds of relationships require new attitudes, skills, and commitments. Such alliances may indeed be more characteristic of the future than church mergers were in the last three decades. A threshold has been reached.

---

14. Douglas Schuler and Peter Day, eds., *Shaping the Network Society* (Cambridge, Mass.: MIT, 2004), 372.

15. John Sidney Brown and Paul Duguid, *The Social Life of Information* (Cambridge, Mass.: Harvard Business School Press, 2000).

Developing Networks: Ten Guidance Statements

These statements are drawn from those who have written about networks, and from the authors' experience in collaborative work.

1. Attention to network purpose is essential. Without the usual authority and accountability systems, networks thrive on the unifying and binding effects of a clear purpose held in common and brought out periodically for public celebration and updating. It is also necessary to translate purpose into work, that is, bite-sized tasks that are understood, supported, and doable. Otherwise, purpose may become an abstraction that does not unify and inspire.

2. Define network membership. Are members individuals, groups, or institutions? Are some *members*, with others defined as *partners*? Are there different kinds of membership? Missed expectations of participants in a network can lead to confusion, disappointment, and even dissolution of the network.

3. Honor the independence of network members. Networking does not cancel out the independent status of participants. Networks are not thinly disguised arrangements for institutional mergers or takeovers. Three Lutheran church bodies in the African nation of Namibia are forming a cooperative system guided by a council of representatives to move toward greater unity, perhaps to form one Lutheran church. The purpose, however, is clear, supported, and "on top of the table." In the meantime, the three churches do not lose their independent identity and operation. They are *choosing* to seek greater unity because they believe it is God's will and consistent with their self-understandings as churches. Perhaps the oft-used term "interdependence" needs revisiting. What is interdependence? The loss of individuality? A blurring of identity? Perhaps only truly independent persons and institutions can create greater unity, including participation in networks.

4. Communication within the network is very important and is a major way the network develops. While this statement is obvious, it is included because it is so easy to neglect. Who is responsible for information sharing within a network and how and when it will be done become important questions.

5. Networks need rules, roles, and identity formation. Contrary to popular perception, networks do not operate as amoeba-like creatures, changing shape or form in a haphazard manner. Rules help create mutual expectations and provide a basis for arbitration and negotiation. No rules means no expectations. Rules

can be oppressive, but agreed-upon rules are actually a source of freedom. Roles likewise create the "glue" that holds things together. Groups sometimes assign roles to individuals like convener, note-taker, timekeeper, and evaluator. Networks need similar roles to function well. Identity formation is too large a subject for our purposes here. What can be said is that unless the identity of participants includes the network reinforced by beliefs and values of "love for neighbor" or possessing a "place of responsibility," then the life of the network will never achieve its potential.

6. Gather guidance and support from the larger environment in which the network exists. This observation has two parts. First, if possible, build on the encouragement and/or permission from the larger environment. Second, models of networking need to already exist on which to build, extend, and draw wisdom. Is the larger environment network-friendly or network-hostile? The support of the larger environment becomes critical because, as noted earlier, networking "involves the creation of new forms of action and interaction—new kinds of social relationships, and new ways of relating to others and oneself." Without support, the old ways of relating will recur.

7. Process and structure must be developed to keep pace with network development. The organizational charts of the future will look less like this:

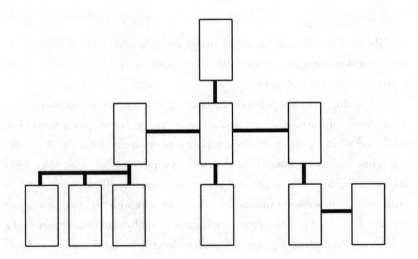

and more like this:

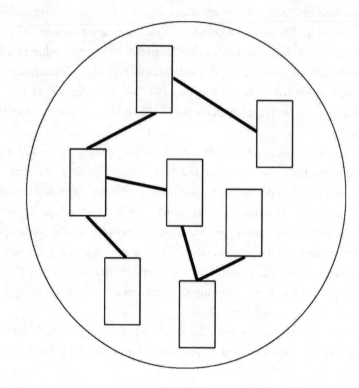

The need for *structure* (the ways things are organized) and *process* (the way things are done) will not go away, but what they look like is changing as more experience is gained with networks.

8. Develop an online presence representing all key network processes to create a shared information source and a climate conducive to networking. How much and what kind of technology supports network development? A website that is interactive for members and is a place to which members want to go regularly for benefits helpful to network activity is a necessity. Then online development will, like process and structure, need to keep pace with network growth and use. The future of this online presence is determined by careful attention to the needs, goals, and plans of network members. Interviews, focus groups, and surveys can be used to gather, understand, and appreciate members' views and needs for online technology.

9. A dynamic testing process is needed to identify, evaluate, and develop new opportunities for projects among network members. There is a creative tension between the need for a way for network members to decide together what common action should be taken, on the one hand, and the goal of flexibility and individual initiative, on the other. For example, a network of theological seminaries may decide to develop continuing education programs as a network activity or affirm the separate programs of each seminary, perhaps with increased consultation for mutual learning. Each model is networking, but a common decision is made about which direction to take.

10. Leadership in a network is a crucial variable in achieving effectiveness. Who leads, and how? If five congregations of the same denomination or across denominational lines decide to form a network, who provides leadership? The normal (there is not much normal in networking, partly because of its newness) pattern is for existing leaders (pastors or staff) to rotate in leading the network. This approach seems to work initially. There comes a point, however, when the demand is too great on persons who already have full-time jobs. The network has reached a critical juncture. If someone other than an existing leader is appointed, whether volunteer or paid, the direct communication to and connection with the independent groups are lost. This step, however, may become necessary to keep the network going. Some of the network literature calls this person an "orchestrator," meaning the person does not play an "instrument," but makes it possible for all those who do to make their contributions to the creation of beautiful music together!

Our speech is ahead of our practice. We talk networks but are still learning how to live them. These ten guidance statements, while tentative, may help to shape a future that is increasingly networked.

The Church for Others: How Long Is Your Reach?

In this chapter we have presented some theological and organizational ideas and advocated for certain ways of relating to the external environment. Embracing the *other* is part and parcel of faith, church, and administrative responsibility.

After learning of the failed third and last attempt on Adolph Hitler's life, Dietrich Bonhoeffer wrote from his prison cell:

> A transformation of all human life is given in the fact that 'Jesus is there only for others.' His 'being there for others' is the experience of transcendence. . . . Faith is participation in the being of Jesus (incarnation, cross, and resurrection). . . . The transcendental is not infinite and unattainable tasks, but the neighbor who is within reach in any given situation. . . . The church is the church only when it exists for others. . . . The church must share in the secular problems of ordinary human life, not dominating, but helping and serving.[16]

What is the church? A cave? A sanctuary? An open-air market? An extended blended family? The church resembles all these metaphors and many others as well. The point is this: external relationships are not an add-on to church related institutions or congregations. Relating to those outside the walls is an expression of Christian identity, which practices at the same time in-reach and outreach, gathering and scattering, neighbor love of those at hand and those far away.

The above quote from Dietrich Bonhoeffer is from the outline of a book he never had time to write, or if he did, no copy was ever found. The words represent his gift to the future church, to the end that it would avoid the traps into which his church fell. Bonhoeffer experienced a church that, in his words, was so bent on its own "self preservation" that it sold out to empty promises, afraid to venture out for the sake of those suffering and the victims of gross injustice, extreme cruelty, and murder. The manner in which he cast his gift to the future church ("The church is the church only when it exists for others") sounds like a diminishment of worship, prayer, teaching, and nurture. It is not, but what he did leave with us is a disturbing question, "Do you love the neighbor within your reach?" How long is your reach? How long is your institutional reach? Tending to external relationships, loving thy institutional neighbor is packed with promise.

---

16. Dietrich Bonhoeffer, *Letters and Papers from Prison*, enlarged ed. (New York: Simon and Schuster, 1997), 381–83.

CHAPTER 11

When Conflict Comes Calling

Church conflict is a growth industry!
—*George Parsons*

Where all think alike, no one thinks very much.
—*Walter Lippmann*

Nearly two decades ago, at a workshop sponsored by the Alban Institute, George Parsons spoke confidently of his job security as a congregational conflict consultant. Indeed, both formal surveys and anecdotal evidence suggest that conflicts in congregations and other ministry contexts are still part and parcel of life in the twenty-first century. Few of us live very long in the church without bumping up against conflicts that arise from disagreements about all manner of things—from the relatively inconsequential (what color shall we paint the sanctuary?) to the heavy-duty substantive conflicts that make national news headlines (shall we ordain non-celibate gay and lesbian persons?) While it may strike some as unusual to find a chapter on conflict in a book on church administration, we are convinced that creative positive utilization of the inevitable conflicts that occur in all ministry contexts is in fact one of the key attributes needed by effective leaders.

As prevalent and normal as it is (some statistical evidence will follow), many of us still seem surprised to encounter conflict in congregations and other are-nas of the church's ministry. Both formal research and informal surveys among clergy, bishops, and other church leaders suggest that, despite the predictability of encountering and having to deal with conflict throughout their careers, there is a widespread sense that "they never taught me that [dealing with conflict] in seminary." From both seminary courses we have taught and conversations we have engaged in, we find that the greatest anxiety felt by many if not most aspiring ministers is the prospect of having to deal with conflict in their future parishes or other ministry settings. Why this is so merits some reflection at the outset of this chapter on coping with conflict.

That life is full of conflicts is no surprise to anyone. All human beings are aware that daily life—for us as individuals, communities, and nations on the global scene—is replete with disagreement, differing points of view, and distinct perspectives on all manner of things. An astute reader of history books or the daily newspaper soon discovers that what makes the pages noteworthy usually contains some element of conflict and tension. Individuals, families, or communities who live out their days in a high degree of harmony and tranquility seldom make the headlines. "Happy Family in Harmonious Community" is not likely to be a feature story in a major national news magazine anytime soon!

So why is it then that when conflict occurs in church contexts it has a tendency most places to send a shudder throughout the faith community? Why do new ministers recoil upon discovering conflict in their first parishes? How is it that many elected or appointed bishops or other ministry overseers are surprised to discover that a huge portion of their time is spent counseling with congregations, clergy, and other leaders who find themselves in the midst of conflict? There are undoubtedly manifold reasons for such widespread conflict-aversion in the church. Chief among them may be a piety (as opposed to theology—more about that later) based on an idealistic image of the church as a lofty harmonious, tranquil, and tension-free community engaged with unanimity in pursuit and promotion of the universal peaceable kingdom.

In the Bible, story after story, image upon image seem to point toward such a vision of a conflict-free community. In Genesis, the Garden of Eden was apparently a conflict-free environment prior to the serpent's tempting the human ones to place themselves in conflict with God's desires and commands. After the Hebrews' deliverance from bondage in Egypt, for forty years they wandered in the desert with the promise held before them of finally inheriting an un-conflicted and uncontested land flowing with milk and honey. Many of the Old Testament prophetic visions hold up idealized images of a future time when conflicts endured in the present will be transcended. Prominent among them are such images from Isaiah: the rough places shall be made plain or level, the wolf shall dwell with the lamb, and swords shall be transformed into plowshares and pruning hooks.

The New Testament appears to join the Old in chorus, singing even more melody lines that communicate the image that authentic Christian community is a place of harmony and conflict-free peacefulness. The Gospels are replete with pastoral images that bring to mind pictures of amicable relationships amidst peaceful settings. Jesus is the Good Shepherd who cares for a contented flock of sheep that graze harmoniously under his care and protection (John 10). He attends a happy wedding at Cana and, at the first sign of tension over the depletion of the wine, Jesus steps in to rescue and restore the occasion's full festivity (John 2:1–11). The first Christian followers are encouraged not to worry or be anxious about tomorrow, "for your heavenly Father knows that you need all these things" (Matt 6:32). In his great high priestly prayer (John 17), Jesus beseeched fervently that his followers would all be one, "even as you and I are one."

Further perpetuating this piety of Christian perfection, the letters of Paul appear to univocally portray conflict as falling short of God's intent. Addressing multiple situations where the first Christians found themselves in conflict over all manner of issues, Paul counseled them to work things out so that harmony would be restored in short order. In his most famous passage, frequently read at weddings, Paul exhorted Christians to follow the more excellent way of love, which is always patient and kind, never envious, arrogant or insisting on its own way. Here in 1 Corinthians 13 there appears no room for dissent or disagreement, for asserting one's own needs and desires if they conflict with those of others.

Beyond the Gospels and letters of Paul, there are many other New Testament texts that reinforce an idealized piety suggesting that Christians should avoid conflict at all costs. In the first of the so-called Pastoral Epistles, the writer of 1 Timothy urges supplications, prayers, and intercessions for everyone "so that we may lead a quiet and peaceable life in all godliness and dignity." Christians are further exhorted by the author to avoid anger or argument (1 Tim 2:1–2, 8). In the letter by James to the twelve tribes in the dispersion, conflict is regarded as abhorrent: "Those conflicts and disputes among you, where do they come from? Do they not come from your cravings that are at war within you?" Conflicts result from sin, from "friendship with the world" which is enmity from God, and from giving way to the devil (see James 4). The New Testament ends with Revelation's ultimate vision of a new heaven and new earth, in which all the conflicts, struggles, and pains of the past are forever left behind. God's final gift, the new Jerusalem, will be a place of harmony and peace: "God will wipe every tear from their eyes. Death will be no more; mourning and crying and pain will be no more . . ." (Rev 21:1–4).

Taken together, therefore, many of the biblical passages that refer to conflict can be understood as portraying all disharmony and disagreement as resulting from sin, as being a less-than-perfect state than is God's intent for the cosmos and for all human communities. A purely uncritical, prima-facie pietistic reading of Scripture readily leads to the conclusion that all conflict is bad, to be avoided at all costs, and if encountered, it should be resolved immediately, regardless of the cost and compromise that may be required.

Beyond Piety to a Theology of Conflict

If our assessment is correct that much of the church's culture of conflict aversion and avoidance results from an overly simplistic and pietistic interpretation of Scripture, then a deeper reading of the Bible may be required as a first step toward developing a theology of conflict. Attempting to imagine what lies behind the texts in many cases is as important as a surface reading of the passages themselves.

The exodus experience, regarded by many biblical scholars as the pivotal event of the entire Old Testament, was a historical incident involving profound and prolonged conflict. Against his natural inclinations to remain comfortable in his secure position, when prompted by God's call at the burning bush, Moses ultimately determined he would take on Pharaoh's entire empire. The plagues leading to the eventual liberation of the Hebrew people provoked conflict and caused widespread anguish among the Egyptians. In the final episode of the great saga of the exodus, the conflict rose to the level of armed combat; the cost in human life as the Egyptians lost the war of the waters at the Red Sea appeared great. And conflict did not end at the other side of the sea; it was not long into the wilderness wanderings when the Hebrew community found itself internally conflicted. Many if not most soon turned against their leader, loudly complaining to Moses that he had led them not into the promised land of milk and honey but rather into a barren desert of starvation and deprivation. In short, the history of the exodus is a chronicle of prolonged and profound conflict.

So it is with the other portions of Scripture cited in the previous sections as constituting the canon for a pietistic perspective on conflict. While the prophets could and did indeed on occasion wax eloquent with their visions of an obedient, harmonious human community of God's faithful followers, more often their oracles and utterances evoked or provoked conflict. The prophets regularly found themselves in opposition to kings and other politically powerful figures; faithfulness to their calls brought them into conflict with other religious leaders as well.

The conflicts recorded in the Old Testament reflect an ongoing state of war between those who named Yahweh as their God and opposing individuals or communities. A good measure of conflicted conversation also took place between God and those chosen to be messengers and agents of the Divine. At the moment of his call, Moses argued vociferously with God. Most if not all the prophets accepted their calls only after disputation with the Divine. The deep and profound tensions within individuals who found themselves internally conflicted likewise fill many pages of the Holy Scriptures. Jacob's wrestling the night long with an angel is but one of many such examples of internally conflicted souls seeking to sort out their desires from God's calling, attempting to distinguish between the tempter's beguiling beckon and the true voice of Yahweh.

A deeper reading of the New Testament reveals that the early Christian community was not immune from but rather awash in conflict as well. While Jesus and the disciples had some high moments of warm, loving intimate community, much of the time they spent together involved arguments and wrangling among themselves. Who was the greatest? Which one was most beloved by the master? Together with his disciples, Jesus was in constant clashes with the Pharisees and others among the Jewish sectarian groups, each believing that it had a corner on perfect obedience to the Law. The great conflict between Jesus and both religious and secular leaders rose to its zenith in the events we remember and relive each year during Holy Week. Above and beyond all its other deep meanings, the cross on which Christ was crucified can be understood as an enduring witness to humanity's destructive, profoundly conflicted relationships. Because we as human beings are in conflict among ourselves, and because we are engaged in an ongoing and intractable contest with God, Jesus was stripped and scourged, despised and denigrated. And amid the menacing mayhem resulting from the ultimate conflict between good and evil, between God and all the satanic forces of the universe, Jesus was murdered. The cross is the ultimate symbol of conflict and its pervasiveness in the world. In what has been referred to as Martin Luther's "combat theory of redemption,"[1] it is in the very conflict between God and Satan waged on the cross that the salvation of humankind and the cosmos is achieved.

A good primer in a theology of conflict is to be found in the second of Luke's great New Testament volumes, the book of Acts. Here are found stories of the bold witness, Stephen, whose unwillingness to mute his missionary proclamation led to martyrdom as he came into conflict with the ruling religious authorities. In Acts we find a record of the profound and prolonged internal conflict within Saul the persecutor until he finally embraced the Christian message, becoming transformed into Paul, the great missionary apostle. Also recorded in Acts are the blow-by-blow accounts of the early church's first heavy-duty conflicts. Fighting over a host of issues—who could eat what meat in which setting; when it was and was not appropriate to allow for speaking in tongues; deportment and comportment in settings where the ecclesial community gathered to share the Lord's Supper; belonging to one's baptizer, Cephas or Apollos; appropriate responses to the plight of the poor; mandatory circumcision versus making the matter voluntary for Gentile Christians—all these and more stories of conflict are recorded in Acts. In every case, the early Christians did not avoid the conflict or allow themselves to become paralyzed by its existence. Rather, they confronted their differences, prayerfully engaged in long informal conversations and more formal prolonged councils until communal stances were adopted.

Exegeting to a deeper level the Pauline epistles and other New Testament writings, we can discover that, as much as pastoral visions of a desired future state of harmony and perfectly peaceful relationships are upheld, the reality of currently conflicted communities is confronted. Throughout Paul's letters, the early Christians were not exhorted to run from conflict or to sweep it under the rug but

---

1. The phrase is cited in the index of *What Luther Says: An Anthology*, compiled by Ewald M. Plass (St. Louis: Concordia, 1959), 3:1641.

to engage it in such a way as to stimulate growth and promote the advance of the church's mission.

Moving beyond a superficial piety to develop a thoroughgoing theology of conflict, therefore, begins with a deeper and slightly more creative reading of Scripture. The Bible chronicles a series of defining events and conversations, most of which involve at least some degree of conflict. Those of us who view the Bible as far more than a book of history—as the living Word of God that reveals the good news of the gospel—will be led to ponder the nature of the God revealed to us in Scripture. Can it not be said that the God of Israel and the God who raised Jesus Christ from the dead is a God constantly engaged in conflict with all the forces of evil in the world around us? The God who became incarnate in Jesus proclaimed, "I have come that you might have abundant life!" (John 10:10). This life-giving, liberating God was and is in ongoing conflict with all the death-dealing oppressive foes and forces at large in the cosmos.

In developing a theology of conflict, we may also ponder more deeply the question whether conflict is always the result and manifestation of sin. In other words, is all conflict bad, destructive, and evidence of the fallen nature of humanity and the whole creation? Or is conflict a part of God's grand design in the creation? Are all instances of conflict signs of human shortcomings and evidence that we have sinned and fallen short of the glory of God? Or may the existence of conflict rather signal on some occasions that we are being true to our authentic created human nature and faithful to our callings as followers of the Creator?

It would seem that certain forms of conflict and tension are indeed inherent to the Creator's design of the universe. In the physical realm, we know that any growth requires a certain amount of tension. The development and maintenance of strong muscles in the human body, for example, requires exercising those muscles, stretching them, and forcing them to be in conflict with their natural tendencies to be flaccid and relaxed. In human interactions the deepening of relationships beyond superficial acquaintance often involves periods of working through differing perspectives and competing desires. Healthy psychological development requires learning that one's needs and desires cannot always be fulfilled, especially as they bump up against the needs and wants of others. Working through multiple conflicts is a key component of maturing and growing. That's probably why so many conflicted and difficult encounters occur between teenagers and their parents and peers!

A fully developed theology of conflict, therefore, should take into account the multi-faceted portrayals of Scripture. Many parts of the Bible do seem to send the message that conflict is always the manifestation of sin, of the creation and humanity falling short of God's intended wholeness and shalom. God engages in conflict with the forces of darkness and destruction. Jesus regularly places himself in conflict with the Pharisees and others whose legalisms enslave themselves and others. Jesus' conflicted engagements are portrayed in the Gospels as acts of liberation, as components of his overall message and meaning. But other wide swaths of Scripture may point to conflict as simply part and parcel of God's activity in the world. Everyday growth-producing nonviolent human conflict between groups or individuals may be positive witnesses to the God who engages and acts in history, and not always manifestations of evil and the power of sin at work in the world.

We hope that these comments will provoke continuing theological reflection about conflict. Our experience leads us to suggest that when church groups find themselves in destructive conflict, some theological reflection together can be a starting point in a process of reconciliation. Moving beyond a pietistic default stance that sees all conflict as bad toward a multi-faceted theological perspective can help groups in conflict begin to reframe issues and see their situation from new perspectives.

Frequency, Sources, and Seasons of Conflict

Often coupled with the pietistic perspective that "all conflict is bad" is a vague and unsubstantiated conviction that conflict in the church is rare and must surely be a sign of unfaithfulness. It can be helpful to conflicted groups or entire faith communities caught up in the throes of a heavy duty fight to recognize the reality that they are not alone, that not only is conflict rampant but it apparently is becoming almost routine in ecclesiastical communities.

How prevalent is conflict in congregations? In the mid-1990s, the Evangelical Lutheran Church in America conducted research on the extent of conflict among its 11,000 congregations. The researchers concluded that over a five-year period, 1990–1994, about 42% of ELCA congregations had experienced serious conflict. How serious? These conflicts were of such intensity that they resulted either in the departure of the pastor or a significant number of congregational members leaving the congregation.[2] A 2000 study published by the Hartford Institute for Religion Research was based upon the most extensive research ever conducted among U.S. congregations across the denominational spectrum. In the Faith Communities Today (FACT) research, which assessed twenty-six surveys of congregations in forty-one different denominations and faith groups, 75% of congregations reported some level of conflict in the previous five years. A high percentage of conflict revolves around decision making, particularly the minister's role and authority in making decisions.

Congregational Conflict

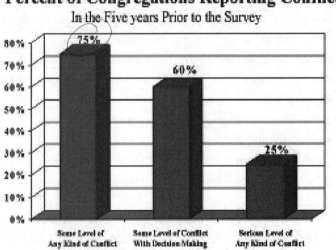

Based on the Faith Communities Today national survey of 14,301 congregations. http://www.fact.hartsem.edu

---

2. *A Profile: Facts about Congregations of the Evangelical Lutheran Church in America* (Chicago: ELCA Department for Research and Evaluation, August 1994).

In summarizing this research, Carl S. Dudley notes that "disagreements were reported in every aspect of church life: from theological beliefs to the way money was raised and spent, from worship practices to mission priorities, from lay decision making to pastoral leadership styles."[3] Within these categories there are as many variations as there are congregational stories of conflict. Even within the same denomination, no two conflicts surrounding the pastor's leadership style will look quite the same. Bishops, judicatory staff, or independent consultants working with multiple conflicted congregations soon learn that, while there may be some similarities in how conflicts are played out, every group of God's faithful find their own unique ways to fight.

Speed Leas, widely regarded as one of the foremost experts on congregational conflict, has conducted research indicating that the ten most predictable times when a church is likely to experience conflict are (1) Easter season; (2) stewardship campaigns and budget preparation time; (3) addition of new staff; (4) a change in leadership style; (5) the pastor's vacation; (6) changes in the pastor's family; (7) when baby boomers join the church in significant numbers; (8) completion of a new building; (9) significant loss of membership; and (10) significant increase of membership.[4]

While congregational conflicts may cause pain and anguish for many members, those who often bear the greatest brunt are the professional staff, especially the minister(s). Beginning a quarter century ago, numerous studies have been conducted regarding what are euphemistically called "involuntary terminations." By another name, these are simply clergy firings. An ecumenical study reported by *Leadership* magazine in 1996 found that 22.8% of responding readers had been forced out of a ministry at some point during their careers. Two-thirds of those reporting being terminated indicated that predecessors had also been removed.[5]

---

3. Carl S. Dudley, "Conflict: Synonym for Congregation," *FACTs on Fighting* data from the Fact2000 Study (http://fact.hartsem.edu/research/fact2000/topical_article3.htm).

4. Speed Leas, "The Ten Most Predictable Times of Conflict," in *Leading Your Church through Conflict and Reconciliation*, ed. Marshall Shelley (Minneapolis: Bethany House, 1997), chapter 4.

5. David L. Goetz, "Forced Out," *Leadership* 17/1 (Winter 1996), 42.

The research indicates there is a high vulnerability during a minister's first three years in a congregation, that some congregations are prone to ruptured relationships with a series of clergy, and that interpersonal difficulties and value-driven conflicts are those most likely to force a minister out of office.[6] Robert H. Welch reports that "in the year 2000, the executive board of the largest Protestant denomination in America [the Southern Baptist Convention] reported that nearly one thousand (987) ministers were considered as 'forced terminations' from their positions. The reasons often given were issues about who will run the church, poor people skills, pastoral leadership style perceived as too strong, the church's resistance to change, and the church was already conflicted when the pastor arrived."[7]

Some General Types of Conflict

At the beginning of his famous novel *Anna Karenina*, Leo Tolstoy declares that "All happy families are alike; each unhappy family is unhappy in its own way." So too, it might be suggested that happy congregations are alike and every conflicted church has its own way of being in turmoil. Nevertheless, many who have studied and been involved in working through conflicts in churches attempt to group or categorize conflicts into various general prototypes. Understanding the nature of a conflict may be helpful in working toward its resolution in the most creative and productive ways.

Conflicts often center in differing views of the roles of key individuals, particularly leaders. Despite the existence of carefully prepared written job titles and detailed position descriptions, sometimes based upon more general provisions in constitutions, bylaws, and other governing documents, there is often broad latitude in interpreting an individual's or a group's true role and function in the congregation or other organization. Central to conflicts resulting from confusion or differing perspectives regarding a leader's role are questions like, "Who's really

---

6. Speed Leas, *A Study of Clergy Firings* (Herndon, Va.: Alban Institute, 1980).

7. Robert H. Welch, *Church Administration: Creating Efficiency for Effective Ministry* (Nashville: Broadman & Holman, 2005), xiii.

in charge here? How broad is her or his authority? Who's empowered to make this decision? What's the role of the entire congregation, the board, the pastor, the Sunday school committee?" If the Sunday school superintendent understands his role to include full authority to spend money up to allowable budgeted amounts and the treasurer believes that all expenditures must be pre-approved by her, a *role-related* conflict is at play. Likewise, if the Christian education committee looks to the pastor for a high degree of guidance on matters related to curriculum selection, calendar planning, teacher recruitment, and other matters, and the pastor sees herself as available for occasional consultation on broad matters of theology, the differing understandings of the pastoral role can lead to conflict.

Another broad type of conflict identified by many experienced consultants and authors who reflect on church fights is identified as *structural*. In this variety of conflict, groups or individuals are brought into conflict by the way the congregation or organization is structured. A common pitfall in organizational design or practice is that those charged with responsibility for an area of work simply do not have the authority and resources to fulfill their charge. A church council's giving a youth ministry director the mandate to plan two significant monthly events for teenagers, but providing no budget and prohibiting the director from engaging in fund-raising, is an example of a structural design guaranteed to result in conflict when the youth minister is unable to fulfill the assignment. Holding the minister accountable for all staff members' performance, while reserving formal supervision to committee chairs in various areas, would be another structural set-up for conflict. When a committee chair and the minister disagree on the measures of effective staff performance, a conflict is bound to result.

There is a vast array of disputes and disagreements in church settings and everywhere that fall into the broad category of *interpersonal* conflicts. A reality of our human community is that some folks just don't like each other. Psychological projections often contribute to bad chemistry between two individuals. A fellow parishioner reminds George of his least favorite and even somewhat feared uncle. No matter how much George may strive to "be adult about this" and set aside his prejudices and projections, he simply cannot bring himself to like this perfectly decent Christian brother. When there are serious interpersonal dislikes, it can be almost impossible for people to work together productively, even though they may agree on the purposes, goals, and ways to conduct an important project.

Simply acknowledging to oneself that such an interpersonal difficulty exists may enable a measure of positive relating to the disliked other. But short of deep and prolonged therapy or perhaps multiple mediation sessions with a skilled third party coach or counselor, such interpersonal conflicts are likely to persist. If they cannot be readily managed, keeping the two parties apart as much as possible may be the wiser course for leaders responsible for a group or faith community's well-being and mission.

As we proceed in examining types of conflict, it should be acknowledged that the further we go, the more difficult resolution becomes. *Substantive* conflicts, as the word implies, are disputes over one or more important issues. No matter how much we may agree on respective roles and responsibilities, align organizational structures, and despite the fact we really like one another and are relatively free of interpersonal conflicts, you and I may flat out disagree on significant issues. As noted above in the summary of sources of conflict, substantive disagreements arise in churches over any number of issues. Some substantive conflicts may fall out along generational lines. Often, younger folks are more willing to go into debt, while the older generation believes the money should be in the bank before beginning a major construction project. People from different backgrounds and of different educational philosophies may have very different approaches to how the religious education program should be conducted. Similarly, backgrounds and personal preferences will dictate preferred styles of music, formal or more informal worship styles, and a whole host of substantive differences over important matters.

Most difficult and emotionally charged are conflicts resulting from core *ideological* differences. In churches these typically involve deeply ingrained theological convictions about the nature of God, human beings, and moral-ethical issues that are considered central to personal and communal identity. The very fact that there are currently hundreds of denominations and church bodies is testimony to conflicts of the past that frequently were of the ideological/theological type. Disputes over the interpretation of Scripture and possible ministerial roles for women perpetuate the existence of two major national Lutheran church bodies in the United States, for example. Almost all denominations currently engage in deep and painful struggles over issues related to human sexuality, particularly homosexuality. The widespread conflict in faith communities over vexing ethical issues like abortion and stem-cell research mirrors that which exists in the broader society. Because the

ideolgical diff.

convictions are so deeply held, and because these kinds of issues touch our very core personal identities and self-understandings, ideologically driven conflicts can be virtually impossible to resolve. Either the parties in dispute find ways to agree to disagree and live together with ongoing differences or they decide there must be a parting of the ways, i.e., that the conflict is a church-dividing matter.

Conflict Administration: Beginning Diagnosis

If a healthy approach to disputes consistent with a biblically based theology of conflict involves living with and attempting to work through disputes and disagreements rather than ignoring them or hoping they'll simply go away, how do those called to leadership in a faith community begin?

How

Let us suggest as a starting point that how a person views her or his work in the midst of conflict is an important matter. If working amid conflict is viewed as drudgery and approached resentfully, such an attitude will be perceived and probably mirrored by others. On the other hand, if engaging conflict is viewed as yet another dimension of one's ministry that, while difficult and somewhat undesirable, is neither unexpected nor overly onerous, then those involved in the conflict may be given hope of growth and eventual positive outcomes. This matter of attitude, self-identity, and how one should act amid conflict is frequently described in articles and books in terms of exhibiting a "non-anxious presence," a key concept and phrase from important work by the late Rabbi Edwin Friedman.[8]

conflict dimension of ones ministry

Much of the literature related to conflict, in ecclesiastical and other arenas, refers to the notion of conflict management. Some who ponder conflict, the authors included, are beginning to question whether it can really be managed. In keeping with the overall spirit of this book, we find more helpful the notion of *conflict administration,* that is, ministering to and with individuals, groups, or an entire community that finds itself in the midst of a dispute, contest, or fight.

conflict admin

A beginning point in any process of conflict administration is to engage in as much dispassionate diagnosis as possible. Just as a doctor cannot begin to prescribe

---

8. See especially Edwin H. Friedman, *Generation to Generation: Family Process in Church and Synagogue* (New York and London: Guilford, 1985).

medicine, surgery, or other needed intervention before conducting a thorough examination of the patient, one who seeks to bring healing in the midst of conflict begins with a thorough diagnostic assessment. Some basic questions that merit research, careful listening, pondering, and conversation with all parties to the conflict and perhaps some neutral third-party observers or co-consultants are:

questions

- Who are the parties to the conflict? Which individuals and groups are involved? What are their formal and informal roles within the community's organizational system?

- What do they say they want? What are the presenting issues about which they are fighting?

- Are there underlying, unspoken (and perhaps even consciously unknown to the parties themselves) concerns that are the real issues?

- What type of conflict is this: role, structural, interpersonal, substantive, ideological (or some other type we haven't thought of yet)?

- Are there patterns, rhythms, or trends observable in the occurrence of conflict in this particular community? Do they, for example, seem to always have skirmishes and squabbles in the Easter season? Or is there a cyclical pattern wherein every three or four years there is a major congregational blow-up?

- Are there dimensions of the conflict that can readily be resolved or eliminated by the simple provision of additional data or information currently unavailable to the parties?

- Are there external drivers that may be causing or contributing significantly to the conflict?

- How bad is it? Can we manage by ourselves, at least initially, or is the immediate involvement of an outside consultant needed to provide objective and neutral refereeing?

With regard to the final question, once again Speed Leas has done a great deal of work on offering tools for analyzing what he terms *levels of conflict*. Often in a conflict, he suggests, one of the disagreements is regarding its severity, with some members and leaders minimizing and others seeing dire catastrophe on the near horizon. Conflicts may range from problems to solve, to disagreement and contest, all the way to full-blown fights, and finally intractable and irremediable conflict where the only sane and humane solution is to separate the parties on a permanent basis.

The stage or level of the conflict often determines the nature of conflict administration called for in a given situation. Lower-level conflict, often requiring a problem-solving approach, may be quite manageable with internal leadership. At their ugliest, some conflicts teeter on the verge of violence, requiring outside intervention and police action to ensure the safety of individuals and a community. Rather than rehearse in depth his several writings on the predictable and progressive stages through which a conflict proceeds, we commend Leas's perspectives for the reader's further study and reflection.[9]

Additional Influencers: Type, Size, Identity, and Polity

The growing body of knowledge and literature in the field of congregational studies has additional insights to contribute in assessing and diagnosing conflicts in faith communities. In addition to other variables, much of the research analyzes congregations in terms of type, size, identity, and how they are influenced by the particular polity of a parent denomination. Many congregational-studies researchers delve into dynamics of conflict, concluding that these several factors will influence the nature of conflicts, how they are played out, and how they may be resolved in congregations of varying sizes and types.

Arlin Rothauge theorizes that membership size has a significant influence in how a congregation carries out its life and mission as well as in how it defines the roles of minister, lay leaders, and others who fulfill functions that often are not spelled out in any documents or organizational charts. Rothauge suggests that congregations fall into four groups by size: family (up to 50 worshipers), pastoral (50–150), program (150–300), and corporate (300 plus).[10] In general, the larger

---

9. Speed Leas, "Conflict in the Parish: How Bad Is It?" *Word & World* 4/2 (Spring 1984), 182–91.

10. Arlin J. Rothauge, *Sizing Up a Congregation for New Member Ministry* (New York: Education for Mission and Ministry Office, Episcopal Church in the USA, 1984).

the church, the more power and authority is vested in the clergy and other paid staff. Particularly as congregations grow or shrink and move from one group to another, it is likely that conflict will be experienced.

In a significant research-based study, *Congregations in Conflict: Cultural Models of Local Religious Life*, Penny Becker concludes that there are four overarching congregational models: house of worship, family, community, and leader. Each of these four types hinges on a core corporate identity and understanding of congregational purpose. The expected roles for the minister and other leaders vary widely among the four. Again, if a faith community is in transition from one to another model, or if a new leader misreads the type of ministry she or he has undertaken, conflict is predictable and usually very painful. Sometimes, amid conflict, a person whose primary image of church is house of worship sits in the same pew as one who sees the church as a leader for social change and community action. Hearing the two describe their congregation, an outside listener may conclude that they are members of different churches. From her research with twenty-three congregations of several denominations in suburban Chicago, Becker concluded that the nature of the conflicts experienced will vary in frequency and nature, depending on the congregational model.[11]

While congregations of all traditions seem to get into more or less the same kinds of conflicts, the process of administration and resolution may vary depending upon denominational polity and resources. Churches in episcopal communions can turn to their bishops for intervention and support in times of conflict. Similarly, in other highly structured denominations that have judicatory executives responsible for regional oversight, congregations often can find skilled (and generally cost-free) assistance in coping with conflict. Churches or ecclesiastical institutions affiliated with more congregational polity communions may be largely on their own, or they may have to hire paid conflict consultants. The authority for ultimate decision making in resolving conflict may also vary depending upon denominational polity. In many denominations, for example, a congregation may not unilaterally fire its clergy leader(s) but can only dismiss her or him following a period of consultation involving the bishop's office.

---

11. Penny Edgell Becker, *Congregations in Conflict: Cultural Models of Local Religious Life* (Cambridge: Cambridge Univ. Press, 1999).

Beginning to Engage: Ground Rules and Staging

After a period of diagnosis and assessment, a course of conflict administration may begin to emerge. Those take on a worthy task who assume responsibility for leading a process whose desired outcome is a combination of stronger congregational health and reconciliation among any estranged by conflict. Any such process will involve a series of conversations—some perhaps one-on-one and others in group settings. Particularly when folks come together who are engaged in fighting each other, establishing and maintaining some ground rules is essential. If at all possible, eliciting such rules of engagement out of a group itself is a good approach. Such an effort immediately engages those at odds in a common task, and there is a much higher degree of ownership of the ground rules than if they are imposed by an outside authority or consultant. A beginning list of such rules of engagement is likely to include norms like the following:

- We remember at all times that we are sisters and brothers in the faith; that God loves each and all of us equally; that "in Christ there is neither Greek nor Jew," etc.
- We commit ourselves to listen attentively and respectfully when another person is speaking, avoiding interruptions or immediate response.
- We pledge to live up to Martin Luther's interpretation of the Eighth Commandment: put the best construction on others' words and actions.
- We seek to avoid posturing ourselves as adversaries; rather together we seek to be problem-solvers and do what's best for our community of faith.
- We agree to receive and ponder new information and objective data that may help us more fully grasp our situation.
- We will attempt to focus on and discuss or debate issues, avoiding personal attacks and disparaging comments about the attitudes and perspectives of others.
- We agree to direct communication, avoiding triangulation (rather than A speaking directly to B, with whom A is in disagreement, A complains to C about B), and talking behind one another's backs.

- We trust that God is at work among us and that the Holy Spirit may enable us to find creative alternatives and arrive at consensus without anyone compromising their core convictions and key values.

The setting and staging of conflict administration often has a powerful influence over ultimate outcomes of a resolution and reconciliation process. Sitting in a circle, assigning chairs to guarantee an intermixing of persons with differing perspectives, providing refreshments, and other dimensions of warm hospitality may contribute to a climate wherein anxieties are reduced and creative problem-solving may proceed. Opening sessions with prayer and singing may enable those who are in disagreement to at least spend some time "on the same page." There's a fine line between skillful stage-setting and manipulation that will make all wary of the leader's motives and ability to create a safe climate.

If You Are the Issue

It's one thing to engage in conflict administration if the fight is about issues or between individuals and groups in a parish or organization. If the real or apparent issue is one's own person, perspectives, or actions, however, the anxiety meter spikes like a thermometer thrown into a blast furnace! As we've noted above, in a significant percentage of conflicts in faith communities the conflict centers on the person and leadership of the pastor/minister.

There are probably few more difficult aspects of ministry than to serve in the midst of conflict swirling around one's own personality, leadership style, or perhaps family situation and other deeply personal matters. Under such circumstances, when one is feeling personally scrutinized, criticized, and even attacked, it is very difficult to maintain a degree of objectivity sufficient to listen carefully and assess clearly all the dynamics at play. Our personal experiences and the collective wisdom of many colleagues who have found themselves in painful conflict situations lead us to suggest a beginning list of coping strategies:

- Seek outside help fast and frequently! Turning to one's bishop, trusted colleague, or someone else in the larger ecclesiastical system may be a live option for many. If the nature of the conflict is highly personal, or if one's anxiety and anger are building rapidly, a few sessions with a skilled therapist/counselor can provide needed support.

• Find stress-relieving activities and practice them regularly. Physical exercise offers a healthy relief valve when the pressure is building amid a difficult conflict. Redoubling one's commitment to devotional life, family activities, and hobbies that take one's mind off a painful conflict can be a lifeline.

• Understanding one's own style of engaging (or avoiding) conflict is important under any circumstances when working amid congregational or organizational stress and anxiety. Particularly if one is the target of personal attacks or at the center of a brewing or fully developed conflict situation, understanding her or his conflict-engagement style can be helpful. The more an individual acts consciously and chooses behaviors, the higher the likelihood of positive ultimate outcomes. Some good tools for self-assessment are available in print.[12] Consulting with a counselor or participating in an experience at one of the various clergy career-counseling centers can provide additional self-insights that may be especially helpful amidst a difficult conflict.

• Consider your options, including the advisability of disengaging from an extremely unhealthy and even life-threatening context. While it sounds extreme, in some cases a prolonged congregational conflict can lead to hypertension, heart attack, or even suicidal feelings. Feeling trapped and doomed can lead to depression and dysfunction. Exploring potential new calls or even a new calling may be empowering for one feeling entrapped and without options amid a heavy-duty conflict.

In Conflict's Midst: Pastoral Care and Preaching

As in many aspects of ministry, those who minister amid conflict must strike a balance between ministering to the entire faith community and its many constituent groups while also providing pastoral care to individuals and families.

12. See, for example, Speed B. Leas, *Discover Your Conflict Management Style* (Herndon, Va.: Alban Institute, 1997).

This can be particularly challenging in a season when the conflict can be all-consuming.

While many if not all the members of a congregation may be drawn into and affected by a conflict situation, some might feel its effects particularly poignantly. If the conflict, for example, is whether or not to allow young children to receive Holy Communion, those children and their parents may have especially strong feelings and need an extra measure of pastoral sensitivity. So, too, if a congregation is in the throes of debates over homosexuality, persons known by the minister to be gay or lesbian may merit special attention. In the midst of a conflict, stepping up rather than reducing pastoral calling, casual one-to-one conversations, and a ministry of presence in multiple venues may be among the most important aspects of one's leadership. While our natural human tendency is to avoid those with whom we are in conflict, those entrusted with leadership in faith communities must make every effort to continue ministering to all members, including those who may be engaging in personal attacks against the minister.

Should I say anything from the pulpit about this conflict that is such a prominent feature of our life together at the moment? That's an important question with which many ministers wrestle when faced with parish turmoil. Should the bishop write a pastoral letter to address a simmering situation in the diocese? Such public communication can be an important ingredient in healing. It can also throw fuel on an already raging inferno. Few judgment calls in one's ministry may be as important as whether or not to "go public" in speaking to conflict that is being experienced in the faith community. One should carefully examine one's motives. Am I going to preach about this so I can use the "bully pulpit" to tell my side of things and seek to sway more people to my perspective? Is some measure of my desire to write a pastoral letter or address the matter in the parish newsletter the intent to shame those who are making mischief through their attitudes and actions?

Not to address a raging conflict may smack of a lack of being in touch with reality or a desire to gloss over matters that threaten the community's harmony and ability to carry out a collective mission. Surely St. Paul did not hesitate to address publicly congregations that found themselves in conflict and turmoil. The pastor who avoids any mention of a conflict situation, even when the scriptural texts for that day seem directly applicable, may be regarded as inauthentic or afraid to let the Word be spoken in truth and power. On the other hand, twisting texts to support one's own point of view or to lambaste certain individuals or groups usually will prove divisive in a volatile situation. Since it is often so difficult to separate oneself and one's own emotions and stances, the old adage, "If in doubt, don't," may be a guiding principle for those debating whether to preach or publish about an ongoing conflict situation. And, of course, as at all times in one's ministry, respecting individuals' privacy and refusing to breach the bounds of confidentiality are absolutely essential when seeking to administer and lead amid conflict.[13]

Why Church Conflicts Are So Powerful and Problematic

People who are not involved in religious communities are often puzzled by the intensity with which adherents and members engage in conflict. Many in the general populace probably shake their heads and wonder, "Why do they fight so hard about such seemingly inconsequential matters?" Even many of us who are faithful church members are puzzled at the intensity of some conflicts in our own or other congregations. Why are church conflicts so powerful?

At the outset of his comprehensive textbook on *Managing Church Conflict*, Hugh F. Halverstadt ruminates on the reasons why fights in faith communities frequently escalate to levels way out of proportion with what's really at stake. Noting that "parties' core identities are at risk in church conflicts," Halverstadt recognizes the centrality of religious perspectives and practices for people of faith. In matters of religion, we deal with ultimate questions and cling to promises that transcend everyday life and hold out prospects of eternity. We do not take such matters lightly. Accordingly, particularly when conflicts involve matters of doctrine, beliefs, and treasured theological perspectives, there is far more at stake than in most other aspects of life where we find ourselves conflicted. Debating which route to a destination is the fastest pales by comparison to deep theological differences over the true pathway to spiritual wholeness and eternal salvation. It

---

13. See Craig A. Satterlee, *When God Speaks through Change: Preaching in Times of Congregational Transition* (Herndon, Va.: Alban Institute, 2005).

should be no surprise that in matters of ultimate concern we often experience the ultimate degree of conflict.

Halverstadt also recognizes that the systemic nature of faith communities contributes to the degree of difficulty experienced in attempting to work through conflicts.[14] As voluntary institutions that lack clear lines of accountability and authority, congregations are particularly vulnerable to individuals who may have weak self-esteem, poor boundaries, or be bent on mischief-making. In many congregations, a troublemaking Sunday-school teacher or jaded volunteer janitor cannot be fired. Lines of authority get blurred, and there are frequently many so-called dual relationships. On Sunday morning the minister declares God's grace and salvation, celebrates Holy Communion, offering the very presence of Christ—that's real power! And then Monday night the parish council meets and the very parishioners who heard the gospel from their minister must exercise their responsibility as the pastor's supervising board of directors. Some individuals seek to wield disproportionate personal power by means of their financial contributions or perhaps through professional relationships involving the minister or her or his family members. A clergyperson probably thinks twice about crossing a parishioner who happens to be the local police chief, or about holding in check disruptive behavior on the part of a member public school teacher who must write a college application letter of reference for the pastor's son or daughter.

Blessed Are the Peacemakers and Covenant-Keepers

The larger global events of recent years and decades serve as a backdrop for some concluding reflections about conflict administration in faith communities, reminding us of the urgency for peacemaking in our world and in local contexts. Much of the violence being perpetrated by terrorists of all persuasions is carried out in the name of a divine being. Religious fervor drives destructive reactive forces within individuals and communities who declare others enemies.

---

14. Hugh F. Halverstadt, *Managing Church Conflict* (Louisville: Westminster John Knox, 1991), especially chapter 1.

Careful administrative work — setting tables for conversation

Just as all politics is local, so all peacemaking begins at home and in the neighborhood. Careful administrative work—setting tables for conversation, facilitating dialogue instead of diatribes, absorbing major measures of anxiety rampant in individuals and organizations—is indeed a holy calling, perhaps now more than ever. If local faith communities led by skilled and courageous leaders can model conflict resolution and achieve more frequent reconciliation among estranged persons and groups, such efforts may contribute to some of their most important lasting legacies.

As perhaps at no other time, in the midst of conflict a faith community has opportunity to witness to its covenantal nature. "Hanging in there together" through a prolonged season of conflict bears witness to a church's self-understanding of being in the world, yet different and counter-cultural as a community where persons pledge themselves to deep and abiding commitments to one another. In most purely social organizations, the glue that holds a group together is its harmonious sociability. When things get strained, or a member gets bored, she or he is free to leave the organization. But in the church, where all are members of the body of Christ, withdrawing or pulling away should never be done lightly. This is not to suggest that members or leaders should stay at all costs, particularly if crazy-making conflict is literally beginning to erode one's mental and spiritual health and well-being. But it is often by means of persistent peacemaking and eventual conflict resolution that a faith community and its members grow to new levels of spiritual maturity.

CHAPTER 12

Life under Law: Navigating Legal Issues in Ministry

> *Just as a pious theologian and sincere preacher is called, in
> the realm of Christ, an angel of God, a savior, prophet, priest,
> servant, and teacher, so a pious jurist and true scholar can be
> called, in the worldly realm of the emperor, a prophet, priest,
> angel, and savior.*
> —*Martin Luther*[1]

A little knowledge is a dangerous thing! Nowhere may that old adage be true more than when it comes to legal matters. Even if we have received advanced first-aid training, most of us recognize our limits, and we avoid dispensing medical advice or attempting to prescribe medicine or perform even minor semi-surgical procedures. When it comes to legal matters, however, we all indeed have some measure of knowledge. In order to procure and maintain driver's licenses, we must master and adhere to a basic knowledge of the rules of the road. As we do many everyday things—open bank and credit card accounts, buy and sell automobiles or other personal property or real estate, or enter into contracts in our personal or professional lives—we engage in transactions that have legal underpinnings and implications.

In recent years it has become apparent to most clergy and other religious professionals that we live at the crossroads where things of God and things of Caesar

---

1. *Luther's Works* (Philadelphia: Fortress Press, 1967), 46:239–40.

intersect. Nowhere does this become manifest more readily than in casual conversations with those among us whom we ask to serve in the office of bishop, superintendent, or overseer. Some who have served long in such ecclesiastical oversight offices say things like, "I used to call an attorney every few years when we needed to execute some transaction related to church property; now I have my attorney's number on my telephone's speed dial and talk with her more frequently than I do with almost anyone else." Denominational headquarters, which used to engage an attorney occasionally or have one on retainer, currently typically have one or more full-time attorneys on their staff as in-house counsel. These lawyers rarely sit around their offices wondering how they'll spend their time! Even those who serve as parish ministers or leaders of small or larger ecclesiastical agencies and institutions find they must often consult with an attorney or other legal professional as they seek faithfully both to steward their office and also to engage in a prudent measure of personal and institutional self-protection and reasonable risk management.

At the outset of this chapter, we, the authors, offer a loud and forthright disclaimer: *We are not giving legal advice!* We are neither qualified nor inclined to offer legal counsel or guidance. Our intent in this chapter is simply to identify in a rudimentary way some broad areas where religious organizational practitioners are likely to encounter sticky issues that are frequently at the intersection of faithful ministerial practice and complex legal requirements and ramifications. In the course of our ministries in several contexts, both of us have been in regular consultation with attorneys who have guided our actions, helped us work through difficult situations, and in the process become trusted colleagues and good friends. While we are certainly aware of excesses on the part of unscrupulous individuals in the legal profession, our personal experiences have also led us to the conclusion that there are outstanding persons of faith who live out their vocations in the practice of law. In our case, most lawyer jokes therefore fall on unsympathetic ears. Relying heavily on what we have learned from some of these wise and faithful counselors,[2] we seek further to offer some guidance on how one might seek to live with a certain degree of grace and even comfort amid the sometimes conflicting and competing expectations of the church and the demands of the law. Finally, we

---

2. The list of lawyers who have shared their insights with us over the years is long. We wish to acknowledge in particular David Hardy and Phillip Harris, former

hope to offer some reflections on the interplay of professional ministerial ethics and constraining legal requirements.

Because we are Lutheran pastors and theologians, our theological reflection on matters of ministry and law as well as of church-state relations is guided by what is often referred to as the doctrine of the two kingdoms. This classical tradition, espoused in varying articulations by Augustine, Luther, and others, asserts that God's activity in the world is by no means confined to arenas typically regarded as "the church." Rather, said Luther and other theologians of note, God acts in both what are often referred to as secular and sacred arenas. In the kingdom of God's right hand, God governs by grace and gospel, declaring forgiveness when individuals go astray and then repent. In the kingdom of the left, by contrast, God's primary way of stewarding the creation is by means of law—including both religious and secular regulations. Under Luther's expansive view of God's way of working in the world, no qualitative distinction is made between ministry in one realm or the other. A Christian, argued Martin Luther, can exercise a priestly ministry in the courts or arenas of commerce as much as by serving as an ordained priest who preaches, presides at the sacraments and offers pastoral consolation among the saints and in the broader community. There are, nevertheless, specific responsibilities and stewardships that pertain to particular offices.[3] A minister who has taken vows of allegiance to God and to her or his communion's commitments and expectations must seek to fulfill those obligations, even at the pos-

---

and current general counsels of the Evangelical Lutheran Church in America. Additionally, a series of columns on legal issues in ministry in the newsletter of the Northeastern Pennsylvania Synod of the Evangelical Lutheran Church in America by Blake Marles provided insights particularly on matters related to clergy confidentiality and privileged communication. Finally, as acknowledged at the book's outset, we are indebted to Emried Cole, Vice President for Seminary Advancement at Gettysburg Lutheran Seminary and a practicing attorney for more than thirty-five years. Both Cole and Harris offered helpful suggestions following their review of this chapter in draft form. None of these attorneys is responsible for statements in the book.

3. For a comprehensive explanation of Luther's doctrine of the two kingdoms, see *Living the Faith: A Lutheran Perspective on Ethics*, Session 6: "The Lutheran Church in Society" (Chicago: Evangelical Lutheran Church in America, Division for Church in Society, 1999).

sible cost of violating the civil law and bearing the consequences of such disobedience or transgression.

Church-State Relations: Navigating the Boundary Waters

In northern Minnesota and across the border into Canada, there is a vast interconnected network of lakes known as the Boundary Waters area. In summer, this broad region attracts many tourists who want to navigate the pristine waterways and enjoy the breath-taking vistas that go on for mile after mile as a canoe wends its way on the interwoven lakes, streams, and rivers. All who seek permission to launch their vessels in the Boundary Waters region are forewarned to plan carefully and give unceasing attention to their navigation, lest they become lost in the vast wilderness territory of the northland.

For both novice and veteran ministerial practitioner, navigating the complex, often unseen, and frequently confusing boundaries of church-state relations is no less daunting than casting one's canoe on the Boundary Waters that join our two friendly nations. One common area of confusion may be caused by the seemingly neat distinction summarized in the oft-quoted phrase "separation of church and state." Does such total separation exist in reality? Absolutely not! If a fire breaks out in the church building, most congregations will dial 911 and expect the municipally funded fire company to respond. Likewise, if there's a robbery in progress at a church function, an alert observer will call the police, and the community of the faithful hope that an officer in uniform—an agent of the state—responds promptly. Members of the clergy may themselves become agents of the state by being elected to public office or when authorized by state laws to officiate at weddings and execute marriage licenses. Churches and religious groups are generally permitted to lease or to meet on public property that is available for secular gatherings.

The perception of an absolute and impenetrable wall of separation between church and state is further fueled by glib and simplistic notions that the First Amendment grants absolute freedom to churches and their agents from normal legal constraints that bind all other individuals and organizations. To be sure, there are broad First Amendment guarantees against intrusion by the state into the internal affairs of faith communities. The gray areas emerge as one begins to exegete the constitutional provision that the government "shall make no laws concerning the establishment or free exercise of religion." To what extent is a church or church-related organization engaging in the free exercise of religion in, for example, matters of employment? In general, in selecting its clergy, a religious community is exempt from federal, state, and local laws prohibiting discrimination. A church can insist that those who serve as its public representative ministers adhere to its creeds and doctrinal positions, and may exclude from service those who cannot so declare. Absent a specific statutory exemption, it may be more difficult for a church to assert this right to theologically based discrimination in the process of hiring a custodial or maintenance-staff person, whose work, it can be argued, is not affected by religious perspectives, although even that kind of religiously based employment qualification has been upheld by the U.S. Supreme Court.[4]

A flurry of court decisions in recent years has established broad legal precedent for areas in which churches are clearly not held to be "above the law" on the basis of First Amendment guarantees against governmental intrusion into doctrinally based ecclesiastical practices and policies. Like all nonprofit corporate entities with tax-exempt status, most faith communities do not have to pay federal or state income taxes on contributions received or real estate taxes on properties used for worship and other spiritual activities. Nevertheless, a church or church-related institution will be bound by many federal, state, and local employment laws, such as overtime payment to nonexempt staff. (The Fair Labor Standards Act classifies employee positions as either "exempt" or "nonexempt." Exempt employees are salaried personnel who are exempt from the minimum wage and overtime provisions of the FLSA. Exempt employees include such positions as directors, managers, and professional staff. See the precise definitions of the Internal Revenue Service.)[5]

---

4. *Corporation of Presiding Bishop of Church of Jesus Christ of Latter-day Saints v. Amos*, 483 U.S. 327 (1987).

5. While not exhaustive, the following are basic federal employment-related laws that merit attention: Title VII, Civil Rights Act of 1964; Equal Pay Act of 1963; Family and Medical Leave Act of 1993; Age Discrimination in Employment Act of 1967; OSHA Act of 1970; Privacy Act of 1974; Americans with Disabilities Act of 1990; Immigration Reform and Control Act of 1986; Welfare Reform Act of 1996.

Church-related educational and social service institutions have been held liable for age or gender discrimination in hiring or firing practices, with investigations, citations, and damages assessed by the Equal Employment Opportunity Commission or courts. In addition to compliance with many federal and state laws, such agencies frequently also are held accountable to regulations and standards established by accrediting bodies whose credentialing is critical for their public reputations and funding eligibility. Their leaders, accordingly, must constantly be attentive to multiple and sometimes contradictory requirements and influences that exist within what is often called the "accountability triad."[6]

In general, broad First Amendment latitude is granted churches and other faith communities with regard to their teachings and declarations. Preachers are not likely to face civil action or criminal charges on the basis of statements in sermons, for example. But even in this arena, there are limits. Because of certain legal constraints attendant to granting churches tax-exempt status, a minister who endorses and promotes a partisan political candidate from the pulpit or in a church publication will have crossed a line that could jeopardize her or his church's exemption. Nevertheless, a minister is not precluded from personal involvement in partisan political activity as long as it is not done in her or his official capacity on behalf of the church. Nor is a preacher in jeopardy of crossing this line by taking a strong public stance, including from the pulpit, with regard to issues.

Another area requiring careful stewarding on the part of church leaders is a congregation's or religious institution's tax-exempt status. In general, federal, state, and local taxes are not levied on the real estate or other assets of an entity granted exemption by virtue of its religious purposes and not-for-profit status (commonly referred to as a "501(C)(3) organization" as defined by the IRS classification). All such organizations, however, may engage in activity that goes beyond their fundamental purposes and results in substantial income, which may be regarded by the IRS and other taxing agencies as subject to "unrelated business income taxation"

_____

6. William L. Baumgaertner, "Accountability to Church and State," in *Good Stewardship: A Handbook for Seminary Trustees*, ed. Barbara E. Taylor and Malcolm L. Warford (Washington, DC: Association of Governing Boards of Universities and Colleges, 1991), 47.

(UBIT). Rental of unused office space to another nonprofit agency for a modest fee may not be problematic, but weekday rental of a church parking lot for commercial purposes, generating monthly income of thousands of dollars, is another matter. When considering all such issues of facility rental, for-sale activities and the like, consultation with a Certified Public Accountant, attorney, taxing agency representative, or other expert is essential. If at all possible, seek a written ruling or advice document, which can be helpful if there should be accusations of tax code violations.

Perhaps as nowhere else, the delicate dance of stewarding church-state relations must be engaged by clergy who serve in the military as chaplains. Both pastors and officers, these servants of both God and Caesar live on a daily basis at the intersection of church and state. Bearing symbols of their faith tradition on military uniforms, they must constantly decide where ultimate allegiance lies and how far they can go in serving the state's purposes without compromising the integrity of their ministerial office. Those who serve currently or are veterans of such chaplaincy ministries can be valuable resources to colleagues in other ministerial arenas.

Clergy Confidentiality:
Fraught with Conundrums

On a blustery wintry evening, Jane and John arrive for their appointment in your church office. In requesting the session by telephone, Jane said simply that they wanted to discuss an important personal matter with you as their pastor. After exchanging pleasantries, you ask, "So how can I be of help to you?" Between sobs, first John and then Jane blurt out painful stories of their troubled marriage, which include John's involvement with other women. As the hour progresses, John states at one point, "Knowing that you have to keep what we say totally confidential, pastor, I'm confessing and seeking God's forgiveness and your absolution for having been sexually aroused and acting out with one of the teenage girls during last year's youth group overnight lock-in, which Jane and I chaperoned. But I forbid you to tell her parents or anyone else. And, by the way, I've discussed this with my lawyer, who assures me we have 'privileged communication' with you." As Jane and John talk on, you find your mind swirling with questions about how to respond. Can and should you grant John absolution? Can you guarantee not to pass along disturbing information you have been told in this "confessional" conversation?

Sooner or later, most clergy and other religious leaders will experience internal conflicts and potential legal complications in the broad and murky arena of confidentiality. Age-old expectations, as well as current policies, establish for ministers, rabbis, imams, and leaders in most faith traditions a high standard of holding in their hearts or "keeping under the stole" information transmitted in the confessional by penitents or in counseling sessions and conversations with parishioners and even members of the general public. Many denominations state such expectations on the part of their clergy explicitly in constitutions, books of order, or documents outlining clerical ethics. For example, the governing documents of the Evangelical Lutheran Church in America set forth expectations for ordained ministers regarding clergy confidentiality:

In keeping with the historic discipline and practice of the Lutheran church and to be true to a sacred trust inherent in the nature of the pastoral office, no ordained minister of this church shall divulge any confidential disclosure received in the course of the care of souls or otherwise in a professional capacity, nor testify concerning conduct observed by the ordained minister while working in a pastoral capacity, except with the express permission of the person who has given confidential information to the ordained minister or who was observed by the ordained minister, or if the person intends great harm to self or others.[7]

7. *Constitution, Bylaws and Continuing Resolutions of the Evangelical Lutheran Church in America*, 2005, 7.45.

While ecclesiastical codes of ethics may be quite clear and specific regarding expectations for clergy, it is not a given that civil law upholds the same standards and grants protection from legal intrusion into the "seal of the confessional." With some exceptions, in the United States, this is one of many areas of civil law governed by states rather than federal legislation, and such state laws vary considerably. As one begins ministry, therefore, or moves into a new jurisdiction, it is important to understand the extent of protection granted a clergyperson under what are typically called "privileged communication" statutes or case law decisions.

Contrary to what is often assumed by the clergy, statutory protections that allow a minister to avoid revealing confidences and that preclude being forced to testify in a court proceeding often are quite limited. They may be defined in terms of "clergy-penitent" or "confessional" or "spiritual advice" contexts. Pastoral counseling likely will not be construed by a court as constituting such a context, *unless* the subpoenaed clergy can prove that there was a penitential or explicitly spiritual aspect to such counseling. A counseling session with a non-member, even if it includes a confessional dimension, may not be construed as legally protected from later disclosure. In some jurisdictions, privileged communication may be narrowly defined as pertaining only when there are no more than two persons in the room—the clergy and one penitent/parishioner. Under such limitations, a minister subpoenaed as a witness in a divorce or child custody proceeding, for example, would not be afforded the privilege for counseling sessions with both partners in which an attempt at reconciliation was being made.

Most if not all jurisdictions now also set forth legally binding expectations for doctors, psychologists, social workers, clergy, others in the helping professions, and sometimes all persons, regarding mandatory reporting to state or local agencies when suspected or confessed abuse of minors is encountered. If discovered or revealed in the context of a penitential counseling or confessional context, it may be legally as well as morally incumbent upon a minister, priest, or other religious leader to report an individual whose past and possible future actions endanger the safety and sanctity of a child's well-being. It is incumbent on a ministry practitioner to know what is expected and be clear in her or his own heart and mind how to respond *before* an actual incident is encountered.

Even if clergy are not explicitly cited in laws requiring mandatory reporting, a minister's and church's moral scruples and internal obligations should tilt heavily in the direction of protecting children and vulnerable adults. In this regard, Pamela Cooper-White's wise counsel should prevail:

> The dilemma of competing duties is perhaps solved by asking the question: To whom is my primary commitment? The purpose of confidentiality is to protect not the clergy or, for that matter, the church, but the vulnerable and those served.[8]

A ministry practitioner needs to know whom to call and how to report child abuse, domestic violence, and other forms of dangerous (and probably illegal) behavior. When dealing with such very difficult situations, which for the minister may include competing "claims" of confidentiality, safety for victims, and imposing appropriate discipline upon perpetrators, it is always wise to seek consultation with a supervisor or professionally trained expert.

In conducting the pastoral calling and counseling dimensions of one's ministry, it is important to strive for transparency and to clarify mutual expectations at the outset of a session or visit. If a minister senses an individual is heading down a road that may lead to a confessional revelation, stopping and clearly establishing or refusing to establish a penitential relationship may be important. Or one might say something like, "While I am willing to hear your confession, you should know that in our church and in this state certain types of revelations are not protected and cannot be kept confidential." In the current era of clergy sexual misconduct, for example, many bishops feel bound to intervene when they sense a minister has approached them for confession and absolution. In such a context the bishop may be well-advised to say, "I need to clarify that if you confess to me a violation of your clergy ethics and ordination vows, then I can no longer be just your pastor but must fulfill my responsibilities of ecclesiastical discipline and protection of the vulnerable." The dilemma of such preemptive disclosures on the minister's part is, of course, that they may prevent a person from unburdening herself or himself and cause the counselee to stop short of revealing information that might enable helpful therapeutic and/or restraining interventions.

---

8. Pamela Cooper-White, *The Cry of Tamar: Violence against Women and the Church's Response* (Minneapolis: Fortress Press, 1995), 223.

Another area of consideration regarding matters of confidentiality and privileged communication involves potential differences between verbal exchanges and statements in writing. A minister may be able to argue that a conversation with a parishioner was of a penitential and spiritual nature, and hence privileged. But unless specifically stated at the top of a file memorandum summarizing the counseling session in question, that minister's written notes may be deemed subject to subpoena. In general, it may be unwise to commit certain matters of a sensitive nature to writing, without clearly designating what is confidential and then keeping the documentation safe from prying eyes. Similar great caution is to be exercised in any and all email correspondence, especially as multiple cases in recent years have established that electronic communications are subject to subpoena and admissible as evidence in legal proceedings.

Because of the challenging nature of navigating the murky boundary waters surrounding confidentiality-related matters, even the most experienced ministry practitioners often need assistance. Conversations with seasoned colleagues and one's own or other judicatory officials, attendance at workshops and seminars on ministerial ethics, and personal consultation with attorneys well-versed in a particular jurisdiction's laws pertaining to confidentiality and privileged communication can all be helpful. There are also some fine books and other printed resources that can aid a minister in this critical area of stewarding the mysteries of God, upholding the highest ethical standards, and simultaneously adhering to the laws of the state.[9]

9. In addition to Cooper-White's helpful treatment (ibid., 220–27), see, e.g., William W. Rankin, *Confidentiality and Clergy: Church, Ethics and the Law* (Harrisburg, Pa.: Morehouse, 1990); sections on confidentiality and privileged communication in Richard R. Hammar, *Pastor, Church and Law*, 3rd ed. (Matthews, N.C.: Christian Ministry Resources, 2000); and Richard B. Couser, *Ministry and the American Legal System: A Guide for Clergy, Lay Workers, and Congregations* (Minneapolis: Fortress Press, 1993).

Prudent Preventive Measures: Boundary Reinforcement and Background Checks

"Pastor, why in the world are you insisting that we attend this silly child-abuse prevention workshop sponsored by the diocese next Saturday? I have taught Sunday school here at St. Mary's for 30 years and this is the first time anyone has ever questioned my integrity or my love for these precious little ones who I teach about God's love. It's offensive to me that the vestry has established this unnecessary policy which actually goes so far as to say I have to quit teaching if I don't participate in this phooey seminar. I think that anyone who ever lays hands on one of God's little ones or does other sick things should be locked up forever!"

"Well, Ethel, I can appreciate your feelings. Our new policy is not meant to call into question your integrity or that of anyone else who is employed or volunteers here at St. Mary's. We simply want to make every reasonable effort to safeguard all our members and everyone else served by or in contact with the parish. If it helps, let me share that just last month I participated in the diocesan clergy abuse prevention seminar. Like you, I have never violated my professional boundaries; fortunately, I've never even been seriously tempted. But you know, Ethel, I gained some new insights and was fortified talking about these difficult matters with my colleagues. And the parish is protected as well by having on file my certificate of completion."

We debated the placement of the following material in this chapter on legal matters. We do not want it construed that abuse and harassment prevention, boundary reinforcement, background checks, and other such matters should receive attention only or even primarily because of legal requirements or to avoid lawsuits. At their core, these are deeply theological, ethical, and pastoral issues.

Giving them the most careful attention flows from our conviction regarding the sacredness of human persons created in God's image, worthy of the highest respect and honor, especially from those entrusted with ministerial stewardship of the mysteries of God. Nevertheless, there are legal ramifications and growing requirements in these areas as well. Since sexual harassment often occurs in the context of mixed-gender working relationships, it is treated in chapter 9, above, on ministry teams.

Sadly, as a spate of newspaper headlines in recent years attests, both members of the clergy and other professional church employees, as well as volunteers, have crossed boundaries, violated a sacred trust, and thereby caused enormous pain and damage. Moreover, the repeated testimonies of victims and countless verdicts in lawsuits have established that ecclesiastical authorities too often have abdicated their responsibility to exercise discipline against offending clergy and to offer support to those harmed by abuse.

Amid all this pain and scandal, summarized succinctly under the broad umbrella of clergy sexual abuse, signs of hope have been lifted up by many courageous victims and their advocates as well as by a growing cadre of informed leaders and learners committed to make faith communities safe places. Their advocacy efforts, writings, and testimonies have resulted in widely available workshops, seminars, and materials (including a growing body of good quality available on the Internet) to assist church leaders and those responsible for governance and policy setting. In order to stem the tide of ministerial abuse and ensure greater safety in parishes and other settings, many judicatories require mandatory attendance by all clergy at what are often called "professional boundaries" workshops. Whether or not such abuse-prevention training is required by external authorities, it should be engaged in recurrently (at least every few years) by all who serve as leaders in congregations and other ecclesiastical organizations. It is important upon completing any such training to keep a record of attendance in church personnel files as well as one's own resume file.

Beyond assuring that there is abuse-prevention and boundary-keeping training for clergy and other key leaders, a congregation, agency, or institution should make every effort to foster an organization-wide climate of safety and respect for the integrity of all persons. Offering classes or workshops for youth and adults on issues of personal boundaries, publishing newsletter articles on appropriate pastor-parishioner relationships, and addressing these important matters in staff performance reviews are ways a faith community can seek to reinforce a healthy and abuse-free climate. Key leadership groups, including the staff and board or council, will do well to engage in more in-depth communal reflection, using excellent resources like the booklet *Safe Connections*[10] published by the Evangelical Lutheran Church in America.

Not only are careful initial scrutiny and screening important in selecting clergy or lay staff for a congregation or church agency but such care in selection, coupled with ongoing preventive training, is essential for volunteers as well. No longer is it satisfactory to issue a blanket "y'all come!" invitation recruiting Sunday school teachers or youth group volunteer leaders. Especially for staff and volunteers working with children and youth, conducting a reasonably thorough background check is helpful to ensure the safety of those served. The church that discovers after a tragic incident of child abuse that the gregarious new Sunday school teacher has a criminal record will experience immeasurable remorse and regret, as well as possible legal liability with attendant financial consequences. In such a case, an ounce of prevention may have prevented tons of grief and pain. At the same time, it must be remembered that background checks cannot ensure that all prior conduct, even criminal conduct, will be revealed, and they do nothing to uncover behavior that is not a matter of public record. Nothing can substitute for the hard work of personally verifying resumes and checking with references and prior employers or supervisors.

With growing attention in our society to protecting and safeguarding children as well as adults, it is becoming relatively routine to conduct background checks regarding an individual's history of criminal convictions, motor vehicle accidents or violations (especially those involving alcohol or other substance abuse), and financial malfeasance. Depending on the nature of a church paid-staff or volunteer position, requiring and requesting one or all of the above may be prudent.

---

10. Janice Erickson-Pearson, *Safe Connections: What Parishioners Can Do to Understand and Prevent Clergy Sexual Abuse* (Chicago: Evangelical Lutheran Church in America, 1996), available online at http://www.elca.org/safeplace and also from Augsburg Fortress. Many fine additional abuse-prevention resources for congregations and organizations are available at the ELCA website.

While it may not be critical to ask a new treasurer to provide documentation of a clean driving record, it surely is prudent to investigate whether or not she or he has any history of embezzlement or declaring multiple bankruptcies! And for the vacation church school van driver, a motor vehicle record review as well as general background check will be essential. If not performed, the church's motor vehicle insurance protection may be nullified, and the congregation or organization may be deemed negligent and culpable in the case of an accident.[11]

Conducting and periodically updating background checks is another layer of work to place upon already-overworked church leaders. Fortunately, in recent years, a number of commercial enterprises have sprung up who will conduct such checks at a variety of levels for reasonable fees.[12] Policies setting forth who will be subject to background checks, the nature of those investigations and reports, and how and by whom they will be received and retained should be developed and adopted by a church's or organization's governing board or perhaps a personnel committee. Likewise, policies should spell out the nature and extent of preventive training and orientation to be undergone by, for example, all who will work directly with children. Some denominations, as well as community service organizations, colleges, and other educational institutions, are offering an increasing array of training programs, and churches may avail themselves of such opportunities rather than designing and fielding their own. Engaging in such communal sessions with others can reinforce for participants a positive sense that "we're not in this alone."

Regardless of what may be required by law, insurance policies, or ecclesiastical expectations, faith communities should be proactive in their abuse-prevention and boundary-reinforcement efforts. In legal proceedings, the "reasonable person standard" is generally applied. If a reasonable person in leadership would insist upon basic child-abuse prevention training for all Sunday school teachers, a leader who does not may be held liable for contributing to damages suffered. Again, in the spirit of witnessing to God's love and justice and promoting God's *shalom,* will

---

11. For excellent resources, including a guide, "Screening Interview and Background Check Procedures," see the Episcopal Diocese of Chicago website: http://www.epischicago.org; also, see the background-check chart in Appendix I.

12. For background-check provider referrals, see the ELCA website: http://www.elca.org/safeplace.

we not strive to surpass minimal standards that may be dictated legally? As good stewards of our sacred trust, ministers and other church leaders will seek to uphold the highest standards, doing all within our capacity to make faith communities places of safety for all.

Conflicts of Interest: "What's the Matter, Don't You Trust Me?"

Over the course of several months, a college faculty held a series of lively discussions regarding a new policy being considered by the trustees regarding "conflicts of interest." Basically, as all such policies do, it reinforces the notion that board members and employees owe a duty always and everywhere to act in the college's best interests, and to avoid competitive posturing that might in any way work against the school. Such policies also set forth the expectation that if a board member or employee stands to benefit personally from some contract or financial transaction (for example, if the food service director purchases supplies from a family member who owns a local grocery), such external factors and relationships will be disclosed in writing.

Eager to establish its straightforward standards requiring disclosure of any possible conflicts on the part of its own members and senior administrators, the board of trustees debated whether or not the new policy should also apply to the faculty as "key employees" of the school. While some faculty members felt comfortable with the proposed policy and even had signed similar declarations while serving on boards outside the institution, others felt that such a policy held the potential for constraining their academic freedom. And some read into the new policy a lack of confidence in their personal and professional integrity, asking in effect, "What's the matter, don't they trust us?" In the end, at the president's urging, the board expressed

> its high trust in the faculty, excluding them from signing an
> annual disclosure and simply including in the faculty hand-
> book a clause requiring immediate disclosure to the president
> or dean of any anticipated conflict of interest.

Matters such as criminal background checks, standards for limiting the number of pastoral counseling sessions, and carefully thinking through when, where,
and with whom one meets behind closed doors are relatively new considerations
for many church leaders. So too is the whole notion of pondering and revealing
potential conflicts of interest.

A conflict of interest exists whenever a professional or person in a leadership
capacity has competing or conflicting personal interests that may affect her or his
decision making and ability to act solely in the best interests of a client, parishioner,
patient, or organization. Any time one hires a family member, for example, there will
be a degree of conflicted loyalty, particularly if the employee's performance proves
unsatisfactory. In hiring a spouse, child, sibling, or parent, an employer should face
squarely the difficult question, "If things don't work out, can I really fire him/her?"

Conflicts of interest normally do not involve inappropriate actions or unethical behavior. They simply arise when an individual is involved in multiple arenas
that may overlap or cause competing claims on her or his loyalties. One of us, for
example, heads an organization that recently had the opportunity to acquire as a
subsidiary another entity on whose board he was serving at the time. As merger
possibilities began to develop, he declared to other board members the conflict of
interest, and recused or "sat out" all votes pertaining to the matter. There is normally nothing inappropriate about having a conflict of interest; it is only in failing
to disclose it openly that a line gets crossed.

A church's or organization's context and culture will inform whether or not to
require that those involved in governance as well as staff persons with decision making and contractual authority execute a conflict of interest disclosure statement. In
tight-knit, family-oriented faith communities where everyone knows everyone else,
it may be manifestly apparent to everyone that Brother John who runs the local
construction company stands to benefit if hired to repair the roof of the fellowship
hall. On the other hand, in large metropolitan congregations where many members
will not even know one another's professions or affiliations, it may be prudent and

help avoid potential misunderstandings or unfounded accusations if all involved in major decision-making bodies execute an annual written disclosure.

For church-related institutions or agencies, there may be external accrediting or regulatory bodies that also set forth expectations regarding conflict of interest policies. In their periodic comprehensive accreditation reviews, for example, colleges and universities must give evidence of the existence and enforcement of conflict of interest policies. Likewise, accrediting bodies for nursing homes or hospitals periodically scrutinize a facility's policies and practices, including those self-imposed by governing boards (see Appendix A for a sample conflict of interest declaration).

Insurance Coverage and Other Risk-Management Measures

Almost any time we seek the counsel of an attorney, we are involved in some form of risk management, seeking to minimize threats to our personal or collective well-being and reputation, as well as enhance our chances of avoiding lawsuits or other disputes and preserving our good name in the community. While some congregations and ministers might boast that even in today's litigious context they never deal with lawyers, even those who so declare likely are in fact engaged in prudent risk management simply by virtue of seeking and maintaining insurance coverage. There may still be a few faith communities who rely on self-insurance, but most churches and organizations carry at least basic insurance coverage against risks of losing the church building to fire or other catastrophic causes, and protecting drivers and passengers in any church-owned or operated vehicles. Similarly, most comprehensive church-insurance packages offer liability coverage that protects the organization and its assets against claims resulting from accidental injuries incurred on the premises, or other causes deemed to be the church's fault by way of negligent or other non-criminal behaviors or inactions.

Even with reasonable standard insurance protection, however, ministers and other church leaders should not become overconfident or assume an attitude of invulnerability. Insurance policies should be read carefully to understand and appreciate fully both the protections afforded, and the accompanying conditions specified. The congregational president might sleep soundly at night in full confidence that the church van has adequate liability coverage against all accidents, only to discover after an accident that was caused by a brake system failure that the coverage was nullified as a result of the failure to seek and pass an annual state-mandated safety inspection. Allowing an individual with a record of DUI conviction, undetected due to the absence of a background check, to drive the van may also void coverage. Likewise, as noted above, failure to conduct criminal background checks on employees or volunteers and/or the absence of anti-abuse training for these individuals may void the insurance policy's coverage against claims of child abuse. The failure to conduct regular audits or financial reviews may render invalid protections against fiscal malfeasance.

Another pitfall that many churches create for themselves is that of inadequate insurance protection. Sure, it only cost $500,000 to build the new church two decades ago, but today's replacement costs are five or ten times that amount. As a result of inadequate current coverage, in the event of total loss by fire, the congregation may find itself unable to rebuild. Insurance liability limits also should be periodically reviewed, perhaps in consultation with an attorney familiar with recent claims levels awarded by judges or juries. A caution in this regard is that it may be prudent to avoid broad public dissemination of overall liability coverage limits.

Securing a comprehensive insurance policy through a denominationally sponsored plan or broker who specializes in church insurance offers the advantage of greater likelihood that all bases will be covered. Particularly if working with a local insurance agent whose primary business is not with large organizations and specifically churches, it is well to get expert assessment of the adequacy of coverage. Are church council members and others involved in governance, for example, afforded what is commonly known as "directors and officers" insurance that will mitigate against their being held personally liable for their governance decisions made in good faith? Is there likewise adequate protection for both those who handle money and for the congregation in the event of alleged or actual financial malfeasance? If the treasurer leaves town with a major endowment or savings account in tow, will the congregation have reasonable hopes of recovering the bulk of its loss?[13]

---

13. For an excellent comprehensive treatment of risk management in congregations, see Richard B. Couser, *Managing Risks: First Steps in Identifying Congregational Liability* (Minneapolis: Augsburg Fortress, 1993).

It's Mine, Not Yours! Intellectual Property Laws

It is twenty minutes before the Saturday wedding is set to begin. At the rehearsal last evening, the bride reminded you of the couple's request to invite the entire congregation to join in singing one of their favorite hymns. You recalled that this particular song is not printed in the hymnal, but has been distributed occasionally as a Sunday bulletin insert. As you hear the organist begin playing wedding prelude music in the sanctuary, you are furiously photocopying the requested hymn after downloading it off a music source on the Internet. As it was printing, you noticed on your computer screen the warning: COPYRIGHTED MATERIAL: MAY BE REPRODUCED ONLY WITH PERMISSION AND FOR FEE. With no time to inquire further, you clicked off the website, wondering who had requested permission for previous usage in the congregation. "Oh, well, gotta' run," you say to yourself, and dash off to perform the wedding, turning your thoughts from copyrights to 1 Corinthians 13 and your homily, which will be centered on verse 6: [Love] "does not rejoice in wrongdoing, but rejoices in the truth."

"A person with a computer or photocopy machine can be a danger to self and others!" This characterization applies not only to gossips or troublemakers bent upon spreading the latest salacious half-truth or unfounded damaging rumors. These wonderful technological tools for ministry can easily enable an otherwise scrupulous and law-abiding citizen to unintentionally tread all over another's rights—and even violate the law. Scrupulous attention to copyright laws and what are frequently called "intellectual property rights" is but one more dimension of ethically stewarding one's office of ministry in a congregation or organization of any kind.

Citing the words and work of another person in a written document, sermon, or speech without giving proper attribution is quite simply a violation of the Seventh Commandment, "You shall not steal." Likewise, copying material from a book, journal, or magazine and presenting it as one's own is fraudulent activity that most ministry practitioners will scrupulously avoid. Few of us are tempted to engage in such outright plagiarism or illegal activity. Where things become complicated, however, is when it comes to determining what constitutes legal and ethical "fair use," and when, in addition to an appropriate credit line, a formal request for permission must be made and granted prior to using someone else's publication, music, or information. As in other areas treated in this chapter, the area of intellectual property, its ethical and legal ramifications, is complicated and may vary by changing societal norms as well as evolving statutory and case law.

One broad generalization embraces the commonly acknowledged arena called "the public domain." Some frequently quoted written or spoken material has been used so often by so many that while general quotation is important, neither specific citation nor permission is necessary. In a sermon, newsletter article, or more formal permanent publication, Abraham Lincoln's introduction to the Gettysburg Address ("Four score and seven years ago . . .") need not be further acknowledged. Such familiar prose has been quoted so often in so many venues that no one other than Lincoln "owns" it. Likewise, many familiar hymns, popular songs, poems, and biblical quotations have been used so often that mere general reference will suffice.

The legally recognized concept of "fair use" allows quotation and publication or other distribution of another's copyrighted material without permission. Four factors govern its applicability: (1) the intended use, (2) the nature of the material, (3) the amount or length, and (4) the effect of use on the potential market for the material.[14] Brief quotation of a small portion of someone's work in printed or published material generally requires only a reference in one's text or a footnote. Extended quotes, however, or reprinting an entire journal article or book chapter normally requires formal permission, either written or by personal statement or telephone confirmation (if the latter, be sure to document date and time, as well as the name of the person granting permission). In some cases fees may be charged for permission, particularly in reproducing a chart or photographs. Sometimes

14. Evangelical Lutheran Church in America, "May We Use Copyrighted Material in Our Congregation?" (http://www.elca.org/worship/faq/music/copyright.html).

permission to reproduce will be denied: "No, you may not photocopy that choir anthem; we'll be glad to sell you as many copies as you need."

Many authors, composers, and publishers will grant limited or unlimited reprint or photocopy rights or license for a modest one-time or annual fee. A wealth of contemporary hymnody and liturgical material, for example, is for sale by independent or denominationally affiliated publishing entities. Lacking either explicit permission (including from one's own denominational publisher) or a reprint license, copying songs from a hymnbook or Sunday school materials from a textbook likely constitutes a violation of copyright law, as well the Seventh Commandment.

A whole new generation of copyrighted or generally available materials has been born with the recent advent and phenomenal growth of the Internet. Given the cut-and-paste technology at our fingertips, it is so easy to lift text and images off the Web even when there are clear indications that material is copyrighted. Mere appearance of material on websites conveys to some users the impression that it is in the public domain, which is not necessarily the case. New formats for footnoting material have been created for citing World Wide Web–based works. As with other matters treated in this chapter and throughout the book, when in doubt about how to give proper credit or when permission must be acquired, seek help! Many governmental, denominational, and college or university websites offer guidance related to intellectual property, copyright laws, what constitutes "fair use" (for example, limited classroom usage), and related matters.[15]

Can't Live without One: Life with Your Lawyer

If you are convinced by now that the practice of ministry and leadership in ecclesiastical organizations of all sorts, shapes, and sizes will bring one into the boundary waters of church-state relationships and involve the stewardship of office within a society where legal requirements and constraints are ever expanding, you may also have the dawning recognition that sooner or later you probably have to get

---

15. See especially guidelines from the U.S. Copyright Office: http://lcweb .loc.gov/copyright.

involved with attorneys and even courts or regulatory bodies. Just as it is a good idea to seek and establish a relationship with a personal physician before you get sick, so having a personal or organizational attorney before you need one may be prudent.

In many cases, a congregation or organization will have within its membership one or more attorneys, and maybe even a judge or legislator. Is it a good idea to ask a member attorney to serve as one's personal lawyer and/or the congregation's legal counsel of record? As with most questions raised throughout this book, our considered and inconclusive answer is: It depends! If the attorney in question is with a huge law firm and specializes in one narrow field of law, it may not be wise to ask her or him to offer advice or represent the congregation in a legal proceeding. A good attorney will tell you right up front, "That's not among my areas of expertise." But just as some clergy have difficulty seeing their own weaknesses and being self-critical, so some attorneys may have a tendency to overrate their own competence and deem themselves wise in all areas of the law.

If a member attorney offers legal counsel and services without cost (pro bono, as it is commonly called), it may be particularly inviting to accept such generosity. Beyond questions of competence and expertise, there are other considerations to be weighed in selecting personal or organizational legal counsel. Asking forthrightly, "Can this person be my/our attorney and can I still be her pastor?" is important. While disclosures to an attorney member of personal or professional details relevant to a legal matter will be protected under attorney-client privilege, will you feel comfortable revealing such matters to one who is also a parishioner? Could such information be used against you if down the road the relationship with the attorney member becomes conflicted? Perhaps the most difficult of all questions to pose is, "If I or we become convinced that our member attorney is not representing us well in important legal matters, can we dismiss her or him without irreparably damaging relationships and perhaps even resulting in the member's leaving the congregation?"

Another consideration in contemplating how one relates to legal counsel involves some honest self-scrutiny regarding attitudes and disposition. While surveys indicate that public esteem for most professionals has waned from earlier eras, and while the all-pervasive lawyer jokes seem to rain down widespread disparagement on those living out their vocation in the legal arena, many people still hold attorneys and judges in considerable awe and treat them with undue deference. An important question to ask oneself is, "How do I regard the opinions and advice of our lawyer?" Both of us worked for several years with an in-house general counsel whose bombastic delivery would have been well-suited for movies requiring the voice of God! When this devout attorney offered his opinion on any and all matters, by the sheer sound of his voice and physical demeanor, he spoke with authority! His knowledge and talents were extraordinary, and we were usually in agreement with his recommendations. But we had to remind ourselves that our organization's actions finally had to be determined by the bishop and church council, not by the office of the general counsel.

"Listen to and heed the advice of your attorney; then do the right thing" is good advice to all who finally bear responsibility for navigating and steering a faith community in the directions we believe God is calling us to go. As in a theological debate among ten theologians one likely will hear ten slightly different opinions, so also on many routine or critical legal issues an individual or organization will receive conflicting advice from competent and well-informed legal advisers. Like everyone else, lawyers' professional practice is influenced by their natural personality traits. Some tend to be of a cautious nature and will urge prudence and avoidance of risk to the maximum degree possible. Other more adventurous types will encourage a minister or congregation to forge ahead boldly into uncharted waters, not unmindful or heedless of potential risks but also avoiding paralysis or inaction out of undue concern for potential legal minefields lurking below the surface.

Fear Not, for God Is with Us!

While serving with a denominational churchwide organization, both of us bore significant responsibilities for the orientation and support of multiple leadership groups. One of us organized and helped staff an annual series of orientation briefings for newly elected bishops of the synods or regional judicatories. In the early years of these briefings, we began the first day with what came to be known as "Legal Seminar 101." By the end of the day in which the general counsel's office offered a whirlwind overview that might have been entitled "Fifty Ways a Bishop Can Get Sued," the neophyte episcopal leaders' enthusiasm to assume their new calls had waned considerably. Some began asking questions like, "Should I remove my name from my home's title and transfer it exclusively to my spouse in case I get sued personally in a claim against my synod?" Others who embraced their new callings with high enthusiasm to exert strong strategic leadership and lead their synods to new heights worried that most of their time would be spent dealing with painful situations of clergy sexual misconduct and other manifestations of sin in the church. Still others expressed fears that the very existence of the synod or entire denomination could be threatened by huge financial judgments that surpassed insurance liability limits and could force it into bankruptcy.

A dozen years after these early bishops' briefings, their initial worst fears have proved unfounded. To be sure, many have indeed had to invest considerable portions of their time and psychic and spiritual energy into fielding complaints of clerical misconduct or matters like financial malfeasance on the part of parish or even synodical fiscal officers. A number of bishops have resigned in disgrace as evidence was brought to light of their own failure to live up to ordination vows, either while in office or at previous times in their ministerial careers. But most have gone on to enjoy strong episcopal ministries in which they spend the major portion of their time and energy doing what they feel called to do—preaching, teaching, visiting parishes and pastors, and advancing the mission of the church in their areas. Oh, and yes, after those first couple of years we learned to defuse the initial anxiety by changing the new bishops' orientation agenda, offering the legal seminar at the end rather than the beginning!

Seminarians or ministers at all stages of their careers may feel the same trepidation as did those fledgling bishops in their Legal Seminar 101. "In view of all the pitfalls and my limited training, do I dare do any pastoral counseling at all? Will I get sued if I make even a few minor mistakes in my interactions with parishioners? How likely is it that I will fall victim to false accusations of abuse or harassment? Can I ever be behind closed doors counseling with a person of the opposite sex without placing myself in danger?" To be sure, such concerns are not totally unfounded. But the reality is that lawsuits involving clergy remain relatively rare rather than rampant. By exercising due diligence, establishing and abiding by good personnel practices, giving proper attention to basic legal matters, and consulting frequently when feeling "over one's head," most pastoral practitioners and religious leaders will find rewarding rather than onerous their ministries that are carried out in both realms—law and gospel.

As we navigate the confusing boundaries of church-state relations and encounter the challenges at the intersection of the two kingdoms, it is our conviction that ministry remains an exciting and rewarding calling. With a reasonable measure of common sense, continuing education in areas where we discover our weaknesses, and a healthy spiritual life coupled with collegial and professional support persons and networks, we need not be overly concerned about matters of legal liability. Embracing concepts like reasonable care standards and responsible professional ethical behavior based upon our religious convictions, we can approach our callings with grace and good courage.

Afterword: The Church Administrator as Person

Who am I: This or the other?
Am I one person today and tomorrow another?
Am I both at once?
—Dietrich Bonhoeffer, 1944[1]

The preceding chapters are a topical presentation of church administration. Church administration is a collection of encounters with governance, boards, personnel processes, legal issues, planning, fiscal matters, resources, conflict, communication, teams, and external relationships. But what of the administrator, especially the ad-minister (administration as holy calling) who time-travels all these engagements? What is worth noting about the *person* behind it all, more personally put, you and us? We finish with three thoughts: taming the untamable, the importance of self-awareness, and the attitude toward learning.

Organizations-R-Crazy (Including Church Ones)!

Much of the writing on administration delivers an oh-so-rational view of organizations and the world in which they exist. Administration, then, is not so difficult because the world holds still while administrators apply their calculated steps of

---

1. Dietrich Bonhoeffer, *Letters and Papers From Prison*; enlarged ed. (New York: Simon and Schuster, 1997), 347–48.

observation, analysis, decision, and action. We hope we have not fallen into this trap. Each chapter has tried to be realistic about how these administrative tasks play out in everyday organizational life. The sub-theme "Riding Time to the End," set forth in the Preface, acknowledges the need for courage and persistence in confronting the unpredictable and fading character of all things. The prophet (known as "Second Isaiah") says:

> *All people are grass,*
> *their constancy is like the flower of the field.*
> *The grass withers, the flower fades*
> *when the breath of the Lord blows upon it;*
> *surely, the people are grass.*
> —Isa 40:6b-7

Administration is not rationalizing the irrational, ordering disorder, or taming the untamable. It is *effort* (with expected outcomes) undertaken with others in the face of irrationality, disorder, and the unruly nature of things.

Equipped with a degree of understanding and corresponding skills, it is possible to do administration and do it well, with full knowledge that it won't be neat and without pain. Planning serves as a good example. Preparation for planning (see chapter 4) includes confronting the aftermath of previous planning episodes that may carry the seeds of disappointment, skepticism, and even anger, to sufficiently cleanse the past, enabling new and effective planning to proceed.

When someone says, "I am not an administrator," even though she or he is doing administration, they may mean, "I have been disappointed with my efforts to do administration," or, "I am disillusioned with human nature's propensity for self-centered behavior that works against teamwork or pursuing common goals," or, "I was taken in by a belief in the inevitable triumph of rationality." Notice that the entire field of administration was seduced by the false promises of pure rationality (see chapter 1). This led finally to a discovery of the social side of human nature as expressed in groups and collectives, and the necessity of thinking of institutions, their governance and administration in systems terms and images to comprehend their dynamic and complex character.

Church administrators should know better than to fall for the rational trap, given such theological assertions as, "For there is no distinction, since all have sinned and fall short of the glory of God" (Rom 3:22b-23); "If we say that we have not sinned, we make him [God] a liar, and his word is not in us" (1 John 1:10); we are both saint and sinner at the same time (Martin Luther); and "Christ died for our sins" (1 Cor 15:3).

Those who work within church systems can attest to the intensification of conflict and the accompanying emotions around important and unimportant issues. Holy matters are at stake! The potential for great good and egregious evil is multiplied. The quote with which this Afterword begins is from the prison writings of Dietrich Bonhoeffer. The poem that contains these words is an honest self-reflection on the degrees to which the Nazi struggle in the nation and *in the church* was taking its toll on him. Bonhoeffer's identity as person and child of God was under siege, as the concluding lines make clear:

> *Who am I? They mock me, these lonely questions of mine.*
> *Whoever I am, thou knowest, O God, I am thine.*[2]

In a similar fashion (though perhaps not as dramatic), the church administrator needs ways to guard against the effects of irrationality, selfishness, and even deliberate assaults on the *personhood* of the administrator. To be involved in the unfolding of the Christian story is to take on the history and future of that story with all its struggles against the forces that oppose it and would like to defeat it. That struggle shows up inside as well as outside the church, even *inside* the administrator if we are to believe the above theological claims.

It is imperative, therefore, to access ways and means to fight against the corroding acids of cynicism and denial that, if untreated, lead to disillusionment, withdrawal, and abandonment. Taming the untamable? Hardly, but being armed with concepts and tools for the doing of church administration at least makes it possible to assist the church and its organizations in fulfilling their mission and being faithful to their calling.

---

2. Ibid., 348.

The Importance of Self-Awareness

Albert Speer was a great builder and industrialist. There was just one problem. His talents were offered to and used by Adolf Hitler in the diabolic attempt to inaugurate a "Thousand Year Reign" of National Socialism in Germany.

Speer's misdirected use of his talents serves as a parable for the church administrator. There seem to be two very powerful forces at work in human beings: the desire to be effective, that is, to have an effect on the world around us, and the almost endless capacity to fool ourselves about what we are really good at doing.

Let's call the first force the *competence motive* (from psychology) and the second, the *capacity for self-deception*. How effective you or we are as administrators will have much to do with how we activate the first and avoid the second.

Psychiatrist Rollo May has studied the competence motive and believes it to be more powerful than even the famous search for identity:

> The old myths and symbols by which we oriented ourselves are gone, anxiety is rampant; we cling to each other and try to persuade ourselves that what we feel is love; we do not will because we are afraid that if we choose one thing or one person we will love the other, and we are too insecure to take the chance. . . . The individual is forced to turn inward, he [sic] becomes obsessed with the new form of the problem of identity, namely, Even-if-I-know-who-I-am, I-have-no-significance. I am unable to influence others. The next step is apathy. And the step following that is violence. For no human being can stand the perpetually numbing experience of his own powerlessness.[3]

One reason why administrative ability is important is that it is one way (not the only or even the most important way) of having an effect, making a dent on the world around us, especially in and through institutions where we spend much of our time. From this perspective, understanding and acting on what we are good

---

3. Rollo May, *Love and Will* (New York: Horton, 1969), 13–14.

at is not just a private search for identity or fulfillment; it is an activation of a basic human need and, if directed toward the betterment of society (unlike Speer), helps to make human collective efforts, like institutions and their administration, more effective and doable.

But a funny (or not so funny) thing happens on the way to competence: self-deception. There is not space in this book to explore the many ways human beings deceive themselves; let it suffice to claim that it happens, especially among those who lead others. This claim is supported by the presence of "self-awareness" or "strong self-concept" on almost every list of leader traits or competencies. A Google search on "leadership" uncovers an extensive study on leadership conducted by a major university in partnership with a well-known public-opinion survey group that identifies nine major areas of interest, including "self-awareness and reflection."

How does one become self-aware? There are many ways: through reflection on major life experiences, listening to others (who will tell you the truth), counseling, and coaching. Three ways of gaining greater self-awareness are feedback analysis, autobiography, and the IRS model (Identity, Roles, and Skills).

1. Feedback Analysis. The grandfather of modern management, Peter Drucker, observes, "The only way to discover your strengths is through feedback analysis."[4] Acknowledging the difficulty of finding persons who know you well enough and will be honest, Drucker suggests an alternate activity he has followed for more than thirty years. After each major life or work decision, write down what you hope to accomplish. After nine to twelve months, reflect on (and write down) what actually happened. Analyze the gap between intention and outcome. What were the forces at work? What did you do or not do to determine the actual outcome? What did you learn about yourself?

2. Autobiography. A second example comes from two theologians who did a study of Albert Speer's life through his autobiography, *Inside the Third Reich*. Their conclusion is that Speer fails the test of overcoming self-deception. Speer explains himself to himself in ways that strengthen self-illusion and avoid the tough requirements of the real story of the Third Reich. The two theological

---

4. Peter F. Drucker, "Managing Oneself," *Harvard Business Review* (March–April 1999), 66.

researchers make the following case for the art of autobiography as an antidote for self-deception:

> The art of autobiography offers the best illustration of how to recheck and test the adequacy of the central story and image we have of our lives. The constraints and requirements of autobiography parallel those of a life well lived. Like the moral person, the autobiographer cannot simply recount the events of his or her life. He or she must write from the dominant perspective and image of his or her present time. If his effort is successful, these images and metaphors will provide the skills to articulate the limits of past images and show how they have led to the autobiographer's current perspective. Autobiography is the literary form that mirrors the moral necessity to free ourselves from the hold of our illusions by exercising the skills which more demanding stories provide. Autobiography is the literary act that rehearses our liberation from illusory goals by showing how to bring specific skills of understanding to bear on our desires and aversions, so that an intelligible pattern emerges. An autobiographer, like a moral person, needs to find a story that gives a life coherence without distorting the quality of his or her actual engagements with others and the world.[5]

For our purpose here, note that autobiography has five features. It:

- is written ("a literary form")
- is more than description ("cannot simply recount the events of his or her life")
- confronts the limits and illusions of old self-understandings ("articulate the limits of past images"; "free ourselves from the hold of our illusions")

---

5. David Burrell and Stanley Hauerwas, "Self-deception and Autobiography: Theological and Ethical Reflections on Speer's *Inside the Third Reich*," *Journal of Religious Ethics* 2/1 (1974), 112.

- prepares for the future ("rehearses our liberation from illusory goals")
- produces a direction both realistic and desirable ("an intelligible pattern emerges"; "a story that gives a life coherence without distorting . . . actual engagements with others and the world")

An illustration: The entry into a doctoral program in public administration includes a required course in self-assessment. The lone requirement is a one hundred-page paper consisting of four parts: exploration of major life themes (especially recurring ones); obtaining feedback from others and analysis; a model to relate self-understanding, feedback, and life choices; and life, family, and doctoral program goals. Cohort student groups are formed based on geography and access for mutual support. Career and self-assessment material is supplied.

At the end of the semester the students gather, turn in their papers, and reflect with each other and the professors on the experience. Four of the twenty-nine students announce they are dropping out but declare this course to be the most valuable activity they have ever experienced. An evaluation conducted three years later shows the extremely high regard participants placed on the course and the strong correlation between course learning and completing graduate study, making work and life choices. The course made a difference. This course increased self-awareness, not in some narcissistic way ("look at me"), but in a productive and positive manner related to society and its need for effective public administrators.[6]

3. The IRS Model. In addition to feedback analysis and autobiography, a third way to enhance self-awareness is the IRS model, that is, to clarify one's Identity, Roles, and Skills.

Identity is the more durable aspects of personality over time. What is constant, recurring not once but again and again? One of us seems to always seek out (or is sought out for) starting up things: a new tutoring program in college, a new congregation, a new national church agency, a new denomination. The other author is best casting a vision and seeking a path forward amid tough situations: a problem solver and solution seeker, not in perennial search of conflict but calm and effective in dealing with it. The life themes of the autobiographical work in

---

6. Robert N. Bacher, "Autobiography—Learning Plan," unpublished manuscript, 1975.

the previous example are a good way to capture identity. Answer the question, "Who am I?" ten times, and an identity narrative will develop.

Roles are not a popular concept, probably because of the connotation of "playing roles" being non-authentic and manipulative. We do, however, tend to fulfill certain roles in a situation or organization. Small-group research was one of the early ways roles were discovered. Regardless of personality, gender, and race differences of group members, tasks undertaken, environment, or any other variables, certain group roles develop, and are filled sometimes by different or the same members. In the research these two roles were generalized as *attention to task* and *group maintenance*, that is, some persons concentrate on getting the job done, while others care for the ways the group works together. Try these two simple exercises. Complete the sentence "I am . . ." twenty times. Your roles as husband, mother, child, executive administrator, neighborhood counselor, congregational pastor have a lot to do with how you function and what you seek out to do. Or look at the list of roles related to running a machine (see Appendix K). The three you check as "most like to do" or "do not like to do" are windows into your identity and represent the ways you tend to exercise your effectiveness.

While individual strengths and preferences shape the roles taken by church administrators, there are three general categories that emerge, given the nature of administrative work. They are:

- Interpreter. "And how are they to hear without someone to proclaim him [the Lord]?" asked Paul in his letter to the Romans (10:14c). And how do people who associate with organizations know what's going on without an interpreter? Rumors rampage, bad news is exaggerated, good news is ignored, the past is wrongly remembered, the future is uncertain—all these realities of organizational life need interpretation in ways neither "Pollyanish" or "doomsday" but honest, direct, and enlightening.
- Integrator. The church body of the authors declares itself not to be top down or bottom up but interactive. The parts (congregation, synod, churchwide office, related institutions) work together to fulfill an identity and carry out a mission that assigns ultimate authority only to God. In such a church and in almost all organizations these days, administrators are expected to be integrators who bridge and connect groups, both

informal and formal. In fact, the work of administration today increasingly takes on the central role of connector, especially as groups develop around passionately held positions creating more and more we's and they's. The administrator integrates hardened lines that otherwise morph into dividing walls.

• Innovator. Hopefully, with more than personal ego at work, the church administrator often is dissatisfied with policies, procedures, and systems that seem to have outlived their usefulness. Changing things is an art, as people often resist, partly because change creates uncertainty. Yet the role of innovator goes with church administration, not innovation for its own sake, but to improve, to increase effectiveness. Research on exemplary leaders has shown that they "challenge the process," "search for new opportunities," and engage in "experimenting."[7]

Skills are capacities to achieve effectiveness, some skills are technical in nature, others involve working with people, and some are symbolic, that is, developing vision, or defining the situation, or offering motivation to get from here to there. A newer word for skills is *competencies*. Either way, it is important for a church administrator to (a) be aware of what skills or competencies she or he possesses or needs to develop, and (b) which ones the congregation or church-related organization requires to carry out its mission. A broad set of competencies provided in the *Dictionary of Occupational Titles* of the U.S. Department of Labor is shown in Appendix L. This list, organized by data, people, and things, can be used by individuals (to determine strengths), or by organizations (to develop expected and needed competencies to achieve organizational goals and effectiveness). Finally, a set of eight questions has proved helpful for individual and group reflection and assessment in following the IRS model (see Appendix M).

Self-awareness is a key to doing effective administration. Three examples have been described for increasing self-awareness: feedback analysis, autobiography, and the Identity, Roles, and Skills model.

---

7. Jay A. Conger, *Learning to Lead: The Art of Transforming Managers into Leaders* (San Francisco: Jossey-Bass, 1992), 86.

Learning to Learn

The third and final aspect of the administrator as a person is the call to continuous learning. Reflecting on his seminary experience, one graduate reported that the best gift the seminary gave him was teaching him how to keep learning.[8]

A church administrator's continuous learning involves attitude and style. The attitude is formed from the belief that one does not know it all, others (colleagues, partners, board members, constituents, donors, clients) have something to teach, and life is a sequence of learning opportunities because change is a constant companion.

Style in its simplest form refers to three ways of learning: reading, writing, or talking.[9] Great leaders exhibit one of these three modes for learning. For example, Winston Churchill and Ludwig van Beethoven kept copious notes and sketchbooks. Talking is often not well understood by those around a leader who learns that way, as it may appear the leader is changing his or her mind when what is actually happening is talking through the options available. An additional factor for the church administrator is response to the ongoing guidance of God in changing situations: "O sing to the Lord a new song" (Ps 96:1a), or "The wind blows where it chooses, and you hear the sound of it, but you do not know where it comes from or where it goes. So it is with everyone who is born of the Spirit" (John 3:8).

The administrator who ceases to learn is in danger of being overtaken by developing events and emerging needs. Part of being on top of things involves an open attitude toward learning that never stops.

A Final Word

In his first inaugural address (1861), Abraham Lincoln wrote, "I do not consider it necessary at present for me to discuss those matters of administration about which there is no anxiety or excitement." We have tried to follow President Lincoln's lead

---

8. Susan Wilds McArver and Scott H. Hendrix, *A Goodly Heritage: The Story of Lutheran Theological Southern Seminary, 1930–2005* (Columbia, SC: Lutheran Theological Southern Seminary, 2006), 27.

9. Drucker, "Managing Oneself," 68.

by discussing those matters of church administration about which there is anxiety or excitement. The ministry of administration is too easily dismissed as marginal to the real work of the church. We have tried to show how integral administration is to the doing of ministry and mission in the world.

In between his discussion of spiritual gifts and their proper role in the church and his poetic proclamation of love as the more excellent way, the apostle Paul wrote to those assembled in Corinth about who they were and who was to do what among them. Paul begins with a declaration, "Now you are the body of Christ and individually members of it" (1 Cor 12:27). Not, "I would like you to be the body," or, "I hope you want to be the body," but "you *are* the body!" Body is carnal, fleshly, and from a theological point of view in-carnational: "You are the body *of Christ*."

Our reasoning behind this book is that the church is called to exist and minister in the world. The church "occupies space," to use a Bonhoeffer phrase. The world is constituted by space and time coordinates. The church, if it cares at all about incarnation in time and space, must employ the gifts given by the same God who calls, in as response-able manner as it can possibly muster.

And that is what Paul's next sentence to the Corinthian assembly is about, namely, the use of gifts in response to the call to be the body of Christ. "And God has appointed in the church first apostles, second. . . ." We quarrel with a translation. The Revised Standard Version (1952) includes "administrators" among those who use their gifts for the sake of the body of Christ. The New Revised Standard Version (1989) does not. The Greek word in question is *kybernēsis*, rendered in early translations as "governments," "governings," or "administration."[10] As mentioned in chapter 2, this word literally means the work of a ship's pilot who steers the ship through rocks and storms to safe harbor. One commentator claims, "The people to whom Paul is referring are the people who carry out the administration of the Church. It is supremely essential work."[11]

---

10. William F. Arndt and F. Wilbur Gingrich, *A Greek-English Lexicon of the New Testament* (Cambridge and Chicago: Cambridge Univ. Press and Univ. of Chicago Press, 1957), 457.

11. William Barclay, *The Letters to the Corinthians;* The Barclay Study Bible (Edinburgh: Saint Andrew, 1959), 129.

Our protest over translation is mild and beside the point. The point is that Paul's assertion that, as the called body of Christ rides time to the end, it is gifted beyond belief. As Paul wrote elsewhere: "For the gifts and the calling of God are irrevocable" (Rom 11:29). If among the revocable things—including the ways the church responds to God's call at different periods of history to meet changing circumstances—there is a good word spoken for *governings* or even *administration,* we are happy.

Thanks be to God for the *call* and the *gifts* (among them the gift of administration)!

Conflict of Interest Certification

Board members owe duties of care and loyalty to _____ and must fully and promptly disclose any situation in which their personal or economic interests may materially conflict with the institutional or economic interests of _____ and its affiliates, or impair independent, unbiased judgment (a "conflict of interest"). Examples of conflicts of interest include, but are not limited to, having a family member enroll as a parish school student; serving on the board of or having a direct or indirect interest in an organization which does business with or competes with _____; and directly or indirectly engaging in a transaction or pursuing an opportunity in which _____ has or may have an interest.

I have received copies of the complete Conflict of Interest Statement and understand its contents as applicable to my role as a director/board member;

I agree to comply with the Conflict of Interest Statement and any applicable federal or state law, including the affirmative obligation to report any violations or suspected violations thereof, and I understand that if I have any questions or concerns about such compliance, I should consult the chair of the board;

I understand that my failure to comply with the Conflict of Interest Statement, including the reporting requirements, will, among other things, subject me to loss of my appointment to the board; and

I understand that _____ is a charitable organization and that, in order to maintain federal tax exemptions, it must engage primarily in activities which accomplish one or more of its tax-exempt purposes.

[ ] I represent that I am in complete compliance with the Conflict of Interest Statement as it applies to my role as a director, OR

[ ] I hereby disclose the following possible or actual conflict of interest or other matter which is or may be a violation of the Conflict of Interest Statement, including without limitation my involvement in any business or organization that conducts business with _____:

_____

_____

_____

_____

I agree to update this certification in writing if there are any changes in the information contained herein, including immediately declaring any possible or actual conflict of interest which may arise.

Signature: _____   Date:_____

Printed Name: _____

APPENDIX B

**Sample General Fund
Revenue and Expense Statement
for the Month and Year-to Date Ending (Current Month)[1]**

Support and Revenue	Month	YTD	Budget	Budget Remaining	% of Budget Rec'd/Spent
Contributions	26,417	247,123	305,000	57,877	81.02%
Interest Income	623	5,112	5,000	(112)	102.240%
Workshop/Events Income	214	600	1,000	400	60.00%
Total Support and Revenue	27,254	252,835	311,000	58,165	81.30%
Expenses (by Program)					
Worship	9,000	77,845	100,000	22,155	77.85%
Education	2,403	9,453	10,000	547	94.53%
Care/Fellowship	925	8,766	10,000	1,234	87.66%
Evangelism	1,613	8,453	10,000	1,547	84.53%
Resources	2,543	28,488	50,000	21,512	56.98%
Community Relief	800	2,475	3,000	525	82.50%
Youth	865	2,776	3,000	224	92.53%
Administration	10,325	111,457	125,000	13,543	89.17%
Total Expenses	28,474	249,713	311,000	61,287	80.29%
Excess of Support and Revenue Over Expenses	(1,220)	3,122	–	3,122	1.00%

---

1. Printed with permission of the Evangelical Lutheran Church in America, Office of the Treasurer. Available at http://www.elca.org/treasurer/congregations/genfund.pdf.

APPENDIX C

**Sample Statement of Revenue and Expense
Year to Date[1]**

Support and Revenue	General Fund	Restricted Funds	Plant Funds	Endowment Funds	Total All Funds
Contributions	309,027	5,472	16,575		331,074
Interest Income	6,132	3,655	640	5,130	15,557
Workshops/Events Income	733				733
Bequests				10,000	10,000
Total Support and Revenue	315,892	9,127	17,215	15,130	357,364
Expenses (by Program)					
Worship	98,541	2,435		5,000	105,976
Education	10,205	750			10,095
Care/Fellowship	9,876	219			10,095
Evangelism	9,545				9,545
Resources	46,723				46,723
Community Relief	3,000	1,934			4,934
Youth	3,025		11,000		3,025
Administration	123,786		11,000		134,786
Total Expenses	304,701	5,338		5,000	326,039
Excesss of Support and Revenue Over Expenses	**11,191**	**3,789**	**6,215**	**10,130**	**31,325**
Fund Balances at Beginning of Year	**41,730**	**72,158**	**446,995**	**55,370**	**616,253**
Fund Balances at End of Year	**52,921**	**75,947**	**453,210**	**65,500**	**647,578**

---

1. Printed with permission of the Evangelical Lutheran Church in America, Office of the Treasurer. Available at http://www.elca.org/treasurer/congregations/genfund.pdf.

APPENDIX D

Sample Congregational Balance Sheet
Year to Date[1]

ASSETS	General Fund	Restricted Fund	Plant Fund	Endowment Fund	Total All Funds
Cash and Cash Equivalents	62,533	32,947	16,210	8,500	120,190
Accounts Receivable	1,768				1,768
Pledges Receivable			72,000		72,000
Other Current Assets	4,765				4,765
Land, Buildings and Equipment			525,000		525,000
Investments	10,000	43,000		62,000	115,000
TOTAL ASSETS	79,066	75,947	613,210	70,500	838,723
LIABILITIES AND FUND BALANCE					
Accounts Payable	3,621			5,000	8,621
Payroll Withholding	524				524
Deferred Revenue	22,000				22,000
Current Portion Long-Term Debt			10,000		10,000
Long-Term Debt			150,000		150,000
Total Liabilities	26,145	–	160,000	5,000	191,145
Fund Balances					
Unrestricted	52,921				52,921
Temporarily Restricted		75,947			75,947
Permanetly Restrricted				65,500	65,500
Net Investment in Plant			453,210		453,210
Total Fund Balances	52,921	75,947	453,210	65,500	647,578
TOTAL LIABILITES AND FUND BALANCES	79,066	75,945	613,210	70,500	838,723

---

1. Printed with permission of the Evangelical Lutheran Church in America, Office of the Treasurer. Available at http://www.elca.org/treasurer/congregations/genfund.pdf.

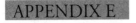

Sample Statement of Cash Flows
Year to Date[1]

Operating Cash Flows	General Fund	Restricted Fund	Plant Fund	Endowment Fund	Total All Funds
Excess Revenues (Expenses)	11,191	3,789	6,215	10,130	31,325
Adjustments					
Depreciation	2,796				2,796
Change in Prepaid Expenses	(1,248)				(1,248)
Change in Accounts Payable	1,525				1,525
Change in Payroll Withholding	(78)				(78)
Change in Deferred Revenue	(6,525)				(6,525)
Net Operating Cash Flows	7,611	3,789	6,215	10,130	27,795
Financing Cash Flows					
Proceeds from Borrowing					-
Repayment of Debt			(25,000)		(25,000)
Net Financing Cash Flows			(25,000)		(25,000)
Investing Cash Flows					
Fixed Asset Sales (Purchases)	(5,755)				(5,755)
Purchase of Investments	(10,000)	(75,000)		(50,000)	(135,000)
Proceeds of Investments	-	60,000		47,000	107,000
Net Investing Cash Flows	(15,755)	(15,000)	-	3,000	(33,755)
Net Increase (Decrease) In Cash	(8,094)	(11,211)	(18,785)	7,130	(30,960)
Transfers	(10,000)		10,000		-
Cash and Cash Equivalents:					
Beginning year	80,627	44,158	24,995	1,370	151,150
End of year	62,533	32,947	16,210	8,500	120,190

---

1. Printed with permission of the Evangelical Lutheran Church in America, Office of the Treasurer. Available at http://www.elca.org/treasurer/congregations/genfund.pdf

Sample Position Description*
Minister of Youth

Basic Assignment

The Minister of Youth is responsible for providing ministerial leadership to develop a comprehensive youth ministry that is consistent with the mission of the church.

Staff Relationship

The Minister of Youth is responsible to the Senior Pastor who will supervise, evaluate, and provide a report of evaluation to the Personnel Committee.

Qualifications

A. Shall be a mature Christian, ascribing to the vision of Our Church.
B. Shall have completed the necessary seminary courses or the equivalent to lead in the area of youth ministry.
C. Shall have at least two years' experience working with youth.
D. Shall have received a clear five-year background check prior to employment.

---

*The position description is a modified version of one found in Larry Gilbert and Cindy Spear, *The Big Book of Job Descriptions for Ministry*, 2002; available from ChurchStaffing.com; 9401 Courthouse Road, Suite 300, Chesterfield, VA 23832

Principal Duties

1. Develop and implement programs that support youth members and attract other young persons to Our Church, and promote their spiritual growth in a holistic Christian faith.

2. Plan and coordinate special events (retreats, camps, mission projects and trips, etc.) that touch all youth at various levels of spiritual maturity, within the goals and objectives of evangelism, worship, fellowship, discipleship, and ministry.

3. Lead the Youth Committee in preparing an annual budget that is reflective of the goals and objectives of the ministry.

4. Develop healthy relationships with parents and guardians of all youth, providing resources for them to assist in their growth as Christian parents.

5. Keep abreast of youth trends and resources needed in order to serve as an advisor to the church on adolescence.

6. Review and evaluate all materials used in the area of youth ministry.

7. Be a visible support to the students and parents whenever possible.

8. Develop and administer programs to recruit and equip adults to work within the youth programs. Serve as an ongoing resource to adult leaders for materials, ideas and coordination.

9. Develop and administer a program of active outreach to the youth of the community.

10. Develop and administer a program for follow-up with youth visitors and their parents.

Performance Evaluation and Development Report

NAME: _____

TITLE: _____

Rating Identification

O - Outstanding - Performance is exceptional in all areas and is recognizable as being far superior to others.

V - Very Good - Results clearly exceed most position requirements. Performance is of high quality and is achieved on a consistent basis.

G - Good - Competent and dependable level of performance. Meets performance standards of the job.

I - Improvement Needed - Performance is deficient in certain areas. Improvement is necessary.

U - Unsatisfactory - Results are generally unacceptable and require immediate improvement.

N/A - Not Applicable or too soon to rate. (Note in the "Comments section.")

GENERAL FACTORS	RATING		COMMENTS
1. **Quality**. The extent to which the staff person's work is accurate, thorough, and neat	O____ G____ U____	V____ I____	
2. **Productivity**. The extent to which an individual produces a significant volume of work efficiently in a specified period of time. Consider use of time and ability to meet schedules and to prioritize tasks.	O____ G____ U____	V____ I____	

GENERAL FACTORS	RATING		COMMENTS
3. **Job Knowledge and Skill**. The extent to which an individual possesses/is able to acquire the practical/technical knowledge required on the job. Expertise in doing assigned tasks and utilization of background for job.	O____ G____ U____	V____ I____	
4. **Availability**. The extent to which an individual is punctual, observes prescribed work break, meal periods, and has an acceptable overall attendance record.	O____ G____ U____	V____ I____	
5. **Reliability**. The extent to which an employee can be relied upon regarding task completion and follow-up.	O____ G____ U____	V____ I____	
6. **Adaptability/Versatility**. Consider ability to meet changing conditions and situations; ease in learning new duties and assignments; ability to be innovative and creative; and willingness to seek opportunities for improvement.	O____ G____ U____	V____ I____	
7. **Independence**. The extent to which a staff person performs work with little or no supervision.	O____ G____ U____	V____ I____	
8. **Creativity**. The extent to which an employee proposes ideas, finds new and better ways of doing things.	O____ G____ U____	V____ I____	
9. **Interpersonal Relationships**. The extent to which an individual is willing and demonstrates the ability to cooperate, work and communicate with co-workers, supervisors, subordinates and/or outside contacts	O____ G____ U____	V____ I____	

GENERAL FACTORS	RATING	COMMENTS
10. **Judgment**. The extent to which an individual demonstrates proper judgment and decision making skills when necessary. Ability to anticipate upcoming events/potential problems; and ability to organize and prioritize tasks and set realistic goals.	O____ V____ G____ I____ U____	
11. **Communication**. Consider oral and/or written communications with co-workers, supervisor, and others.	O____ V____ G____ I____ U____	
12. **Attitude**. Consider interest in the job, cooperation with others, receptiveness to suggestions and constructive criticism, enthusiasm in attempts to improve performance, and initiative.	O____ V____ G____ I____ U____	

Accomplishments or new abilities demonstrated since last review: _____

_____

_____

_____

_____

Specific areas of improvement needed: _____

_____

_____

_____

Recommendations for professional development (seminars, training, etc.): _____

_____

_____

_____

COMMENTS:_____

_____

_____

_____

Ways I (as supervisor) can better support this colleague and enhance our work
together: _____

_____

_____

_____

Rate: Overall evaluation of staff person's performance in comparison to position
and responsibilities.

_____ **OUTSTANDING**   _____ **IMPROVEMENT NEEDED**

_____ **VERY GOOD (Above average)**   _____ **UNSATISFACTORY**

_____ **GOOD (Average)**

Discussed with staff person on _____

Employee's Signature_____

Evaluator's Signature _____ Date_____

Sample Timed Meeting Agenda

Our mission in response to God's gracious gift in Jesus Christ is to share the gospel, ourselves, our possessions, and our love with thousands of God's people in Ourtown and around the world. In partnership with others in the Greater Church, we will praise and proclaim, share lavishly in service, and engage boldly in advocacy for greater justice.

hold mission in forefront

Prayer and Faith Development

7:00 P.M.	Devotions (a reflection on gifts of the Spirit)
7:10	Learning Time: Trends in Contemporary Theology (Prof. Jane Jones)
7:25	Discussion with Dr. Jones

Setting Our Work in Context

7:45	Approval of previous meeting minutes
7:50	Review of Treasurer's report
8:00	Discussion of Pastor's report
8:15	Concerns of the Chair
8:20	Questions or discussion of committee reports

Major Monthly Decision Items

8:30	Youth Outreach project and launching search for Youth Minister
8:45	Official parish response to diocesan request for increased benevolence

Wrap-up and Looking Ahead

8:55	Meeting summary and vision for next month's meeting
9:00	Adjourn (followed by fellowship time for those who can remain)

Sample Background Check Chart for Lay Church Workers[1]

R = Required S = Strongly Recommended N = Not Required	Level 1 Training: Preventing Child Sexual Abuse	Level 2 Training: Preventing Adult Sexual Harassment & Exploitation	5 Year Background Reference Check	Driving Record Report	Credit Report
Parish Staff — Employed & Volunteer					
Custodial Staff	R	R	R	N	N
Secretarial Staff	R	R	R	N	N
Parish Administrator	R	R	R	N	S
Treasurer (volunteer)	R	R	R	N	R
Tresurer (paid)	R	R	R	N	R
Children & Youth Program Volunteers					
Acolyte Director	R	R	R	S	N
Church School Teacher	R	N	R	S	N
Director of Religious Education	R	R	R	S	N
Nursery Workers	R	N	R	N	N
Youth Group Leader	R	R	R	S	N
Youth Group Volunteer	R	R	R	S	N
Car Pool Driver	R	S	N	R	N
Adult Program Volunteers					
Adult Education Teachers	R	R	N	N	N
Church Bus Driver	R	R	R	R	N
Committee Chair (of non-children/youth activities)	R	S	N	N	N
Guild Director	R	R	R	N	N
Lay Eucharist Visitors (LEV or LEM)/Stephen Ministries	R	N	N	N	N
Chalice Bearers/Lay Readers	R	R	S	N	N

---

1. *Diocese of Chicago Requirements and Recommendations for Prevention Training and Background Checks of Parish Workers Who Are Not Clergy*, printed with permission of Episcopal Diocese of Chicago, 65 East Huron Street, Chicago, IL, 60611. Telephone 312-751-4200. http://www.epischicago.org.

	Level 1 Training: Preventing Child Sexual Abuse	Level 2 Training: Preventing Adult Sexual Harassment & Exploitation	5 Year Background Reference Check	Driving Record Report	Credit Report
Lay Pastoral Care-giver/Counselor/Spiritual Director	R	R	R	N	N
Licensed Lay Readers/Worship Leaders	R	R	R	N	N
Lay Preachers	R	R	R	N	N
Parish Nurse	R	R	R	N	N
R = Required **S = Strongly Recommended** **N = Not Required**					
Parish Musician/Organist/Choir Master	R	R	R	N	S
Vestry Member	R	S	N	N	N

Sample Screening Interview and Background Check Procedure

The Diocese of Chicago requires screening interviews and background checks of all clergy and paid employees. Volunteers who work with children and youth, and those who perform para-pastoral ministries must also consent to screening interviews and background checks. The period of time to be reviewed is at least five years.

Abusive perpetrators, especially preferential perpetrators, are drawn to environments that enable them to carry out selection, grooming, and abuse. Responding to a steadily growing awareness of the link between past behavior and present actions, in 1998 President Clinton signed into law the Volunteers for Children Act, giving organizations that deal with children, elderly, and the disabled access to national criminal history records. When we take diligent advantage of this legislation, abusive perpetrators are made clearly aware that the Diocese of Chicago insists on an environment that is not conducive for abuse.

The screening interview and background check conducted for clergy (priests and deacons) covers a period of at least fifteen years. Those investigations are of a more specialized nature and are coordinated through the Office of Pastoral Care and the Office of the Bishop. The procedures for the investigation of clergy are not outlined in this manual. The following description applies to screenings and checks conducted for lay employees and volunteers.

The Screening Interview

A screening interview is conducted before the background check. During the interview the applicant should be asked:

- The task or type of task that interests the applicant, and why he or she is interested in this task
- A description of previous experiences, both generally and those that relate to the desired task what are his/her expectations of the church/agency, as related to this task
- Has he/she been charged with or convicted of any felonious or criminal offense, especially one of a sexual nature
- To complete the Dicoese of Chicago's standard application form

During the screening interview, the appliccant should be provided with a copy of the *Keeping God's People Safe* manual.

The Screening Application

A background check is initiated by the completion of a standard application form. The work provided by a volunteer is as valued as the work provided by a paid staff member. For this reason, both paid staffers and volunteers are expected to complete the same application.

Gathering Background Information

The success of the screening and check procedure depends on following up and conducting the reference checks listed on the application. The easiest way of conducting the check is to engage the services of a professional investigation firm. However, that route can be costly.

With the assistance of the Internet, it is possible to conduct the investigation for a very low cost, using present office staff or reruiting a knowledgeable volunteer. Of key importance is to be aware that the records produced as a result of the check are to remain confidential. The screening application, and the replies resulting from the reference checks and reports, must be kept in a locked cabinet. Records stored electronically, on a computer or similar data storage system must be protected by a password and/or stored in an encrypted file format.

The first step is to send out the reference letters. As a precaution, make copies of the original reference letters, to be stored in the applicant's confidential file.

Next, check the State of Illinois Sexual Offender Registry. The Internet gateway to the registry is found at http://www.isp.state.il.us/sor/. IF you agree to terms listed in the Disclaimer and Terms of Use statement, you will proceed to the look-up page at http://www.isp.state.il.us/sor/sor.cfm. Look for the column labeled "Offender Search." An individual can be researched using his/her last name, address, or county.

It is possible to access the National Sexual Offender Registry from the Illinois site. However, only twenty-three states and the District of Columbia are linked through the common Department of Justice site. For individuals who have lived outside of Illinois, the more cautious search would be to check each state's separate registry. A list of each state's registry can be found at the FBI's State Sex Offender Registry Website.

The Sexual Offender Registry only lists individuals convicted of sexual offenses. In Illinois, the State Police manages the state's criminal records through the Bureau of Identification (ISP-BOI). The state provides two types of records, with and without fingerprinting. For the Diocese of Chicago's purposes, the non-fingerprint report is sufficient. At the present time (8/2005), the state assesses a $16 fee for processing a mailed in non-fingerprint request. The fee is set by the State of Illinois and is subject to change.

Information requests need to be on ISP-BOI's specially coded and numbered forms. Payment, in the form of a money order or check drawn on an US institution, must accompany the request. Electronic, Internet filing is possible if an escrow account has been established. Please contact the Office Pastoral Care to find out if an escrow has been set up.

The ISP-BOI forms are available by contacting the Bureau of Identification Supply Room at (815) 740-5216. The form may also be requested on the Illinois State Police Home Page, http://www.isp.state.il.us/crimhistory/crimhistoryhome.cfm. **Please be cautious when completing the request form**; incomplete or mis-completed forms will be returned to the sender, with the application fee forfeited.

Other states have the capacity to provide similar information. Please check with the separate state police offices for information on conducting a criminal record check. The Office of Pastoral Care will also assist with identifying investigative resources.

Specialized Checks

Driving Records: A check of an individual's driving record is indicated if the applicant will include driving, especially transporting others from one place to another. The process of acquiring driving records is described on the Illinois Secretary of State's Frequently Asked Questions webpage (8/2005):

> An abstract of a driving record can be purchased in person at a Driver Services Facility or by writing the Secretary of State, 2701 S. Dirksen Parkway, Springfield, IL 62723.
>
> The cost for a certified abstract of a driving record is $12.00. If you are purchasing another person's driving record, you must provide the driver's full name, sex and date of birth or driver's license number. Before any information will be released, notification will be sent to the person whose record has been requested, giving the date and name of the person making the request.
>
> Disclosing an address or other personal information about a license is prohibited. However, information about convictions, withdrawals, and crashes will be furnished.

Credit Reports: indicated if the applicant will be handling or overseeing significant amounts of money. A merchant member of your congregation or agency might be your best source for advice on the simplest, yet most productive way of researching an applicant's credit history.

Young Adult and Teen Applicants: it is very likely that a young adult or teen may not have a list of previous employers and volunteer activities. School references are an acceptable subsitute.

Of Special Note

The Diocese of Chicago does not wish to entirely preclude those who may have criminal records from participating in a congregation's or an agency's community. At the same time, it is imperative to be cautious. If the returning background information raises questions of the applicant's appropriateness, the issues should be discussed with the Pastoral Care Officer, 312-751-4209.

Source: Diocese of Chicago Requirements and Recommendations for Prevention Training and Background Checks of Parish Workers Who Are Not Clergy, printed with permission of Episcopal Diocese of Chicago, 65 East Huron Street, Chicago, IL, 60611. Telephone 312-751-4200. http://www.epischicago.org.

Roles Identification Exercise

Here are ten things persons could do. The example of a machine is not important, but the roles are. First read all ten. Then select and check the three things you like most to do. Then select the three things you like least to do and check the appropriate blanks.

Most   Least

_____   _____   Develop the theory of operation of a new machine (e.g., an auto)

_____   _____   Operate (manipulate) the new machine

_____   _____   Discover an improvement in the design of the machine

_____   _____   Determine the cost of operating the machine

_____   _____   Supervise the manufacture of the machine

_____   _____   Create a new artistic effect (i.e., improve the beauty of the machine)

_____   _____   Sell the machine

_____   _____   Prepare the advertising for the machine

_____   _____   Teach others the use of the machine

_____   _____   Interest the public in the machine through public addresses

Role Identification Exercise

Competencies Survey Instrument

Data

Conceptualize, interpret. Developing concepts and expounding interpretations after analyzing available data. Structuring problems for solution or resolution.

Innovate, adapt. Modifying and/or revising designs, procedures, or methods to meet specifications, conditions, or standards of effectiveness.

Coordinate, plan. Determining time, place, and sequence of operations or action to be taken on basis of analysis of data.

Analyze, diagnose. Examining and evaluating data. Presenting alternative actions in relation to the evaluation is frequently required.

Research, investigate. Examining systematically. Finding new information or discovering new facts by experimentation or study.

Compile, classify. Gathering, collating, or placing in order information about data, people, or things. Codify. Catalogue. Inventory.

Compute, estimate. Performing arithmetic analysis. Calculating. Making reports and/or carrying out prescribed action in relation thereto.

Audit, bookkeeping. Keeping, examining, or certifying claims or accounts.

Copy, record. Transcribing, entering, or posting data.

Compare, observe. Judging the readily observable functional, structural, or compositional characteristics of data, people, or things. Assessing quality and utility to assign value.

People

Advise, counsel, guide. Dealing with individuals in terms of their total personality with regard to problems, which may be resolved by application of professional principles.

Negotiate, arbitrate. Exchanging ideas, information, and opinions with others to formulate policies and programs and/or arrive jointly at decisions, conclusions, or solutions. Bargaining.

Instruct, teach. Imparting subject matter to others or training others through explanation, demonstration, or supervised practice. Informing.

Expedite, monitor, liaison. Contacting others to make evaluations and audits and to clarify timing and status of operations. Clarifying details relative to workflow.

Supervise, manage. Determining or interpreting work procedures for workers, assigning specific duties, maintaining harmonious relationships, promoting efficiency. Administrating.

Motivate, lead, coach. Acting as an incentive. Animating or filling with ideas. Giving guidance by going ahead or otherwise showing the way. Non-directive.

Perform, demonstrate. Acting, singing, playing a musical instrument, using audial or visual aids. Presiding, public speaking, exhibiting skill.

Persuade, sell. Influencing others in favor of a product, service, or point of view with talks or demonstrations. Convincing.

Communicate, talk, write. Relating with persons in formal or informal manner. Conversing, lecturing, extemporizing, authoring.

Serve, wait on others. Attending to the needs of people or animals or to the expressed or implicit wishes of people. Service in a servile sense.

Things

Design, envision. Creating plans and/or specifications for buildings, furnishings, or machines.

Setting up. Installing machinery or equipment; repairing or restoring machine or equipment breakdowns; responsibility for proper functioning; accuracy.

Do precision work. Patiently and accurately making or repairing objects, materials, or tools; intricate operations and close tolerance or extreme accuracy are involved. Craftsmanship.

Artistic presentation. Paint, draw, portray through sculpture, drama, film, music, the graphic arts, etc.

Drive, control. Starting, stopping, steering, and maneuvering moving machines; requires continuous alertness and readiness of response.

Operate, control. Activating, stopping, monitoring, readying, and adjusting office or shop equipment and machinery.

Manipulate, use tools. Working, digging, moving, guiding, handling.

Maintain, caretaking. Keeping buildings, equipment, or supplies in useful condition. Gardening.

Collect, arrange, display. Gathering or exhibiting things.

Tend, monitor. Starting, stopping, and observing machines or equipment with no significant set-up.

The IRS Model
(Identity, Roles, and Skills)

1. Three things I *do well* are:

2. Three *values* I hold dear are:

3. Two recurring *themes* in my life are:

4. *Roles* I play in society and church are:

5. Imprisoned like the apostle Paul, I would have written to my friends in Philippi about:

6. Three ways I stay *vital* are:

7. Complete the sentence, "My church organization . . ."

8. *Others* tell me that I . . .

INDEX